FEAR

08

sarai READER

SARAI READER 08: FEAR
Produced and Designed at the Sarai Media Lab, Delhi

Sarai Reader Editorial Collective: Monica Narula, Shuddhabrata Sengupta, Ravi Sundaram, Ravi Vasudevan, Awadhendra Sharan + Jeebesh Bagchi

Edited by: Monica Narula, Shuddhabrata Sengupta and Jeebesh Bagchi

Assistant Editor: Shyama Haldar Kilpady
Cover + Design: Amitabh Kumar

Translations: Shveta Sarda

Back Cover Image: Mohammed Khidar (sourced from the collection of Sameena Siddiqui)

Published by The Director,
Centre for the Study of Developing Societies, 29 Rajpur Road, Delhi 110054, India
Tel: (+91) 11 2394 2199 Fax: (+91) 11 2394 3450 E-mail: dak@sarai.net, www.sarai.net

Delhi, 2010

ISBN 978-81-905853-2-3

Sarai Reader 08 http://www.sarai.net/publications/readers/08-fear

Printed by Impress, Delhi
312 pages, 14.5cm X 21cm
Paperback: Rs. 350, US$ 20, Euro 20

CONTENTS

PREFACE

Modernity's great promise – the freedom from fear, now lies in ruins. One can argue that this vision was always compromised – modernity (especially in the form that emerged in the West, under Capitalism) always hid its own fears, and hid from its own fears - the fear of epidemics, of urban panic, of the homeless multitude and of criminal activity. This led to a drive for transparency: for separating the civic from the criminal, the civilised and the barbaric peoples, the human from the non human, life from the machine. With the advent of the mass slaughters of the 20th century, where more died than ever in recorded human history, this promise lay shattered. Today, the drive for transparency has been rendered doubly difficult, with new mobile populations, new networks, new previously unimagined terrors. Sovereignty seems an antiquated slogan of the past, and in the wake of the financial shocks of 2008, there seems to be some substance in the contention that Western capitalism has entered a phase of possibly long term decline.

Today's opacity brings with it a new sense of enduring fear. Not necessarily the terror of sharp and sudden shocks alone, but of the slow mutation of our lives and our times into mine-fields of uncertainty – personal, social and political – that we try and side-step blindfolded. This gingerly navigation across surfaces that might slowly erode to suddenly give way under our feet marks almost every aspect of our lives. Our world has become a nervous system.

We do not trust the weather, the air, the water we drink, the food we eat, the blood that courses through us. We even have misgivings about the experts who reassure us on prime-time television about the trustworthiness of the value of our money or the colour of our dreams. Everything, from the small talk that lubricates sociality to the small print that pads contracts, comes laden with disclaimers. We are always, everywhere, from bedrooms to classrooms to laboratories, offices, fields and the street, taking cover.

Here, now, in the debris of the late, lamented 20th century, which layers the foundations of our 21st, we are building the future with the bric-a-brac of yesterday's terrors, today's anxieties and the fear of what tomorrow may still bring to pass, naked, or disguised as hope. As in every nightmare, what is scary is often the most mundane or banal of things. In our cities, garbage bins may be bombs and the rain may have acid in it. The tennis coach and policeman may be a molester, the portly neighbourhood businssman may harbour cannibalistic fantasies. Fear makes everything we know and take for granted laced with uncertainty. We do not necessarily know what it is that we fear. And yet we know fear with a concrete certainty.

Some live longer, perhaps in the main many live better, but we fear death more. The short sharp shock of panic and the incessant rhythm of worry alternate to produce the counter-point that defines the pulse of our times. Fear is as much a part of the working culture of the stock exchange as it is of the battlefield. We use the fear of what we know to insure us from the fear of what we do not, or cannot, know. Our every step is preceded by precaution. A careful analysis of risk hedges the frontiers of every dream. Yet, all too often, to little avail.

And today, while the fear of a world war may have somewhat receded, the perils of rogue nuclear attacks, of a sudden and lethal outbreak of a virus, of flash floods and freak storms, of forest fires and stampedes, of road rage and suicide bombers, of turbulence in the economy and accidents in the air, constitute the counterpoint to the confidence of progress. This *Sarai Reader* is interested in these phenomena, not as empirical facts (not in whether or not the world is closer to nuclear disaster), but as cultural processes. We want to ask how fear and anxiety shape individual and collective dispositions, how lives and social processes are designed around or against them, and what effects they have on politics and the economy. We are especially interested in fear as language, as mode of communication, as a way of ordering and rendering the world.

The transmission of fear today relies as much on the subtle, almost epidermal contact between human beings as it does on whispers, rumours and panic attacks orchestrated through television and the internet. The effects of these transmissions are visible in a spectrum of situations and processes, ranging from the sovereignty of unstable sentiments in the economy to urban myths about malevolent androids and psychopaths to apocalyptic cults to the robust return of the supernatural in popular culture in the form of new urban horror genres in cinema, gaming and comics. Lacing all this is the salt of terrorism and the so called 'war on terror' – the two forces that have done more to generate discourses of anxiety on an everyday basis than anything hitherto known or imagined. Fear also generates its own industries, which stretch from medicine and pharmacology to engineering and architecture to insurance, surveillance and security.

The *Reader* gathers to itself texts and contributions in the form of image-text assemblages that look at the transmission, generation and processing of fear on an intimate as well as on an industrial scale. They encompass mechanisms designed either to allay or intensify fear or ratchet up and down levels of anxiety and feelings of security. We see this as a beginning, and a broad range of questions and areas of interest, some of which have been touched upon in this book, still remain to be accounted for. While *Sarai Reader 08* does not claim to be exhaustive, it does aim to straddle a wide territory.The form that contributions to the Reader have taken is as varied as the content. While there are stand-alone essays, there are also reports, interviews, photographs, image-text combinations, comics, art-works, personal journal entries, research and commentaries. We believe that this diversity helps the Reader evoke responses to the idea of fear in all its myriad dimensions.

We have always viewed the *Sarai Reader* as a comfort zone for new and unprecedented ideas, as a space of refuge where wayward reflections can meet half-forgotten agendas. This is why we see it possible to imagine *Sarai Reader 08* as setting the stage for a productive encounter with the demand for an account of the limits, margins and edges of our times.

Especially when thinking about fear, we need, as always, fearless speech.

The Editorial Collective
Delhi, 2010

FACING FEAR

Ventilator

IVANA FRANKE

Fear is a Hieroglyph Fractal Repeated on Different Scales

CLAUDIA ROSELLI

Fear in the 21st century is a fractal.

Definition of Fractal

Fractal refers to a geometric object that shows two properties: the property of self-similarity, i.e. the composition and structure of any of its parts is also featured in each detail of the part itself (for as many enlargements as you want); and the property by which the constant ratio between the whole object and each part is continually updated. In a game of zoom-in-and-zoom-out with the observed object, the part can be the whole object and vice versa.

Approaches and withdrawals, balances,
possible readings
affected by viewing distance and by multiple
interpretations.
Groping to interpret and understand fear
in the XXI century.

Appoint fear.
Let's give it a face,
a symbol,
a trajectory,
a luminous trail.
Fear of fear.
Every day on this earth.
Fear of fear.

Fear in the **XXI** century.
In the **XXI** century, fear of suicide bombers,
In the **XX** century, fear of war;
In the **XIX** century, fear of.............
In the **XVIII**.............
In the **XVII**.............

FEAR of agreements and disagreements,
of those other to us, of the different and the non-aligned.
A precise fear of those who deviate from the line, who are not the same.

Signs, lines, faces, symbols, dreams in black-and-white and colour.
Fear, a voice painted on the walls, which animates and gives body to the lines of cities. Walls, lights, transform themselves and become more than that for which they were drawn.
Interpreting fear along lines undefined by boundaries, be they physical, drawn, etched, carved, real or imaginary forms.

Smell the air, trying to identify the cavity, the ravines, the corners where fear was sleeping, resting and preparing to wake up.
Imagine it as a snake coiled in his lair, or as a spore that is near opening.
An entity capable of self-production, regeneration and independent diffusion.

The shape and interpretations of fear are indefinite: first, because it is in perpetual transformation, and second, because it is completely subjective and uncertain.

These features have made fear – in fractal form – capable of crossing borders, crossing thresholds, filtering secret places; have given it the ability to wait asleep behind doors and inside drawers. Powder in envelopes arrived in mail from across the sea. Anthrax spores, daughters of Dr Bruce Edwards Ivins, father of universal bioterrorism.[1]

"Powerful political forces can manipulate public opinion to the point where the mass is convinced that black is white and that war brings peace, that ignorance is strength and freedom slavery. A Pandora's Box of parapsychology and metaphysics, opening the door to the display of a struggle between opposites and polarities.

"The universe is the product of intelligent design, a creature defined by holographic and fractal properties – from the quantum level to the universal – that to be interpreted must be studied and observed at different scales".[2]

Fractal geometry describes nature with a hierarchical language.

Every natural element:
Clouds,
Cliffs,
Rivers,
Trees,
Mountains.................

is described using fractal shapes.

See fear mixed with the forms of nature, camouflaged within them and even capable of changing and transforming.

Fear in crystallisations.
In healing.
In inventories.
In cracks.
In the corners of the walls of the city.
In the interstices of sidewalks.
In the places of the Tiers Paysage of Gilles Clément.

Fear inhabits places not encoded.

Gilles Clément, writer, entomologist, French landscape architect and engineer, finds important resources in residual places. Reserves of diversity:
"Diversity refers to the number of distinct living species of animals, vegetables and simple organisms (bacteria, viruses, etc.), humans being comprised in a single and unique space whose diversity expresses itself in ethnic and cultural variety".[3]

Residual places may contain within themselves more kinds of fear; they are generators of viruses, in unregulated territory; but they can also be caravanserais for diversity.
Terrains vagues open on to new languages often not easily interpretable – and for this are seen as threatening and frightening.

In these areas occur the biological mutations,
the adjustments needed for survival,
that Gilles Clément considers hypothetical moulds or matrices for future global landscape.

Fear lives in diversity,
the non-codified pen,
urban anomalies,
the gaps between the rails.

(in this sense, residual places appear to have been lined up, flattened out, cleaned up, destroyed...)

"Among these fragments of landscape, none have any similarity of form. Their one point in common: all constitute a territory of refuge for diversity. Everywhere else, it is hunted.
"This makes it justifiable to collect them under one term. I propose 'the Third Landscape', the third term of an analysis that has grouped the main observational evidence in shadow on one side, in light on the other. 'Third Landscape' refers to the third state (and not the Third World). A space that expresses neither power nor the submission to power".(Clément,2004)

The antidote to urban fear seems to have been identified as control

Baumann in *The Society of Uncertainty*[4] identifies three categories of fear: those arising from the physical body and the mind, namely those related to pain and anxiety; those resulting from the world, from external objects and their interaction with the human being; and those triggered by other people during the course of life.

The greatest fear is that of uncertainty, insecurity and ignorance, the absence of knowledge of the present and the future.

In this respect, salvation is equated with the concept of control, for which one may cite examples from Foucault and Bentham. Jeremy Bentham suggested and designed a structure called the Panopticon (from the Greek, the all-seeing eye), a circular building in the centre of which was a tower that accommodated the figure responsible for the supervision of all other beings who, in turn, were located in concentric circles divided into cells. Individuals – students, crazies, prison inmates or workers – would live in a state of perpetual subjection to being checked, to being seen without ever seeing.

Foucault also talked about identifying "factories of order" – prisons, psychiatric hospitals, hospices and industrial settlements – as a method of restoring all order to forge the will.[5] Panoptic power as power to control can also, in a sense, be interpreted as the power of approval.

Control as standardisation, as normalcy and therefore safety. Normalcy is security.
Checks and tests to be passed before entering a closed, controlled community give security; they calm, they are the barriers necessary to cross the fencing beyond which another dimension exists.

Exceeding the threshold, the gate, the passage, crossing a border, are symbolic acts which enable and ensure that once beyond these, all will be in accordance with certain behavioural and existential codes, which are shared and are not frightening and would not generate new and unknown anxieties.

In response to this fear:
fear of what differs from the social code for membership of a certain tribe,
of the unexplored,
of the non-coded,
of the hard to label.
Fractal fear,
unstable and changeable, lurks in the minds of people as well as in inanimate objects and can turn itself into anything.

It can ignite currents between physical space and society,
energy dynamics set in motion by single telluric upheavals
a single electric shock passed from person to person,
from animate object to inanimate object
that grows in intensity to culminate in an event so powerful and definitive
that it cannot pass unnoticed.

An example of a fractal that can come close to this interpretation is the physical and geographical 'butterfly effect', derived from chaos theory.

Chaos theory is based precisely on the idea that the conduct of any action may be conditioned by the initial stages of its evolution and the unpredictable dynamics that can occur during its development. To understand this, one can think of smoke spirals from a cigarette or the movement of flowing water: both trace lines, circles, variations, always different from themselves. Everything is, therefore, in part dependent on infinitesimal variations in initial conditions and marginal conditions, which correspond to changes in output but are completely unpredictable; this could be the approach of a particle in a circuit whose entry activates a series of movements capable of transforming all the actions in the pipeline, therefore also changing the process in its final stage.

From this point of view, even the smallest changes in a system of peace are recognised as potential activators of changes in the system, not in an immediate time frame but over a longer time range. This phenomenon may become interesting if projected and applied in a time frame. That is obtained by imagining hypothetical changes in relation to tiny variations of the same scenario.

DEFINITION OF THE BUTTERFLY EFFECT

By **'butterfly effect'** is meant the production of huge variations in the behaviour of a system, considered over a large time frame through small, infinitesimal changes in its initial stages. It gets its name from a story by Ray Bradbury: "Tale of Thunder".

The day after presidential candidate Keith wins the election, a man starts on an experience of time travel in the office of an adventure travel agency which organises safaris that culminate with the trophy killing of animals. The man is, however, warned that it is very important to take care not to kill any living being except those on the point of death by natural causes – animals normally hunted during these expeditions are identified and recorded through a temporal and geographical mapping of the exact time and place at which they will die. The time machine then brings travellers back in time to the exact moment before the death of the beast, or to just those moments needed to kill it.

In the story, the man kills a dinosaur and only upon his return to the office of the agency does he realise that he also killed a butterfly. He sees it under his shoe: a little dead butterfly mixed with mud. Speaking with the man in the agency, he realises that the involuntary killing of the butterfly has led to a semantic shift in language and also to the victory of Keith's sinister rival in the presidential election.

> The butterfly effect seems to be able to change events.
> Not immediately but in the future.
> Who knows what a beat of wings could cause today, here,
> in a week, maybe a month or a year,
> here where is now found,
> the person who is reading these words.

We speak, therefore, of the paradox of time and intention.

The paradox of paradoxes is the 'Grandfather Paradox'.

This represents the possibility of travelling back in time and killing one's ancestors in a more or less fictitious manner, an action that would involve the denial of one's own identity, the self as it is today, bringing about a near de-structuring of the ego back in time (and this explains why there is already talk of paradox!).

In the micro scale: a denial of its existential structure.

Fear is a virus that escapes the rational understanding of most, that is rationally understood by few, understood by even fewer, and therefore feared by most.

Fear is a virus that, having germinated in some location, changes shape and consistency, spreads like liquid, permeating places and modifying them in its wake.

Its representation is a fractal in the formula:

$$d(f^\tau(x), f^\tau(y)) > \delta$$

Contained in the sense of signs that have meaning in the eyes of the person who shows them, based on which scale the interpretation is applied.

From the satellite to the microscope,
microcosm to macrocosm,
matryoshka ecosystems interconnected with each other.
In macro scale, the paradox of the grandfather could correspond to denial forgetfulness and denial of one's personal history.

Wanting to kill/deny one's past, which means what was lived as the collective memory, removing the roots of why certain facilities and cultural dynamics exist, dismantles the memory and essence of a civilisation.

In this sense, reserves, residual spaces, can be identified almost as sacred spaces.

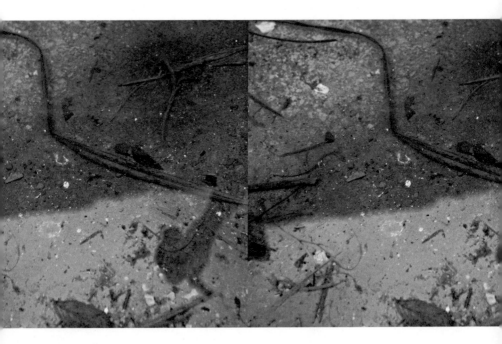

Sanctity, in its potential to perpetrate a freedom, can give breathing space to the other, to the non-approved, in a sense to evolutionary spaces, generators of habitats uncontrolled, spontaneous and hence potentially interesting as true and real. In *terrains vagues*, it is possible to dance the fear and turn it into a sublimation of contemporary identity.

Contemporary identity is often torn between accepting the evolutionary necessities of unstoppable change in society, and its negation.

Refusal and non-acceptance may, in fact, as a reaction, create new fears and forge even stronger ones because they were born from the ashes of those previous.
The fear of difference is the fear of acceptance, knowledge, fear of the consequences of encountering, discovering, new sides of one's selves. (Which would involve a new interior order.)

In the macro scale, fear takes the form of an Other Self, of a cultural melting pot, which could lead to social evolution and transformation, causing subconscious areas and non-coded, unknown places of the imaginary collective to emerge more strongly.

Yona Friedman, architect-urbanist, writer and sociologist, in his *The Complicated Order*, traces aesthetic images of the world not along physical rules universally known, but along the search for harmony and balance between different sensory perceptions.[6]

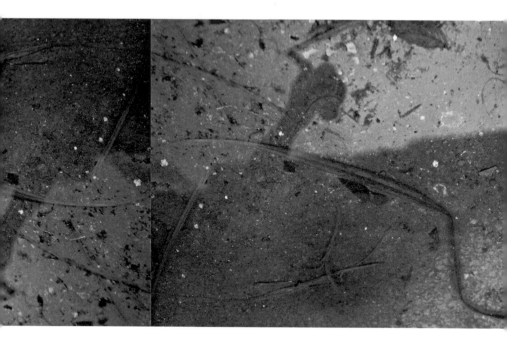

In a drawing representing space and time in granular form: particles, small grains, granules, close to each other. One possible reading of the interactions between the two entities, space/ time. Between grain and grain, there are identifiable spaces/areas/sites, spots that are also recognised as non-spaces, non-continuous fields that form, by virtue of this composition, a network that spans all the granular space.

And the existence of the void that gives meaning to the full, forming a network, is precisely the existence of this empty space between granules, within which filled spaces can develop alternatives to connect with each other, leaving open the possibility of a new interpretation of the relationship between the spaces. Friedman identifies this as a thread, an undulation, the impulse necessary for connectivity and processing.

As is the idea expressed through the concept of the fractal butterfly effect and micro earthquakes resulting in a wave of earth tremors of great magnitude.

The existence of VOIDS or RESERVES or OTHER SPACES can create the possibility of alternative languages. (Here, we could open up the abyss of the possibility of speaking of the limits of and the ambivalence between fear, risk margin and the likelihood/possibility of salvation.)

Other spaces, ambiguous and not identified, not labelled and therefore frightening and awful for most people, are themselves (at least potentially) carriers of the possibility of renewal and the experimental results of the probable adjustments of profit and saving of and in contemporary society. Space bubble reserves as possible responses to change. Yona Friedman's theory introduces the concept of impermeability and the wandering harbinger of positivity, not of fear.

Impermeability forced to seek alternative solutions.the inability to cross a wall forces us to develop other methods of communication with those who are beyond.

Each grain represents individuality and the ability of any person to trigger a hypothetical global transformation, starting with the uniqueness of the individual and the interrelationship that allows for each person to connect with the whole network and with each single individual grain.

It isn't possible to predict what will happen in the present and in the present next, one can only depend on the activity which is immediately before one.

How to say: everything is in the eye and in the bodies of the beholder, and in the transmissibility of perceptions.

Notes
1. On 6 August 2008, ten days after his apparent suicide, United States federal investigators charged Bruce Edwards Ivins as the sole culprit in the 2001 anthrax attacks. The attacks killed five people and are said to have infected nearly 70 others. Ivins was a senior biodefence scientist and an anthrax vaccine co-inventor, listed on two US patents.
2. From YouTube: words spoken in a video recorded under the heading 'Fractal'. In the video, a man sits behind a desk talking like a robot of the relationship between political forces and power and a possible interpretation of the universe conceived and read as a complete fractal emanation.
3. Gilles Clément, **Manifeste du Tiers Paysage**, Copyright © 2004, Copyleft: This work is free; you can redistribute it and/or modify it under the terms of the Free Art Licence.
Available at:
http://www.gillesclement.com/fichiers/_admin_13517_tierspaypublications_92045_manifeste_du_tiers_paysage.pdf (accessed 18 November 2009).
4. Zigmunt Bauman. **La società dell'incertezza** (Il Mulino, 1999, Bologna).
5. Michel Foucault [1975]. **Sorvegliare e punier: la nascita della prigione**, (trans. it.) A. Tarchetti (Einaudi, 1993, Torino).
6. Yona Friedman. **L'ordre compliqué et autres fragments** (Editions de L'éclat, 2008, Paris/Tel Aviv).

Temporary Authoritarian Zone

JOHN ARMITAGE

Consider Virilio's (2002) conception of the contemporary American territorial assemblage, of lines of territorialisation and deterritorialisation and, in particular, the narrative he constructs in *Ground Zero* around the series of events that happened on September 11, 2001 in New York City and Washington DC. Before us, we had a repetition of the first attack on the World Trade Centre in 1993, and the ushering in of a frightening escalation of the new era of terrorism. Indeed, the exceptional aspect of the second attacks in 2001 was that al Qaeda's two primary hijacked airplanes did bring down both of the World Trade Centre buildings. So, September 11, 2001 was yet another strategic event which further corroborated for Americans their passage towards new military assemblages in the 21st century. Thus, with the September 11, 2001 attacks, we had relayed before us acts of 'total war' (Virilio, 2002: 82; original emphases), which were extraordinarily conceived and performed, and with a bare minimum of means. Certainly, as acts of total war, they were very 'simple' manoeuvres. By contrast, the damage inflicted on the Pentagon by the third hijacked airplane was of comparatively little import because "what exploded in people's minds was the World Trade Center, leaving America out for the count" (Virilio, 2002: 82). American capitalism, "the apparent economy of the planet", hence found "itself lastingly affected by the dystopia of its own system" (Virilio, 2002: 82). This, Virilio (2002: 82) tells us, meant that, on September 11, 2001, "the Manhattan skyline became the front of the new war".

To substantiate his claim, Virilio (2002: 82; original emphases) argues that the "anonymity of those who initiated the attack merely signals, for everyone, the rise of a global covert state – of the unknown quantity of a private criminality – that 'beyond-Good-and-Evil' which has for centuries been the dream of the high priests of an iconoclastic progress". But this is where the contemporary problems of the American territorial assemblage arise. For, according to Virilio (2002: frontispiece; original emphases), "the events of September 11 reflect both the manipulation of a global sub-proletariat and the delusions of an élite of rich students and technicians who resemble nothing so much as the 'suicidal' members of the Heaven's Gate cybersect". Undeniably, in today's "American megalopolises", there are increasingly deterritorialised assemblages, sub-proletarian frontiers and movements, areas and districts which are forbidden territories "occupied by an ethnic group foreign to the others, clashing over a building or a street corner" (Virilio, 2002: 77). As Virilio (2002: 77; original emphases) puts it, such machines, such 'resettlement territories', are "urban zones where the margin becomes the mass, a lawless world of deterritorialized destabilization, deception, joblessness, and social de-regulation".

These are the contemporary problems of the American territorial assemblage, and of the American inhabitants of an ever more deterritorialised landscape. Yet Virilio (2002: 78) maintains that Americans have no possible way of escaping the fact that "the terrorist phenomenon begins in everyday life" or the fact that, as Gregory Clancey (2006: 49-76) has written, for much of the 20th century, American 'de-urbanisation' has had its origins in war or warlike conditions and the emulation of the battlefield, which, according to Virilio (2002: 78; original emphases), was "essential to the fanatical advocates of techno-scientific Progress" who "saw that progress as an assault on nature". Furthermore, do not the fantasies of al Qaeda's élite of rich students, by virtue of its acknowledged breaking of the 'civilised' rules of war, and by way of its 'suicide missions' into the heart of global finance capitalism, also abrogate to itself the right and power to drive people in all directions at will, from the September 11, 2001 massacre on the 'battlefield' of New York City to slaughter in the strategic bombing of Washington DC? It is hardly surprising, then, that America's 21st century emblematic spaces are not variations on the city but mutations of the camp, that experimental yet 'Temporary Authoritarian Zone' outside the law involving the quarantine of 'suspicious elements', concentrated yet deterritorialised multicultural populations on the periphery of urban centres, new and diverse resettlement procedures undertaken not far from American towns and cities; camps such as the one built by the American military as part of the 'War on Terror' for detaining 'enemy combatants' in Guantánamo Bay, Cuba. Americans must therefore learn to fear their own territorial assemblage as it inaugurates newly deterritorialised assemblages of civil war within America's own porous borders, within its own, perhaps fatally weakened, democracy. For the continued rise of terrorism alongside multinational drug and human trafficking mafias and so on forge their own forms of militarised movement, panicked immigration, emigration and displacement. Contemporary mechanisms of American 'de-urbanisation', then, are nothing if not the emergence of a global battlefield where sub-humanity is controlled not by technoscientific progress but by organised crime's military assault on the city.

References
- *Clancey, George. "Vast Clearings: Emergency, Technology, and American De-Urbanization, 1930-1945". In* **Cultural Politics** *2 (1), pp. 49-76 (2006).*
- *Virilio, Paul.* **Ground Zero** *(Verso, 2002, London).*

Politics, the State and the Tragedy of Fear
Connected Fragments from Europe to South Asia

ATUL MISHRA

The political promise of modernity was to reduce the influence of fear across social spheres and to eventually conquer it – that this has not happened needs no retelling. Fear has displayed a fantastic durability, and its lingering ubiquity influences, if it does not indeed determine, much of the form and content of contemporary politics. As has become evident, the more modern politics has tried to capture fear, the more it has helped unleash it. This essay probes the dimensions of this contradiction in two main parts. The first outlines the conceptual and historical trajectories of the modern Western state and the problem of fear located within it. The second maps the contours of this contradiction in the politics of India-Pakistan relations. The first part becomes necessary to understand the second because it is through colonialism that the idea and the institution of sovereign statehood were introduced in the South Asian subcontinent. This essay concludes on a pessimistic note.

I

Howsoever one may wish it, the story of the modern non-Western world cannot begin in the non-West. It must start from Europe. Europe, as Dipesh Chakrabarty puts it, is both "inadequate and indispensable" for understanding the modern history of the rest of the world (Chakrabarty, 2000). In the 15th century, especially after the Ottoman forces wrested Constantinople from the Byzantine Empire in 1453, European maritime explorers left the Iberian shores in search of trade routes to the East and for exotica elsewhere. The entrepreneurial romanticism of adventurers like Christopher Columbus, Ferdinand Magellan, Vasco da Gama, Pedro Álvares Cabral et al. gave Europe its Age of Discovery, and the 'discovered' world the age of colonialism. As the Renaissance, the Reformation and the Enlightenment moved Europe away from mediaeval feudalism towards the modern state system, mercantile capitalism acquired colonies for its own survival. Colonialism and the European state system emerged simultaneously. Colonies became Europe's vast experimental laboratory where institutions of modernity, chiefly those of the state, could be tested without pretensions to liberal moderation. How colonialism was justified is often a less important question than the purposes it served.

We must have a glimpse of this history because it is European colonialism which intro-duced modern sovereign states to the rest of the world. Scholars of the inter-discipline of

International Relations (IR) lazily ascribe 1648, the iconic year of the Peace of Westphalia, as the beginning of the state system and modern international politics. The reality is far more complicated. Sovereign European states did not suddenly emerge from the Westphalian big bang. The process – long, gradual, violent, unsettling and terribly uncertain – could have begun as early as the 12th century with the Concordat of Worms of 1122; it culminated in the 20th with World War II.

It would not be misleading to suggest that fear fuelled the development of the European state. The intellectual history of sovereign states in the European tradition deals fundamentally with violence. The crumbling away of the old order made thinkers confront anew the problem of violence and the fear of its consequences. This is evident with the early theorists of state sovereignty. Jean Bodin, the 16th-century French political philosopher and jurist, advocated consolidation of absolute sovereignty as the solution to the civil war-like conditions then prevalent due to the conflict between the Calvinist Huguenots and the Catholic monarchy in France. In *Leviathan*, published in 1651 (three years after Westphalia), Thomas Hobbes invoked the fear of a human life that is "solitary, poore, nasty, brutish and short" to reiterate the desirability of creating an absolute sovereign to rule the state. Hobbes was born prematurely when his mother heard of the coming invasion of the Spanish Armada. "My mother gave birth to twins: myself and fear", he is supposed to have remarked. For a thinker of his fearful times, Hobbes' writings reveal a consistent struggle to overcome them. Two subsequent thinkers of the social contract tradition – John Locke and Jean Jacques Rousseau – give us more relaxed theories of state. But they do not, because they could not, resolve the problem and fear of violence.

Why?

The social contract tradition of theorising the state has arguably been the most influential in so far as the impact of an intellectual tradition on modern states is concerned. What it tries to do with the problem and fear of violence is roughly this: it takes away the right of individuals to indulge in violent activities and assures them a peaceful life in return. It promises a life and society devoid of fear of minor harm and/or unnatural death. The collective potential for executing violence is converted into a right reserved exclusively for the state. The state's police, paramilitary and defence forces become the realised facts of an abstract bargain. The state is accorded the licence to terrorise and kill. And in being able to claim its monopoly over the legitimate use of force rests the state's reason for existence. Put another way, the state appropriates major agencies of fear to itself and promises conditions for what is common-sensibly understood as civil society. But the state must, every now and then, unleash this apparatus of terror to preserve that very civil society from domestic and foreign threat. It ceases to be a state if it cannot do so. It is a tempting contradiction. Because its inherent privileging of order over justice (or any other political ideal for that matter) means that each time the state feels its sovereignty is under threat, it unleashes the forces of fear to, ironically, control fear. No liberal theory of state has successfully managed to resolve this contradiction.

And precisely why is this important for our concern? The fear-state relationship presents itself at both domestic and international levels of politics. In international politics, power differentials are supposed to be the key drivers of fear – of the strong in the bodypolitic of the weak. Thucydides' dictum from the Melian Dialogue of *The History of the Peloponnesian War* – "the strong do what they can and the weak suffer what they must" – is an example of this, to echo a long-cherished habit, the 'timeless wisdom' of realism. In the domestic realm, it is the state's concern for the collapse of order and the possible reign of anarchy which creates and sustains the regime of fear. Bodin and Hobbes both wrote in that tradition. Machiavelli's advice to his prince-ruler, Lorenzo 'the Magnificent' de Medici, that he must instill fear into the minds of the ruled in order to rule without fear of usurpation, was an honest, and for that reason excessively condemned, reflection on the transient nature of politics.

But this division of politics into domestic and international spheres is largely a prop for intellectual convenience. It does not so much reflect reality as it distorts it. In reality, what are generally understood as the domestic and international arenas of political activity collide and collude frequently to blur the neatly-supposed distinctions of within and without. Fear operates and influences politics at both levels. The French Revolution could be an example of this tendency. After the initial momentum had been achieved, the keepers of the Revolution had to save it from counter-revolutionaries at home and from the conservative dynasties of Europe. The Reign of Terror was unleashed to defend the values of the Revolution domestically. The Revolutionary Wars were fought to preserve it from external assault – these became the Napoleonic Wars after 1799. In all, it took seven coalitions of European powers to defeat the revolutionary and republican impulses that had begun in France. The settlement of 1815 was driven by the fear of values that would have revolutionised European politics had they been allowed to succeed. Nearly no assessment of this period can separate the play of violence into neat domestic and international spheres. The guardians of the Revolution feared losing momentum and the Revolution's post-1789 achievements. Fear of the power of the French state (and later Empire) compelled opposing European coalitions to arrest its march. Additionally, the appeal of revolutionary ideas would have caused multiple crises of order in the conservative kingdoms of Germany, Russia and elsewhere. Such domestic-international linkages are more common than scholars of IR generally assume.

II

It is time to move from the West to the Non-West, from Europe to the South Asian subcontinent. The story of India and Pakistan does not begin in 1947, though how far back it can go is best left for historians to debate. The political psychology of fear in India-Pakistan relations has its roots in the same colonialism which grew simultaneously with sovereign European states. Like many things European, colonialism too reached the sub-continental shores early, perhaps as early as the summer of 1498, when a ship from Portugal docked at Calicut. It would take a little over a century for the English East India Company to be formed, slightly more than 250 years for Plassey and three-and-a-half centuries for the Mutiny, or the Revolt. Processes set in motion after the Queen's Proclamation of 1858, when the Crown took over from the Company, became the genesis of the subcontinent's future partitions and, consequently, of a pervasive regime of fear.

After 1858, colonialism began introducing institutions of modern statehood which had by then emerged as the most stable and normatively desirable form of political organisation in Europe. "European ideas take strange forms outside Europe", writes Ashis Nandy (Nandy, 2009). And this was so for the fate of the state in the tropics. (India, thanks to the Tropic of Cancer, is tropical only in the south and temperate in the north. But we are talking metaphor here and not meteorology or geography.) The colonial state's attempt to modernise the individual and collective lives of South Asians produced divergent trends. It fixed the identities of communities and slotted them for the small mercies of representative institutions. Soon, and we are still in the 19th century, cracks began to develop within the colonial state's two communities – Hindus and Muslims. Some who claimed leadership of South Asian Muslims asserted that democracy, reduced to a mere game of numbers, would make Muslims a permanent minority in a predominantly Hindu India. The speeches of Sayyid Ahmad Khan, especially after the late 1860s, reveal this fear of a community supposedly under siege from the political machinations of a modernity born elsewhere.

Once the element of fear entered political relations between Hindus and Muslims, attempts at erasing the recurring lines of distrust returned disappointment. The rulers of the colonial state balanced the fears of both political communities to their advantage. British rule could continue only by keeping the Muslim leadership fearful of the Hindu majority and its consequences. The continued existence of separate electorates hardened hostilities and created differences, even where none existed. There was little the secular nationalists could do to assuage the fear of the Muslim community other than reiterate elements of India's composite culture and petition the colonial state for inclusive policies.

By the late 1930s, the distrust had intensified. The result of the 1937 elections and the politics of the Hindu Right seemed to confirm the fear of minority persecution. Under Jinnah's new leadership, the minority proclaimed its wish to not remain a minority. It wanted to become a separate and equal nation. As much as was declared with categorical certainty in March 1940 at Lahore. Everything else about the future of this now separate nation was kept vague and imprecise, perhaps deliberately so. The political contingencies of the 1940s – when the world was full of fear – could do nothing to reverse the plunge towards partition. When several colonial and some local formulas for power-sharing failed, partition was accepted with the hope that the two communities would exist peacefully in neighbouring states.

But partition merely internationalised an essentially domestic regime of fear. It did not resolve the problem. India and Pakistan, now two sovereign states, emerged dissatisfied from partition. The Indian state was unhappy because Pakistan was the reality of its failure. Pakistan was a stolen geography. Pakistan was a spurious ideology. Pakistan was a successful, even if inadequate, challenge to Indian nationalism during the colonial phase. Pakistan was a nation built out of fantasy. Pakistan was a claimant to a territory (of Kashmir) it never possessed. Pakistan was all that and a state which could not represent itself cartographically without acknowledging India's existence between its two parts. Partition had created a Pakistan inextricably linked to India. It was not an agreeable arrangement at all.

The Pakistani state was unhappy too. It was unhappy because it felt it had gotten an unfair deal. It was "mutilated, truncated and moth-eaten" (Jinnah's words) even before it came into being. Kashmir did not come to it. Neither did all the subcontinent's Muslims. India decided to become a constitutionally secular democracy. The fact of India's secular identity rendered baseless, at least in principle, the fear of minority persecution which had fuelled the Pakistan movement. If Pakistan was the land of the Muslims of South Asia, why did more Muslims choose to stay in India? These were reasons enough for Pakistan to envy India.

Over the past six decades, this mutual dissatisfaction has shaped India and Pakistan's bilateral relations. Wars, territorial disputes, India's role in Bangladesh's independence in 1971, Pakistan's role in fomenting trouble in Kashmir and a host of other issues have kept the enmity alive.

The play of fear in India-Pakistan relations since 1947 has operated at two levels – domestic and international. Internationally, it has been guided by an asymmetrical distribution of material capabilities between the two countries. India was and has been in a position of relative advantage when it comes to material capabilities – geographical expanse, defence infrastructure, demographic strength, size and performance of the economy, etc. – that conventionally make a state powerful. Pakistan is big and powerful. But power is a relative thing. It was and has remained weak when compared to India.

If punitive capabilities are unequally distributed between two countries, as they have been in India's favour, we are expected to see the weak crawl up to the strong for mercy and/or carrots. The weak must do so to survive the existential threat posed by the strong. By this logic, Pakistan, following Thucydides' ancient advice, should submit to India's regional superiority and accept the policies that flow from New Delhi's capabilities. Conversely, the stronger of the two is expected to act the way strong states do: normal and confident, a little pompous and occasionally boastful. India has appeared all of that on occasion. But Indian policies betray the jitter beneath its apparent normalcy. For its size, and, more importantly, that of Pakistan's, India has remained excessively preoccupied with all things Pakistani. This is so despite the fact that Pakistan does not, again because it cannot, pose India an existential threat. On its part, Pakistan knows it cannot win a conventional war with India. It has not so far. It does not have second-strike capability in case of nuclear war either. And yet it has sought to keep pace with India militarily.

None of this makes rational sense. Inherent in this oddity, which would appear endearingly puerile if it wasn't so potentially deadly, is the lingering persistence of fear that marks this relationship. India has remained fearful of the unpredictable actions their asymmetrical capabilities may induce from Pakistan. Pakistan has been afraid of everything Indian that continues to question the very basis of its existence. They share a tragic relation of fear.

The tragic relation of fear is compounded further by a domestic preference for order over everything else. And this is the second level at which the play of fear has operated in India-Pakistan relations. Given the severe crisis of order Pakistan is currently going through, it would be tempting to offer the patriotic suggestion that India has long resolved its own crisis of order. Nothing could be further from the truth. Partition left a permanent scar on the

Indian and Pakistani states. The form of post-1947 nationalism in both countries has contained elements of bashing the partitioned other to keep the domestic house in order. That this tendency has been more pronounced in Pakistan than in India could be explained very substantially by the relative success of Indian democracy and the resources at its disposal. Additionally, Pakistan came into existence in a space that has been a geopolitical nightmare for centuries. All the paraphernalia of the British colonial state could barely infiltrate, let alone tame, the unruly frontier and tribal areas. That the Pakistan state has not performed any better should hardly come as a surprise.

For both states, sovereignty has been the performative tool through which domestic order is sought to be preserved. The sovereignty of one state has very often been asserted in relation to a perceived threat from the other. The politics of nuclear weapons is illustrative here. Both countries have frequently invoked the threat to their sovereignty from each other to justify the possession of nuclear weapons and for increasing the number of warheads they possess. It is not difficult to recall the consistency with which Pakistan's historical and contemporary personages – from Zulfiqar Ali Bhutto to Zia ul Haq, from AQ Khan to Pervez Musharraf – have underlined the importance of nuclear weapons for their country's sovereignty. The temper of expression has been far more sedate and low key in India, which is largely because neither military nor scientific personnel in India are encouraged to voice their wisdom on sensitive political matters. But the general sentiment that nuclear weapons have ensured India sovereignty against all malicious designs originating from Pakistan, or a Pakistan-and-China combine, is reciprocally similar.

Sovereignty, then, has been this hallowed idea, quality or thing that both states have brandished to overcome the underlying fear of each other and of their distinct selves. But because the sovereign states of India and Pakistan remain linked by a common bond of dissatisfaction and enmity, the very project of asserting sovereign separateness runs into the political equivalent of a tautology. The more sovereign the two states try to become vis-à-vis each other, the more mutual insecurity they produce. The more insecure they become, the more they try to overcome it by investing in policies that would strengthen their sovereignty. The circle could go on indefinitely. And it's the people of the two states who bear the cost and consequences of this irrationality.

This failure to establish sovereign autonomy further deepens the tragic relation of fear between the states of India and Pakistan. Are we then condemned to perpetual despair? The answer depends on two things. First, we need to decide whether or not this condition is normatively acceptable. For reasons that cannot be elaborated here, the answer would rarely be a simple yes or no. But supposing it is not. Supposing we find this condition normatively unacceptable, we need to face a second question: is it possible to break out of this regime of fear while retaining the artifice of sovereign statehood?

Again, the answer may not be a simple yes or no. But chances are we cannot break out of this regime of fear without doing away with sovereign states altogether. We have seen earlier how sovereign states are faced with the problem of violence and fear both domestically and internationally, and how they cannot resolve the contradiction successfully. It is essentially the same dilemma that confronts us here. Except that, in postcolonial states like India and Pakistan, the politics of sovereignty assumes an excessively hysterical form. The history of colonial subjugation makes sovereignty a prized possession. The nationalist narrative of hard-earned sovereignty and the problems of existing in a world not of one's making make any meaningful discussion on moving away from sovereignty difficult, perhaps even heretical. This is clearly evident when we consider how nervously sensitive both India and Pakistan become when it comes to any real or imaginary threat to their sovereignty. It's a different matter altogether that sovereignty is effectively traded in nearly every governmental policy, domestic and foreign.

As long as sovereign states remain the predominant and most popular frames for political refraction, we are unlikely to overcome the pervasive regime of fear. Sovereign states are not divinely ordained certainties. They are facts of human creation that have been more durable and more efficient than other competing modes of political organisation. But they are ultimately transient. Indeed, like in the past, Europe *may* be in the process of constructing a new form of political community. But these are early days for that project. It is the paucity of our collective political imagination that keeps us enslaved to the logic of sovereign statehood despite reasonable evidence that it does human beings more harm than good.

Author's Note
I am grateful to Dr Siddharth Mallavarapu for his encouraging guidance and support which allow insurgent theoretical thinking. Thanks to Swapna Kona Nayudu and Shane Boris for promptly and patiently reading and thus improving the essay. Conversations with Shane have produced much meaning and wisdom. I alone am responsible for errors of fact and interpretation.

References
- *Chakrabarty, Dipesh.* **Provincializing Europe: Postcolonial Thought and Historical Difference** *(Princeton University Press, 2000, Princeton), p. 19.*
- *Nandy, Ashis. "Partition and the Fantasy of a Masculine State". In* **The Times of India,** *29 August 2009.*

Symptomatic Values beyond the Romantic

MARKUS MIESSEN

Sometimes, one could argue, in order for democracy to emerge, democracy itself has to be avoided at all costs. To make decisions within any given collaborative structure, network or institution, conflicts can ultimately only be overcome if someone assumes responsibility.

Gustav Metzger once said: "I relate my approach to homeopathy, which puts poison in the system in order to generate energy to defeat the weakness". In this context, let us imagine a post-consensual practice, one no longer reliant on the often ill-defined modes of operating within politically complex and consensus-driven parties or given political constructs, but drawn instead from an understanding of the necessity to undo the innocence of participation.

We are currently experiencing a point of transition within participatory practices: within politics, within the Left, within spatial practices and – foremost – within architecture as its visible and most clearly defined product. Participation, both historically and in terms of political agency, is often read through romantic notions of negotiation, inclusion and democratic decision-making. However, it is precisely this often-unquestioned mode of inclusion that populist politicians use as a mode of campaigning for retail politics. Hence, it does not produce critical results as criticality stands challenged by the conception of majority. Let us instead imagine a conflictual reading of participation as a mode of practice, one that opposes the brainwave of the democratic facilitator, one that has to assume, at times, non-physical violence and singular decision-making in order to produce frameworks for change.

As a next step, let us challenge the idea that – in general – people have good intentions. Conventional models of participation are based on inclusion. They assume that inclusion goes hand-in-hand with a standard that is the democratic principle of everyone's voice having an equal weight within an egalitarian society. (Interestingly, the model of the 'curator', for example, is essentially based on the practice of making decisions and therefore eliminating choice, rather than boosting plurality by inclusion.) Usually, through the simple fact of proposing a structure or situation in which this bottom-up inclusion is promoted, the political actor or agency proposing it will most likely be understood as a 'do-gooder', a social actor or even a philanthropist. In the face of permanent crisis, both the Left and the Right have celebrated participation as the saviour from all evil, an unquestioned form of soft politics. But can we employ the idea of crisis to question our deepest assumptions? Should we rethink our values and devise new principles for action?

Let us imagine a conception of participation as a way to enter politics – proactively and consciously forcing us into existing power-relations by intent – as opposed to a politically motivated model of participation, which tends to propose to let others contribute to the decision-making process. The latter, we might think, is habitually stirred by the craving for political legitimisation. The former may attract attention not from a disbelief in democratic principles per se, but out of sheer interest in critical and productive change.

One could argue that this model inhabits a certain opportunism. Yes and no. It challenges the widespread default that majority equals judiciousness, while arguing for a pro-active citizenship in which the individual outsider to a given, inbred political structure can become a driving force for change, forcefully entering an existing discourse rather than opening it up to the floor. Remaining within the arena of 'the democratic', let us instead bastardise participation into a form of non-democratic practice, an opportunistic model of intervention-ism, in which interference is made possible due to the fact that one is no longer following existing protocols of internalised political struggle. Such a model, we could then argue, is that of Crossbench Practice.

Let us imagine this as an ongoing project. Let us begin now. As a first step, let us attempt to open up a new language of practice, a field of operation, rather than confronting an existing one. Within this frame, let us unleash a series of experiments that shall be conducted over time. Each of those experiments shall be directed towards the undoing of the innocence of participation. Some of them may be text-based, others set up as projects, others again as urban interventions or institutional models – small-scale, local test-grounds for change.

Each one of those projects to come shall be understood as particles within a galactic model in which planets are circulating around an empty void. This void may be loaded with a model for practice by the end of the experiment. The model may present and open questions neither hierarchically organised nor in a field, but in the form of a galaxy – a relational model that challenges political romanticism to open up the potential for a more diffused form of work.

Within a series of case studies conducted over the past years, this essay is intended as part of a pamphlet that is the third component within a tripartite structure that, resulting from increasing gradients of political disillusionment, attempts to question existing notions of participatory practice. The first in this series simply questioned participation.[1] The second kicked it.[2] The third, which may be titled *Crossbench Praxis*, will eventually propose an alternative.

What will be presented as a project in question is a theory of how to participate from outside existing power structures rather than inside-out. Where traditionally participation is understood as a bottom-up practice, the one being examined here sidesteps the democratic invitation process and enters the conversation mid-level, from the side, so to speak, exposing the often-concealed dead end of participation.

What is/are the alternative(s) to conventional confrontation based on the nostalgic notion of the barricade? How can one propose an alternative practice engaging in spatial projects dealing with social and political realities? What could such polyphonic practice potentially be? What is the mode of relevance of such work and does it always necessitate in 'urgent relevance'? But let us not concentrate too much on the urgent as we might forget about the important.

A substantiated mode of 'scattered practice' could put life as practice into a format that uses, as a starting point, the will to act without mandate. Such self-initiated practice, outside of those existing economies in which there is a clear distinction between client and service provider, may enter and in fact produce an alien discourse or field of knowledge productively.

Spatial planning is often considered as the management of spatial conflict. Like the original meaning of the Latin word *conflictus* (fight), spatial conflict represents a clash of interests in using space: who should do what, when and how? The city – and, indeed, the progressive institution – exists as a conglomerate of social and spatial conflict zones, renegotiating their limits through constant transformation. To deal with conflicts, critical decision-making must evolve. Such decision-making is often presupposed as a process whose ultimate goal is consensus. Opposing the politics of consensus, critical spatial practice shall foster micro-political participation in the production of space, and ask the question of how one can contribute to alien fields of knowledge, professions or discourses from the point of view of 'space'. The future spatial practitioner could arguably be understood as an outsider who, instead of trying to set up or sustain common denominators of consensus, enters existing situations or projects by deliberately instigating conflicts between often-delineated fields of knowledge.

To enquire into the role of the architect and the role of the contemporary institution, existing models of participation may be in need of revision, both in terms of the culture of consensus and the ethos of compromise. We may detect a need for actors who operate from outside existing networks of expertise, leaving behind circles of common proficiency and attempting to overlap with other post-disciplinary realities. Instead of aiming for synchronisation, such a model could be based on participation through critical distance and the conscious implementation of zones of conflict. Within such zones, one could imagine the dismantling of existing situations so as to strategically isolate components that could be (mis)used to stir friction. Such practice would help to understand the effects of political, economic and social design components on space. Using the architect's expertise in mapping fields of conflict, we may generate an archipelago of questions that seek to uncover the relevance of spatial and architectural expertise and how, in the remit of institutions, they can generate an alternative knowledge production.

Rather than delivering a recipe, we may lay out a field of potential departures that might allow us to understand what and how an architect can contribute to the questions at hand, tracing some of the above elements in order to create a selective and operational view. What makes an architect's approach to investigating a situation different from the default approaches of other fields of knowledge? What is the value of an Uninvited Outsider, a Cross-bench Practitioner, when juxtaposed to a classical, market-driven consultancy methodology? Why the hell talk to architects in the first place?

Let us try to read the phenomenon of participation through a chain of variable spectacles, depending on the respective and diversified angles of observation. In regard to political science, the core relevant arguments of Chantal Mouffe and Antonio Gramsci may be put in context of and into conflict with the British New Labour model or, indeed, the even more consensus-driven Dutch Polder model. Within the larger remit of late 20th-century philosophy, the writings of Jacques Rancière and Edward Said could be examined, most specifically the latter's *Representations of the Intellectual.*[3] Concerning spatial practices, the practice of soft thinking in architecture could be read through Keller Easterling or Eyal Weizman. We can draw from texts by Marius Babias and Dieter Lesage to open up the field of critical discourse within contemporary artistic practices, as well as from Florian Schneider's thoughts about the notion of collaboration. German politician Joschka Fischer's biography may be hijacked in order to produce a case study to illustrate the intricacies of Gramsci's slow march through the institutions.

Let us hope that this imaginary methodology will constitute evidence for the question at hand. The resulting material may constitute neither a historic survey nor a report from the front lines of activism, but may at best be a self-generated concoction of diversified support-structures to demystify romanticised participatory practices – a confined voice that allows us to further differentiate the existing discourse while stimulating an already-heated debate. In fact, this may not even be a methodology but a nightmare. A nightmare with a productive end. It may be neither approved by academics, nor possibly will it be read by commuters on the train. It will probably not enter the canon of history or be available in a public library. And precisely there may lie the transition-point of opportunity: to produce a condition of politics by considering things before they exist – to speculate with force.

The perhaps autocratic model of participation that I will put up for discussion should not be understood as a blueprint for practice but as a model of departure. It may start to create the necessary friction in order to both stir debate and move practice forward. If there was only a single objective of this experiment, it may be to develop a common understanding and a starting point to begin to disagree from – a theory of how to participate without squinting at constituencies or voters, but by instigating critical debate and, at best, change. There may be two arguments here, one polemical and the other conceptually constructive, both stirred by pragmatic optimism and both, at times, developed through concrete situations and projects, which Simon Critchley would call "situated universality".[4]

Author's Note
This text is based on thoughts that are currently producing **Crossbench Praxis** *(forthcoming, Sternberg Press, 2009).*

Notes
1. (Eds.) Markus Miessen and Shumon Basar. **Did Someone Say Participate, An Atlas of Spatial Practice** *(MIT Press, 2006, Cambridge, MA).*
2. (Ed.) Markus Miessen. **The Violence of Participation** *(Sternberg Press, 2007, Berlin/New York).*
3. Edward Said. **Representations of the Intellectual: The 1993 Reith Lectures** *(Random House, 1996, New York).*
4. Simon Critchley. **Indefinetely Demanding: Ethics of Commitment, Politics of Resistance** *(Verso, 2007, London), p. 42.*

fear/fɪr / ll/fɪe(r)/ n. *uncountable or countable*[1]

ANDRÉS DE SANTIAGO AREIZAGA

Fear as medium, not message.
Fear as economic value, as currency, as exchange rate.
Fear as collateral.
Fear as import and export.
Fear as the force behind progress.
Fear as refuge, as home, as the reinforcer of national pride.
Fear as the potlatch of colonialism and the war on terror.
Fear as President.
Fear as Facebook friend, as Twitter follower, as search engine.
Fear as style.
Fear as character.
Fear as tradition.
Fear as the new Wild West.

The American frontier moved gradually westward decades after the settlement of the first white immigrants on the Eastern seaboard in the 1600s. The 'West' was always the area beyond that boundary...

Through treaties with foreign nations and native peoples, political compromise, technological innovation, military conquest, establishment of law and order, and the great migrations of foreigners, the United States expanded from the coast to the coast (Atlantic Ocean-to-Pacific Ocean), fulfilling its belief in Manifest Destiny. In securing and managing the West, the US federal government greatly expanded its powers, as the nation grew from an agrarian society to an industrialised nation...

As the American Old West passed into history, the myths of the West took firm hold in the imagination of Americans and foreigners alike.[2]

Origins and Convictions

Certitude is Fear, and Fear descriptive discovery. Not just as feeling but as discipline, responsibility and expression. Intolerant to disorder and assertiveness, Fear builds on inherited beauty and the relocation of status and respectability, its foundations nowadays inherent in a denationalised American post-modern dream.

Historically, the use of photographic resemblance (imprinting its new version of reality in series) as metaphor for Western progress, of brand image as friendly guidance and reliable statistic for knowledge, turned the search for the ultimate frontier into a matter shaping national security – masked under the mystified moniker of enterprise and vision. Ever-increasing speed in technology and information alike developed express companies, highway patrols, franchises and correspondents into entities servicing abstract revenue, both in operational terms and consumer influence. The network activated the negative pole of telegraphic machinery, smoke signals were intercepted, and the dreamt paradise faltered.

With horizontal communication widely deployed by then, every threat turned into an offer, and every intimidation into a lobby. The car started sanding the asphalt it itself demanded and heated up (but never financed), and the household became more and more a blog version of the mart – resettling, wiring, specialising, upgrading and archiving.

Staples

Common display of domestic values and the anxiety of possession, accelerated by digitalisation, counterbalance the disorder orchestrated by intranet news and the resurgence of social participation. A neighbour is still labelled an a priori friend and accomplice of the everyday routine space, but keeps being pushed back by e-socialising – the traditionally assumed relationship/association suddenly regarded as insecure and not to be trusted. Why knock on the door when we can mouse click?

Consumerist societies familiar with Fear have not forgotten the potential use of rejection for its own good. The warranty of appliances, electrical gadgets and family products, granted for the consumer's conscience, are presented as improvers of quality and service, but more than offered guarantees, they are hidden ransom demands. It is in this perilous scheme of experience barter (where no bargains are to be made) that Fear consolidates itself as necessary item, as commodity and as unpossessed source of wealth. For, in order to benefit from its powers, Fear neither needs to be owned nor to be too literally controlled, just adequately administrated. And what better strategy to induce this forum of Fear than through its random rationing – driving consumers and producers into surveyed panic, letting go of the wheel just to steer back on track.

Control

The comfort of interacting as part of a hospitable network (supposedly developing to a great extent thanks to its own members and users) facilitates management and rule by media purveyors. What most users do not seem to be able to grasp is that the Internet is in itself content, and that the assumption of freedom of speech powered by accessibility is just an illusion triggered by the medium itself and produced by an instinct of defence and survivalism. Yet safety does not mitigate Fear, as Fear, partly passive and covered, does not expect reflex reaction.

Automated in mode and intolerant in function, Fear operates, creating influences of interrelation and service exchange, entwining a web of multiplied favours against instant transaction. Fear is not a product and does not expect its agents to behave as such. With mechanical serial production and the traditional chain of command surpassed, the channelling of previous organisation charts based on folklore and feudalism into future virtualities has become a matter of the utmost importance to secure boundaries and minimum shelter. Our walled structures, ceasing to be protected (and protective) environments, barricade kin relationships in the distance while, at the same time, making the very spaces they wish to save at home vulnerable by means of fragmented inclusiveness.

The secluded and evading face of anachronisms in ages of anxiety and instantaneousness has finished pushing evolution forward. That is why the experience of danger, the feeling of threat, has survived across the last centuries and has now, with the permanent interrelation and viral accessibility between social networks and platforms at a global level, acquired a quality of permanence and a status of benign chronic disease.

Expedition(s)

Men are moved by two levers only: fear and self interest.[3]

   The domestic securing of one's own entourage by prevention and concomitant warning further motivates Fear to develop itself, to adapt and to prosper. After Fear proved its viral nature for an industrious pulling of the strings in practical anonymity, the scope of the investment and the interest collection predicted lost sole mathematical approach and passed on to the realm of the abstract. Fear was no news, no information, no involved medium. Fear became classified and specialised knowledge and, once founded, looked to become applied and to infiltrate. Following the enclosure of the immediate primeval entourage, Fear expanded to neighbouring territories with no border in mind, looking only to diversify, be implemented and produce an exchange rate to keep in the loop.

   Through blind belief in progress understood and materialised as narrative surplus, dwellings expanded, soil was prospected, transportation got faster, buildings grew taller and men fought and counterattacked harder and harder. Contrary to our economic, industrial and land growth, Fear was not bigger, but it was definitely better. Subsidised and diversified, with franchises and sister companies, Fear shattered the frontier and held the innovations it itself had fostered at stake with the help of human excess: natural resources dried up, crashes were stronger and hijacks more frequent, collapses higher and targets more numerous, everyday relationships harsher and reactions more violent.

The resources of Fear itself, feeling the menace of extinction, led to a new expansion – of Fear as a whole, of the culture, meaning and message of Fear, and the unpredictability of its extremist twin version: terror.

Have Fear, Will Travel

It takes two to make an accident.[4]

As for now, in the aftermath of a non-documented historical event in constant progress, traditions are no longer experienced as traditional in the vicariously age-old world of the West, and the rising of Eastern economies is just a secondhand headline, documenting a drift started decades ago.

One skill that Fear has learnt fast is that once the presence in the arena has been made and running blood has been staged, it is best to act through absence than through exposure, migrating the main body of activities to a third market. In order to carry out this presence without visibility, with no licencing, the forging of partnerships and alliances operating under their original name is key, and a potential creator of new forms of Fear on its own. The Western shareholders of Fear might feel now that some control has to be exercised, that an ownership has to be acknowledged and established. Too patronising for Fear – and too late in time.

Fear is at this very moment playing doubles with The Other and, as usual, keeps winning, no matter the surface, the referee or the opponent. The Other has taken his chance, keeps fit, sweats and enjoys the abundance of serves, scoring the aces. But it is Fear who plays and wins.

Fear caresses. Fear embarrasses. Fear manages. Fear rocks.

Notes

1. Wordreference.com–English-Spanish Dictionary. Available at:
http://www.wordreference.com/es/translation.asp?tranword=fear (accessed 14 January 2010).
2. Wikipedia, the free encyclopedia. "American Old West" (redirected from "Wild West"). Available at:
http://en.wikipedia.org/wiki/Wild_West (accessed 5 August 2009).
3. Brainy Quote: Famous Quotes and Quotations. "Napoleon Bonaparte", p. 3. Available at:
http://www.brainyquote.com/quotes/authors/n/napoleon_bonaparte_3.html (accessed 3 November 2009).
4. Francis Scott Fitzgerald [1925]. **The Great Gatsby** *(Wordsworth Classics, 2001, London), p. 39.*

Just Fear Not Just Reason

RAHUL GOVIND

Fear is already too caught up in the imperative – do not fear – a word enmeshed in its use as negation. This negative imperative captures the autocratic archaic of that which meaning is unable to educt; concealing the content that it lacks. For it appears today a matter of fact that fear – the word – has lost its hold, easily kidnapped by sentences all and sundry. In this it is closest to reason whose use (grammar) is falsely accomplished by banishing precisely that which is germane to it: the certainty and uncertainty of which it can never be certain. In convincing what resists it is unable to ascertain the difference between expression and conversion. To do so would be one or becoming the other. To be it has to possibly not be itself – evidence distinct from and distinctive of the thesis – and so being it can never be characterised or have (be) content. Not dissimilarly, fear is never distinguishable from its possibility which remains indistinct in its imperative negation: sign, locus and invocation of itself. Their exchange value lies in exhibition. Panic as a word – symbolic charge rather than language use – does today what fear never is but whose clue lies in the etymological trenches of the dictionary: "sudden attack or danger, calamity". Overexposure and the loss of resolution – visual and practical – allow panic to take the baton off fear.

With Hobbes standing in for modernity fear is indentured into political ontology. Natural reason – acting as a strong mitigant – designates in its rationality the possibility of differentiating nature from culture as civil/political. However fear as overwhelmingly – not merely – affective effectively pushes in the other direction: it embodies culture as the (vengeful) ghost of nature. Culture as civil political is its awakening and expulsion: how else to capture the former as distinctively different from the latter, a distinction that lies precisely in the possibility of lapsing into the indistinct i.e. nature the body whose boundaries and (thereby) unity is never clear, inherently manifold as it is. What falls through is the distinction between sovereignty by acquisition and sovereignty by institution. Whether we – emerging from nature – come together because we fear each other or whether we subject ourselves in abject – beginning here a long afterlife of the subject in political theory – condition to she who threatens our life and (whom) we fear, it makes little of difference.[1] The calamity of nature is recognisable in the (re)cognition that is capitulation to sense at the cost of an irreducible yet nonetheless timely lag i.e. recapitulation. This is rationality, always but a moment or too late. In being-late it makes amends by emending what it purportedly explains. A failed essay at concealing catachresis: that what is being explained and the fact of explaining are wholly inextricable (from eachother). Fear is justified fear. Just fear as just fear. Taking flight from the reverberation of affect i.e. the vibration of what is embodied – nature as body encrypting sprit at the limit of signifying it – it is let loose into the vacuous rationality of imperative. Now just ise what just does.

Have no fear. (otherwise you will have much to fear voices reason). Is the violence of command – how different from assurance when it is effective – a refuge for sense? Reason has nothing to fear but (fear) itself. If the latter has been said to be rationality, it already infects it with what would have to be left alien. Rationality has to alienate itself – explain itself in terms of what it is not – to evade the charge of vacuity even while it loses ratio. This is the monstrous body, subjective correlate of the 'political' state of nature – since only the body has no ratio as the material and residue of the inference that is one – always a moment away from lapsing into or achieving at a stand-still, the "kingdom of tranquil laws".[2] Pure reason and pure nature have thereby little to distinguish themselves, perpetually fading they cast culture, as their always final card ventriloquising right: how else to (mistakenly) identify one as (universal) subject. In the monochromatic monotony of tone, the president of a country less than 15 years from becoming a nuclear hit man had said, "There is nothing more to fear more than fear itself". This ignited: mushrooming Japanese skies.

Brilliant – and deeply profound – in an age awash with fear. One doesn't have had to have had to have had..../to have traversed the thicket of the Dialectic of Enlightenment to know that nature and culture hardly offer up a self-evident ratio: not merely when held hostage by the bomb. The two terms if discrete alternate only though the self-definition of one; if traced through a third we arrive at an ex-termination i.e. regress, death passing out, passing out... never past out. There fore-defining human nature involves an expulsion whose irrepressible return has been signified as 'second nature' (with an indefinable coefficient). There is a connect between the received wisdom of the president of the country-prior-to-its-becoming- a-nuclear adventurer and a selective rendering of Hobbes that allows crass – cultureless - *real* politik. Counter to Hobbes himself, the hobbessians' effort to construct a state of nature are scarcely aware and callously unaware of the nature/culture of construction. Thereby conceived – as natural – such miscarriage is monstrous pure and simple, impure and confused. Nothing in-between such realism and complete destruction – destruction fanning out catastrophe from the hub of foreign – alien – affairs. The formalism of political philosophy and its mainstream traditions is condensed in the vacuity of the line, "there is nothing more to fear than fear itself". The emptiness within blinds it to the destruction it wrecks 'else'where: where else? Reiterating nature/culture with no ratio determining self and alien is but a unilateral one. In other words, the realism of nature – the primitive insistence that the alien should be possibly exterminated when perceived – is indiscernible from an alienation which has ingested possibility as existence.

Panic one imagines – one cannot be hopeful – is the possibility of conscious fear. It captures a leak gushing across the object continua without limit demanding (and desiring) the subject. Affective it hasn't been subjectivised into an object. It exists for a subject in so far as it is recognised not as known but incurred. This signifies itself only in false embodiment. Objectification can only be the expression – whether vague or inaccurate – of subject-perception. This is feeling which feels itself without self-contradiction in a way that knowledge can never know itself with contradiction. The subject-object polarity of a knowing that can never itself be known iterative displacement as just comeuppance – is transposed into an alternation of subject-object as concatenation: symbolising inadequacy it invokes the adequate. More rational than rationality such an act is conscious of its act and not suicidal – in the form of knowing – when revealing of the so called object: the all pervading inheritance of a naïve epistemology. This records the rage on the part of the latter which knows it can never know and worse feels it to be so: rationality here as always is lapsing affect. Just fear condensing on the brink of nature, a no-body. It just ise.

The *work* – and the (politically) incumbent raw-material – is missing in the political analysis of today which is just rationality, no different from fear. It immures itself from thinking the outbreak – not merely in the form of disease or terror – but the specter and only chance of the subject. This in the meanwhile is documented as naturalised reason: it is reasonable to fear the stranger; we are time and again warned not to befriend the unknown person. (Who else can one *befriend*?). What had induced the need for politics in the first place is reiterated in a state of nature without exit. It is only in this condition that we can speak of justice as fairness referring to 'practices' all the while obliterating the distinction between the two – principle and practice – which can be made only in principle. Practice retracts into the former now emptied of distinction, leaving nothing more (or less) to explain, account for, or investigate. Neither interested in what the State does ('modern constitutional democracies' are axiomaticised) nor in what they are, description, justification and explanation recede into a thought experiment without issue. A return to Roosevelt's motto, not word for word, there is nothing more just than the treatment of justice itself. Veiled ignorance[3] – not unlike the old state of nature – has escaped its laboratory becoming all pervasive. Meanwhile new erstwhile wars mushroom with prediction as justification – this is what time without content can do – that they too will become erstwhile. A blind faith is what just is.

Notes

1. Immanuel Kant. **Perpetual Peace and Other Essays.** *(Trans.) Ted Humphrey (Hackett, 1983, Indianapolis), p. 112. Kant of course famously follows Hobbes here, notwithstanding stated positions. "However a man (or a people) who is merely in a state of nature denies me this security and injures me merely by being in this state. For although he does not actively injure me, he does so by virtue of the lawlessness of his state by which he constantly threatens me, and I can require him either to enter with me into a state of civil law or to remove himself from my surrounding". The state wherein one requires the other to enter into a 'civil state' or remove him is left – and has to be left – indefinite. And, perhaps more importantly, how does one distinguish one from the other, the subject from he who is made an object (of action). As an aside it might be said that Hobbes' autobiography is a biography of fear. In his mother's womb, when she trembled with fear at the approach of the Spanish Armada, Hobbes is claimed to have said, he was then born a twin to fear.*

2. Georg Wilhelm Friedrich Hegel. **Phenomenology of the Spirit.** *(Trans.) AV Miller (Oxford University Press, 1977, Oxford), p. 91. "Consequently the supersensible world is an inert realm of laws which, though beyond the perceived world – for this exhibits law only through incessant change – is equally present in it and is its tranquil image".*

3. There is no need for a veil of ignorance regarding what is being referred to here.

Industrial Landscapes

MEDIA LAB, JADAVPUR UNIVERSITY

The Jadavpur University Media Lab has undertaken a major visual archiving project on the closed National Instruments Limited (NIL) factory in Kolkata. This is the first chapter in the Lab's exploration of the city's industrial ruins. The intention is to explore the relationship between abandoned industrial landscapes, the experience of an urban space in transition and the practice of everyday archiving.

The Lab commissioned ten young filmmakers to shoot for six months on the NIL campus. An archive of about 65 hours of video and 20,000 stills has been created. This is a common pool from which filmmakers and artists are creating blogs, experimental shorts, documentaries, etc.

The factory has been taken over by Jadavpur University, and will soon turn into a new campus. It wears the look of a place teeming with activity, abandoned in haste. Machines, furniture, personal effects, files, telephone sets, workers' overalls, lie in a vast graveyard of what was a once-remarkable site of industry and innovation. Elegant pieces of half-finished products lie scattered on desks and floors. All of this has been captured in detail. Alongside, testimonies of former workers have been recorded.

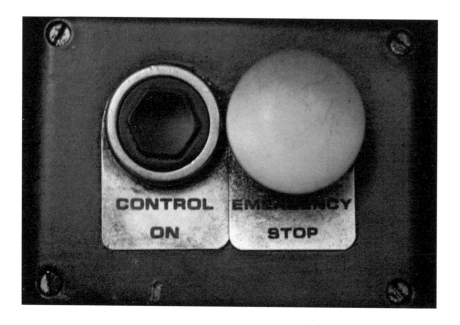

SCARE QUOTES

Who's Afraid of Voting?
The Inexpressible Nature of Some Fears

SUBUHI JIWANI

The dot on my index finger nail has been moving stealthily towards the edge. It is the show-sign of patriotism. I have voted, and this is supposed to make me a good Indian. The television commercials for the *Jaago Re* One Billion Votes campaign, broadcast before the elections, insist that you're sleeping if you don't vote, that you aren't actualising your existence. They're niftily crafted and catchy, and they stirred me. At 29, I had this niggling feeling that I was an apolitical, bourgeois citizen who hadn't exercised her right to participate in democracy.

However, it wasn't the sudden realisation of unfulfilled political duties or steadfast national pride that had awoken me. I'd been awake – wide-eyed, shaken-out-of-my-sleep awake – since late February 2002. I registered to vote because I was afraid of a Hindu nationalist party coming to power in Maharashtra or at the Centre; of Gujarat 2002 happening in Mumbai; of being a number among the riot toll of Muslim women raped or maimed or killed in the streets. This fear had multiplied itself within me and grown another organism: the fear of being on the electoral roll.

I had lived through the 1992-93 riots in Bombay (then the city's name) as a young girl on the cusp of puberty. Initially, I was disgruntled that people in faraway Ayodhya had decided to tear down a mosque on my birthday. After a rather damp morning of Cadbury chocolate distribution, I returned home feeling deprived of an entire day of wishes and attention. I remember taking the Andheri flyover that morning and thinking, 'It's never been this empty before'. There was a perceptible atmosphere of gloom, of confusion, and I felt the beginnings of fear. But it was soon replaced by the thrill of no school for three months and endless games of relay in the building compound. In fact, escaping my building's boundaries became particularly exciting because my parents had strictly prohibited it. I knew that something was amiss because uncles would guard the building at night with cricket bats, and my mother had given me a Christian name, just in case someone asked. But it was not my time for sleepless nights.

Gujarat 2002 has been the most egregious and therefore the most memorable communal carnage of my adult life. I had witnessed it remotely, from my laptop in an overheated apartment in Brooklyn. I had accessed news websites online but hadn't sought out video content. I had read: madly, obsessively, half-shivering, half-crying. At the time, I had just started writing for World War 4 Report, an independent, Leftist press that my editor, Bill Weinberg, ran out of his living room in the Lower East Side.[1] I did mostly secondary-source news collation and spent hours each night after work ploughing through countless Google searches and reading articles about Gujarat in the mainstream and independent Indian press. I had printed out Smita Narula's 70-page report for Human Rights Watch, "*We Have No Orders to Save You": State Participation and Complicity in Communal Violence in Gujarat*, and kept it on my bedside table as necessary reading.[2] I would force myself to read it every night, even though I struggled to get past the first few paragraphs.

I felt like a victim in absentia whose feelings of betrayal echoed those she could hear in the testimonies of Gujarat's survivors. I heard the sounds of my romanticised notions of syncretic India being crushed. I hadn't grown up thinking 'these people' were 'my people', but suddenly I felt like a fish forced into a plastic bag while its bowl was being cleaned. I had waited with as much anticipation for the next episode of *Mahabharat* on Sunday mornings as any other kid in my building. My mother had worn a big *kumkum bindi* on her forehead for as long as I could remember. I had loved the colour and magic and myth of Hinduism and, like a child whose ball is snatched from her, I felt crudely severed from it. I would repeat in my head the clichés one hears from miffed lovers on discovering that their partners have cheated on them: 'I loved you, how could you do this to me?'

The fear that the porous and permeable dotted line between 'us' and 'them' had become impenetrable and double-bolded first made me articulate an ambivalent minority-hood in the diaspora. I was on an H1-B visa and working a dead-end job at a shelter for abused women and children. I eventually decided to leave New York and return to Mumbai, but the fear lingered on: could Mumbai become another Gujarat?

I'd shared these concerns with my mother over the phone in the months before I returned home. She had shrugged them off just as she did my fear of being on the electoral roll. "They tracked down the Muslims in Gujarat from the voter lists!" I'd exclaim in one of our many heated discussions. "I've had my Muslim name on voting lists for 60 years, Subuhi, and nothing has happened!"

If nothing has happened, then my fear must be irrational, an outcome of an over-anxious mind. That's the unspoken refrain I hear every time I confide in someone about this. A Gujarati Hindu friend recently came back with this retort: "You're falling into the trap of minority-hood". She reminded me of the classic argument of how class will protect me. Rioting only happens in the *bastis*, in the slums, to the poor, the uneducated. It is spontaneous, unplanned. It is the result of sudden political upheavals.

I try to explain that cooking gas cylinders were hoarded in Ahmedabad for weeks before the pogrom, which, by all indications, was premeditated.[3] It was the outcome of anti-Muslim sentiment, which has been nurtured and brewed by Hindutvavadi forces. I am met with retorts that point to the planned nature of Islamist violence and its roots in a deeply entrenched fundamentalism. Such arguments devolve into matches of Your Fundamentalism versus My Fundamentalism, and usually end on a predictably liberal note that underlines the tolerance of all religious systems that have been 'corrupted' by politically motivated parties.

I persist with arguments about the politicised nature of everything – religious philosophies, progressive social movements, knowledge systems, interpersonal relationships, etc. This Marxist critique, applicable as it is to most social institutions and structures, takes the discussion away from the particular and into the universal. I am no closer to articulating a sentient theory about the experience of majoritarianism. I fumble, trip, digress and fall over my words.

I've decided to return to my fear to understand before I can extrapolate. I'm cognizant of the fact that I am not overtly marked as Muslim, like someone whose last name is Khan or Sheikh. I don't wear any visible markers of Muslim-ness, and it is not an integral part of my identity, culturally or spiritually. I have gone as far as writing newspaper op-eds about how Eid is uneventful in our home, a date on the calendar like any other. In addition, I have often skirted the 'What are you?' question, and insisted that I am agnostic, disassociating myself from any socio-religious or spiritual history. But the electoral roster, when I finally looked at it, had a number of Mohammed and Sharifa Jiwanis before and after my name. While Islam is just something I inherited, I am Muslim by association on the electoral roll, whether I like it or not.

My decision to vote finally came from the desire to push myself into accepting that, try as I might, I cannot resist being tagged Muslim. It is on my birth certificate, in my passport and my family ration card. Like race and gender, our religious identities cannot be circumvented, however incidental they may be to the construction of our selves. They need not entrap us, however, and perhaps we can, with our particularities, break through their bondage and the essentialisms they force on us.

I landed on a revelation when I finally went to the electoral office in 2009 with a filled-out application form for my voter identity card. The electoral officer said to me in disaffected Marathi, "But, madam, your name is already on the list". My fear had induced amnesia about the time when I was so angry about the Gujarat betrayal that I felt the only way I could overcome it was by voting out the possibility of a saffron government in Maharashtra and the Centre. It was a drizzly afternoon in 2004, a month after I had returned to Mumbai from New York, when I had tracked down the election office in Andheri's concrete maze, handed in my form and was formally written into the voter lists. It had slipped out of my mind, the way an ATM cash withdrawal receipt gets lost in my wallet, in the clutter of bills, Halls wrappers and bits of paper.

Did I simply forget the fear which projected itself as anger, a shudder deep inside my chest that threatened to explode? It ticked time bomb-like each time I passed a Shiv Sena *shakha*, or saw forked saffron flags waved around during Ganapati Visarjan. I lived with it alone, and if I tried to share it, I was reminded of its irrationality. My class, it seemed, was immune to such fears, and the Shi'a Imami Ismaili community was as alien to me as farmers on the American prairie. My self-groomed cosmopolitanism had made me areligious and isolated, and my fear was driven into the ground with a shovel.

In a *Kill Bill II* moment, it re-emerged from its coffin in early 2008. It was my first semester as a Master's student at the Tata Institute of Social Sciences. Journalist Sameera Khan had been invited to speak about Muslim identity. Of the many experiences she shared, I was moved by the story of how her family had to take shelter from a mob during the 1992 riots. They lived at a neighbour's house for four days – hidden, in fear.

This was the first time I had heard an upper-middle class, Western-educated Muslim woman articulate that which I'd quietened so long ago. Images of poor, crying Muslim victims of the carnage were ubiquitous in documentaries and news; these were pictures of affect. The subterranean shivers and exigencies of the 'unaffected' seemed rarely to find voice in public fora.

The events that had spurred on our fears were from different decades; the nature and handling of our fears were different; but fears they were, finally united and echoing each other. Sameera had quite literally tabled her fear, and forced a predominantly Hindu audience to acknowledge a history of communal violence and majoritarianism. I felt less alone in my fear, less convinced of its irrationality, but reminded of it nonetheless.

Fear may be a confrontation with the unknown and the confusion that results from this meeting. In order to grapple with this unknowing, we translate it in terms of the known, in terms of memory. What has been leaves its imprint on us; it makes us and our present. We cannot predict what will be but want to, and this reflects our deep-seated desire to know and control. The impulse that drives institutions to obtain knowledge, classify, taxonomise, experiment and, finally, prognosticate has also trickled down to the individual. If we cannot know what the future will hold, we fill the gaps with our anxieties and extrapolate.

Indeed, un-knowing has inspired my own fears. And the inability to answer the following questions: will a Hindu nationalist party come to power? If so, will it instigate communal violence? Will I be caught up in it and become vulnerable? I've translated the insecurity that results from not being able to predict the future into a self-induced victimisation. This essay grew out of the desire to admit my fears publicly, to share them with an audience and, perhaps, overcome them through articulation. In reality, it has been an attempt to control and rationalise them.

I would like to think, though, that the dot on my nail has brought me a little closer to submitting myself to the unknown. Honestly, though, that's the logical me speaking. These days, I don't get as nervous when I have to answer the 'What kind of name is that?' question. If I am to be categorised, labelled, boxed or stereotyped, that's about as unavoidable as the malleability of water. I do, however, wonder if a communal conflagration can flare up in a snap second. This worry, which inhabits a subliminal space, prevents me from divulging my religious identity to strangers or people I barely know. When the guy who runs a copying shop near my house asks me where I'm from, I usually say "Bombay" (still the city's street name) and end it there. The local Shiv Sena corporators also give him business, and he might, at some point in the future, have to choose sides. In that moment, I'd like to slip though the gap.

Notes

1. *World War 4 Report, http://www.4report.com (accessed 29 December 2009).*
2. *Smita Narula.* **"We Have No Orders to Save You"**: State Participation and Complicity in Communal Violence in Gujarat *(Human Rights Watch, 2002, New York). Available at: http://www.hrw.org/legacy/ reports/2002/india/ (accessed 20 December 2009).*
3. *Arundhati Roy. "Fascism's Firm Footprint in India". In* **The Nation,** *September 30, 2002.*

My Fear Begins Where Your Fear Ends

AMBARIEN ALQADAR

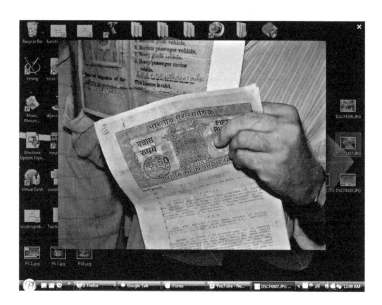

My mother runs a beauty saloon in Zakir Nagar. This is where I lived and grew up. It was inevitable, then, that one was unable to stay away from the vocabulary of the 'inside' and the 'outside' for long. "You live in the Old City", someone on the 'outside' would say and move on to the next bit of conversation, and I would want to say that the 'inside' was not 'the Old City'. That there was more to a 'middle-class Muslim ghetto' than just the generic ways of looking at places like Zakir Nagar, Batla House, Abul Fazal Enclave, Jamia Nagar, Nizamuddin Basti, Chandni Chowk, would be an idea difficult to articulate (the more when stretched as far as, say, Anarkali Bazaar in Lahore). The language in which one could do so would read 'currently unavailable'.

The person who would want to say this would find herself becoming as much an element of exotica as the biryani and kebabs that people from the outside would know these places for, sold, as they are, cheaply on the sidewalk. They would drive in, park their glitzy cars in the middle of the road, eat and go. And so it would always be fixed as Old – pointing towards a way of life replete with food and kitsch.

I imagine the flickering, guilty moment that eating would create. One in which otherness would be embraced, made one's own, the guilt wiped off with a tissue.

But only so long as that plate of chicken tikka lasts.

Soon enough, there would be a transformation. It would 'become' a place where the gangster, the crook, the pimp, the jobless and problem-creating Hyder would be just round the corner, ready to attack. The topography would turn disorienting. GPS systems would go awry and villains from the nooks and crannies of *A Wednesday*[1] and *Aamir*[2] would cloud the screen. A feeling that it would take forever to get out of here, a moment in which all maps and markers collapse, will in any case remind you of the labyrinthesque adventure of K. to get cured in *No Smoking*.[3]

The question has bothered me for far too long now. Where did the 'I am Here' kind of map go missing? It was never there when I grew up, it is not here now. Jamia Nagar is a cluster of colonies. There is one main road and Zakir Nagar, Batla House, Ghaffar Manzil, Abul Fazal Enclave, fall either on this side of the road or that.

I talk to Nilofeur about this one afternoon at the saloon. Like me, she too is an inhabitant of the Old City. She lives in Chandni Chowk and every day takes the Phatphat Sewa (Quick Service)[4] to work. She works at the saloon. This she does every day, except Tuesdays. The same morning, I look up Batla House on Google Maps. It does not help much because it is the ruins, the dilapidated, algae-eaten, broken walls that are the markers through which the place can now be recalled. I don't deny the red, brightly-painted houses and the manicured little green gardens. They are there too. But there is that one image that flickers long after time has passed. The old man looking out of his balcony somewhere on the fifth floor as the khaki men conduct their operation and name it "the L-18 Terror Encounter at Batla House".[5] The place is marked once again as it was some years back. At Muradi Road, when the police had come, toting guns, firing and saying a terrorist was "holed up". A Kashmiri militant. He was killed, and the scene outside the building in which the operation happened was similar to the one outside L-18 a year back. Countless heads chanting *Naar-e-Takbeer, Allah-hu-Akbar*, people crowding the street, people in homes not wanting to go out for fear of being suspected. The police guards gun-toting, macho-posturing, sipping *chai*, looking you directly in the eye and muttering under their breath. Swanky media vans and chic journalists descending for that byte worth millions.

And because the place is marked, the language persists. A language that constantly throws up the Old against the New. The New has the promise of apartments, education, malls, show windows, ATMs, car loans, cake deliveries. The policeman with the boots, badges and paunch who guards its gates doesn't just break inside. Even if he needs to, he does so mindful of those things called 'legality' and 'locality'.

In the meanwhile, the Old City sees terrorist encounters, countless raids and arrests, innumerable people losing their jobs or never getting any because they live in places that hole terrorists. Rahim, the madman, who for the longest while suffered from a fear of stepping outside home, a fear of places he could never describe fully, becomes a man of the streets. He was seen last at Lovely Cloth House, Batla House Chowk. Two women were shouting at him because he had hit them on their heads for being uncovered. My father, like many others, constantly talks about policemen dressed as civilians combing the area, a thought he can't help thinking.

Nilofeur feels this fear can be dealt with. She looks out of the saloon window at the warm, incandescent glow of light bulbs lining the almost similar-looking kebab kiosks and little eating-places. I know she is waiting for the jobless Hyder. It is evening now.

The Old City is her familiar world. There is the comfort of slipping into something known, she says.

Of not being watched as an oddity.

Of being and moving about easily.

For whatever reason, Nilofeur insists on travelling by the Phatphat Sewa. A rickety tempo with six to eight people sticking together, the one on which she travels regularly between Jama Masjid and Batla House Chowk. In the aftermath of the encounter, questions of evidence dominate the conversation inside. For days, she meets the same people carrying newspaper clips, showing each other photographs of the bullet-riddled bodies of those killed, building their versions of what could have happened.

She is still trying to make sense of it all. But this she says with confidence now:

"My fear begins where your fear ends. It is a question of where those boundaries lie."

This she narrates as a thought that comes to her in the Chandni Chowk Metro a day after the 19 September 2008 Batla House encounter. She usually wears versions of the *hijab*. Often wears none, when she and jobless Hyder go for ice cream to the India Gate lawns. But that day she did cover herself – out of whim, maybe.

The woman she was sharing her seat with didn't stop looking at her from the corner of her eye.

Notes

1. *A Wednesday (2008), dir. Neeraj Pandey, Indian thriller drama. A police officer narrates a series of events that lead up to a terror strike being planned by 'extremist elements' in Mumbai. The event unfolds as one that has no record beyond his memory.*
2. **Aamir** *(2008), dir. Rajkumar Gupta, Indian, thriller. A young Muslim doctor returns to Mumbai from the UK and finds himself in a plan to bomb the city.*
3. *No Smoking (2007), dir. Anurag Kashyap, Indian, thriller. K. is a compulsive smoker and needs to be cured of his addiction.*
4. *Phatphat Sewa: A minibus shuttle service, usually packed to capacity.*
5. *L-18 Terror Encounter, Batla House: On 19 September 2008, the Delhi Police Special Cell raided flat number 108 in building L-18 of the Batla House locality in South Delhi's Jamia Nagar, and shot dead two alleged terrorists, Atif Amin and Sajid. Another casualty was Special Cell inspector Mohan Chand Sharma, who was wounded and later succumbed to his injuries. A flat mate of the two alleged terrorists, Mohammed Saif, was arrested from the site; the Delhi Police claimed two others escaped during the operation. The Delhi Police also claimed that the occupants of L-18, all students and all hailing from Azamgarh in Uttar Pradesh, were part of the Indian Mujahideen, supposedly an Islamic terrorist group. Further, the Delhi Police alleged that the deceased and the arrested were the main conspirators and executors of the bomb blasts in Delhi on 13 September 2008.*
The National Human Rights Commission later conducted an enquiry into the encounter and gave the police a clean chit, saying that on the basis of the evidence it was presented, "it cannot be said that there has been any violation of human rights by the actions of [the] police".

When a People Settle/Re-Settle...

ZAINAB BAWA

It was July 2008, my first visit to Traasi[1] rehabilitation and resettlement (R&R) housing colony. I went there with C.

You walk into Traasi, and a number of six- to seven-storey boring, somewhat jaded buildings stand out to greet you. The wide street between them bustles with activity in some corners; in others, groups of boys, seemingly unemployed, stand in bunches, either chatting among themselves or watching people pass by. I feel uneasy as I walk, but I am not afraid because C. is with me. In yet other corners, you notice a lone woman frying potato *vadas* on her cart, and a person or two buying the snack from her.

The second time I went to Traasi, I was alone. This time, I sensed nervousness and tension on my skin. Something seemed wrong/incorrect/out-of-place here. Why the fear? Is it the layout of the space? Or is it the groups of (unemployed) boys standing in the street? Or is it because of the dark and dingy atmosphere inside the buildings that makes you feel uncomfortable when you simply walk into one of them? Or is it the proximity of Traasi to that part of Mumbai city which is known for gangs and crime, and the question of whether moving people en masse into Traasi has changed the social dynamics and networks in, and of, the city? Or is it all of these and more?

Traasi is one of the many R&R housing colonies that have been developed in Mumbai to re-house squatters and slum dwellers residing along railway tracks, on pavements and in areas which were coming in the way of developing roads and railway infrastructure under the Mumbai Urban Transport Project (MUTP) and the Mumbai Urban Infrastructure Project (MUIP). This move was preceded by (and continues to be legitimised by) discourses and policies about security of tenure and housing and property rights – the material and legal tools that are now being deemed as most crucial for poor people and their lives. There is agreement among many individuals and institutions at different ends of the ideological spectrum that poor people should have secure tenures, property titles and housing/shelter, so that they can live their lives without the perpetual fear of demolitions and evictions (World Bank, 1993; De Soto, 1989; Das, 1995).

Property titles and ownership documents, in the manner in which they have been conceptualised, have legal and economic significance (De Soto, 1989, 2000). They (seemingly) establish legal security because the fact of possessing a title is evidence of legal ownership,[2] empowering the owner to move court of law against an 'encroacher' or persons violating his/her property rights. In economic terms, property titles facilitate transfers of property from one person to another, enable poor people to obtain loans from banks on account of their titles,[3] and allow individuals to participate in speculation and notional transactions. This conception of property titles has been interrogated and challenged by researchers and scholars of various disciplines (Benjamin, 2005, 2008; Razzaz, 1993; de Souza, 1999, 2001a, 2001b).

My aim in writing this piece is not to provide a critique/interrogation of property titles. My interest lies in exploring the spectrum of insecurity/security which pervades the lives and experiences of various poor groups[4] as they try to occupy land and start residing in a place, and when they are resettled from seemingly 'informal', 'insecure' conditions into 'formal' housing. In what follows, I narrate a few accounts which individuals who have experienced evictions, demolitions and resettlement have shared with me during my fieldwork. Their life experiences and stories provide important insights for understanding security, fear, the nature of demolitions and life in squatter settlements, slums and rehabilitation housing. I am grateful to them for giving me entry into their lives.

Here we go.

When a People Settle

I was sitting in Amiya's house in Valmiki Nagar, one of the other large R&R housing colonies on the edges of Mumbai city. Amiya was earlier residing on a plot of land near the railway tracks in South Mumbai's Loka area. She has been moved into a building in Valmiki Nagar along with other people living on the same plot. It was felt that the 'community' should not be fragmented/destroyed in the process of rehabilitation, and hence the attempt was made to move people living in shared surroundings into the same buildings.

I met Amiya to understand how her life was in the Loka area settlement and how things were (or were not) different for her now. Amiya began by explaining to me how she started living on the plot of railway land in Loka.

> I have been living here since I was in my teens. My mother got us here. In the beginning, when we occupied the land and tried to build and consolidate our hutments, the demolition squads would come every now and then to move us out of the plot. Opposite the railway land plot we occupied was a large flyover. Below the

flyover, there was place for us to put up our shacks every time we were evicted from the railway land. We moved like this each time the demolition squads came – from the plot to the space below the flyover and then back again. This continued for some years. Meanwhile, NGOs associated with churches started to come to our settlement to help with our children's education and to provide us things like food and clothing. We also developed contacts with a powerful trade union leader, who later contested elections and became a politician. He would speak for us every time there was talk of demolishing our hutments or evicting us from the plot. There were railway employees also living in our settlement; they had given the houses the railway authorities had allotted them under employee housing out on rent to other people. The demolitions stopped eventually. And later, the railway authorities constructed toilets on the plot so we could use those instead of defecating on the tracks.

In 2003-04, we were moved from the plot. This happened because some of our local leaders and committee members went to court to claim ownership of the land. They lost the case in different courts about three times. Their victory enabled the railway authorities to carry out demolitions once again. When these started, we tried to mobilise an NGO to help us remain on the plot. The NGO helped us a few times. But we were constantly facing the demolition squads and kept going to the NGO every now and then. The people from the NGO eventually said that we would be given houses, and they moved us to transit camps while these were being constructed. We did not know where we would get houses – in Traasi or in Valmiki Nagar. Also, not all the 80 families who lived on the plot were eligible for housing because many of them had lost their proofs of identity, such as their ration cards, voter ID cards and other documents, during the demolitions and at other times.

The NGO conducted a survey to determine which of us 80 families would get what and then we were moved into the transit camps...

[To be continued]

Apart from talking to people who were moved into R&R housing colonies, I went to sites and spoke to people who were being allotted land and housing under other government and private schemes and systems. Among these, I visited the Kalhanpur Gate Number 8 site. Kalhanpur is located in a posh area in Mumbai's western suburbs. During my visits there, I met with Baaji. Baaji and others residing on the Gate Number 8 plot had been evicted from the land four years ago because some large commercial builders had purchased it to develop properties for sale. But, even after the purchase, the people residing on the land were unwilling to move. The builders found it difficult to remove them, and so they started putting pressure on the Maharashtra state government to evict the people from the land. I asked Baaji to explain how he came to Gate Number 8 and started living there. Said Baaji:

Around the time of the 1992-93 communal riots in [the then] Bombay, some people found this plot of land and did *ghuspaiti* (trespass/surreptitious occupancy) upon it. They then started subdividing the plots and selling them to incoming people. During this time, demolitions took place on a daily basis. Especially in the neighbouring area, the demolition squads would come each day. One day, I met my friend Yusuf, who resided in that area. Yusuf invited me to his home for tea. When I went over, I saw his wife. Her skin had become pitch black. I knew that she was dark complexioned, but now she appeared darker. I asked Yusuf what the matter was. He told me that the demolition squads were coming each day and breaking down people's hutments in the area. Eventually, people decided that they would build their hutments in the evening, stay in them and then pull the structures down themselves before the demolition squads came back in the morning. They would sit in the hot sun all day on their respective spots with their building material until the demolition squads went away. The idea was to hold firmly to lots people had originally occupied and not leave them. Eventually, the squads stopped coming.

Then, in late 2004, the bulldozers came. This time, they destroyed everything, including the mosques that were built in our area. We were ruthlessly moved out. The land was fenced in, and private security guards were appointed to keep us out. When the demolitions happened, people tried to salvage what little they could of their belongings. We attended rallies organised by an activist who was protesting at that time against the mass evictions of slum dwellers in Mumbai. Later, we approached her to ask her to help us.

In the floods that ravaged Mumbai in July 2005, we used the opportunity to reoccupy the land. We collected around our land, which was still being watched over by the private security guards. The authorities came and asked us what was going on. We told them a survey was being carried out, and that's how we surreptitiously reoccupied whatever little plots we could settle on. Afterwards, we organised protests and meetings outside the state government headquarters in Mumbai to get permission for us to stay. We sent delegations and petitions to the chief minister and the government. The activist continued to support us. In the meantime, the district collector allotted some people plots on the Gate Number 8 land, based on their eligibility and possession of identity cards and proof of residence documentation. Those of us who got the plots built our own houses. Now, we live at Gate Number 8 with some people on plots they got from the collector, and many, many other people still occupying the land. The activist who gave us help is very important for us because her support, even if symbolic, keeps the police away. They are afraid to come here because they say "this is the activist's area and we will not touch it" [meaning, they will not harass the people living here].[5]

Demolitions and Evictions – Security/Insecurity?

The accounts narrated to me by Amiya, Baaji and many other slum dwellers during fieldwork led me to rethink the fear of demolitions and the notion of insecurity. In general, the manner in which we comprehend demolitions and evictions has implications for how we understand and conceptualise security of tenure and property ownership. Demolitions and evictions are usually viewed as violent experiences where people's homes are destroyed and their belongings are either taken away or stolen or strewn ruthlessly around. Yet, much as demolitions are real, they are also symbolic acts which state agencies, police authorities and municipality demolition squads carry out from time to time. In a way, demolitions are carried out to prevent claims of ownership over the space occupied. Demolitions can also be viewed as a form of threat which state agencies issue to occupying persons. In the initial stages of occupancy, demolitions are likely to be more frequent to scare away the occupants, as we can see from the accounts of Baaji and Amiya. Demolitions have also been carried out as part of tenurial arrangements between landlords/owners and tenants (Shetty, 2007). Such demolitions are performed to prevent the tenant from making any ownership claims. This does not necessarily create a condition of insecurity for the tenant. Rather, the tenant agrees to this arrangement in order to secure his/her claims and, at the same time, make the owner/landlord feel secure about his possessions/property.

But the nature of demolitions and their symbolism have transformed in the last one-and-a-half decades. Bhagwati Prasad, researcher at Sarai-Centre for the Study of Developing Societies (CSDS), lucidly explained to me how he comprehended changes in the nature of demolitions in recent times:

> Earlier, in Delhi, demolition squads would come into squatter settlements and simply break things here and there, but would leave the building materials behind after the symbolic act had been performed. This enabled the occupants to reconstruct their houses and rebuild the settlement. Now, not only are the building materials, things and people packed away in trucks, but a fence is constructed around the cleared land, and security is installed as soon as the land is cleared. Workers are immediately called in, and the foundations of the proposed infrastructure are laid down by nightfall. The workers labour day and night to complete their assigned tasks. Within a week or so, the once-occupied land looks completely different and even unrecognisable. This prevents people from coming back and reclaiming it.

In the present day, not only have land values increased enormously, but the pressure on various administrative agencies to clear slums and 'encroachments' on public and private lands has intensified. The pressure on administrative agencies (chiefly municipalities) is applied by chief ministers and offices of the Central government (Benjamin and Bhuvaneswari, 2006), owing to which, these bodies have to execute their orders immediately. Given this climate, the demands for, and the discourse of, housing are only legitimised further.

In Transit

Amiya continued talking to me, this time about the surveys which took place in Loka and about her stay in transit camps.

> We were living in a hutment [in Loka], which we were renting from my maternal uncle. It was his house, and we were living in a part of it. When the NGO said that we would be given housing, they conducted a survey to determine who was eligible. Housing was to be given only to those people who owned hutments and who had identity cards and proofs of residence. The night before the surveyors came, my family and I put up four bamboo poles and spread plastic sheets on top for covering. The next day, the surveyors marked our makeshift dwelling as one house, and so we became eligible for housing. But many people did not get houses because they did not have proof of residence and documentation. Some are still struggling over their unfulfilled claims.
>
> Some time later, we were moved into transit camps. Trucks came and we were loaded into them with our things. In the transit camp, some families lost people because of illness and the trauma of rehabilitation. Others lost some of their documents in the transit camp phase, and they are now in limbo. Then it also happened that people who had been living in the transit camps before us tried intimidating us when we first arrived. They told us that a number of crimes were being committed in the transit camp, including robbery, rape and murder. They were trying to scare us away. But we decided to stay, despite the fear. We lived in the transit camp for six months.

When a People Resettle

Amiya continued:

> Six months later, we were allotted houses in Valmiki Nagar. When we first came here, people who had been living here before we moved tried to frighten us off again. They would tell us that Valmiki Nagar was haunted.[6] But we decided to stay. Nothing happened.
>
> I am happy I got a house here because I can now travel by the easier railway line to the city and not the difficult and uncertain one. But when we first came here, there was no transport to go to the closest train station. We had to ply on the only bus there was, one a *madrasi* [indicating a person from Tamil Nadu or, generically, southern India] was running between our housing colony and the station. Now, we have the public bus service.
>
> Then, also, the water in the taps was yellow in colour and smelly. Power cables were running below the sewage drains. So electrocution would happen. We organised a *dharna* [protest demonastration] to the local ward office and got that straightened out.

During my later sojourns to Traasi, I met with Akshaya and Aaliya, who were also moved into this R&R housing colony from their earlier settlements along railway tracks in cities. They made similar remarks about the initial phase of settling in at the resettlement housing colonies. Akshaya said:

> When we first came here, the land was barren and there were only a few buildings. The plot you see there was a garbage dump – there were no buildings on it then. At first, we used to feel frightened. What would happen? But we continued to live here.

At a later time, Aaliya said to me:

> You know, the people who were moved here, they had to face very rough condi-tions. Some people are worse off now than they were before. Many of them sold the houses allotted to them here, took the money and went off to live elsewhere.[7]

I asked Aaliya how she felt, living in Traasi.

> I was living close to the railway tracks earlier. I loved my life there. Our people did not want to move. We were unsure of when we would be allotted housing and also what kind of houses would be given to us. We have physically fought the police when they came to evict us from our place. We did not want to move. Then, we saw the better-looking state government housing given to some of our people, and so we decided to move. But now, look what we have got – matchboxes with open drains!

It is somewhat well known now that people who were rehabilitated lost employment, and a significant number have only been impoverished further. The question that lingered in my mind was, how does ownership of a house change the lives of people who were perceived to be living in previously 'insecure' circumstances? Amiya said to me:

> I wanted to make some improvements to the house we have been allotted. But then, my husband reminded me that we have not received our registration papers and that the process of registration is not complete. Hence, we should be careful about spending any money on improving this house. **What if we are evicted from here tomorrow?**

On the spectrum of post-resettlement security/insecurity, people like Aaliya and Akshaya are placed in a position where they are forever trying to consolidate the gains they had made with the housing allocation. Said Akshaya:

It is nice that we have this house now. Better than being evicted time and again. I used to miss our former place earlier. After coming here, I have never gone back. I am now looking for space to open a beauty parlour in the area near the railway station.

Aaliya, meanwhile, earns a rental income from one of the two houses that she was allotted in lieu of her two hutments.

While trying to understand the experiences of security and insecurity post-resettlement, I encountered Rose. Rose has rented out her house in Valmiki Nagar and is living on rent in the central city area because she did not want her children's education to suffer. The rent from her house in Valmiki Nagar suffices for the rent she pays on the central city flat she lives in. Amiya also tried to return to the central city area by letting her Valmiki Nagar flat. But:

We came back to Valmiki Nagar. The settlement in the central city area where we rented a hutment for ourselves had no toilet inside. My daughter and I had to go out to use a toilet. My daughter is in her teens. I do not wish for her to go out like that because I am afraid something might happen to her. Hence, my husband and I decided to come back to our flat in Valmiki Nagar. We don't like it here sometimes. But, maybe, down the line, in some years, Valmiki Nagar will become like Loka – posh!

Contestations : Navigating and Traversing Security-Insecurity

The process of resettlement and the fact of being allotted a house do not, as we have seen above, automatically bring security for poor groups. Even when the state allots them a house, they have to negotiate with governments, the city administration, bureaucrats, officials and politicians to secure their possessions and consolidate on them. During fieldwork, Aaliya narrated to me, in a most matter-of-fact way, the contestations which the women living in Traasi were dealing with while trying to regularise (though not in a legal sense) a market they had set up on a corner of vacant land, deemed 'public space', to sell vegetables and small goods in order to earn incomes. The NGO mainly responsible for developing the housing and later supervising the premises initially reported these women's occupancy to the municipalities, on the count that it and their hawking activities were against the rules of use on public space. The municipality officials sent demolition squads to impound the goods the women were selling. They, in turn, tried to mobilise hawker leaders from the central city area to enter into talks with the municipal officials. Says Aaliya:

The municipality eventually allowed us to continue with our market activities because our leader spoke with them, and we also pleaded with the officials and made claims of life and livelihood before them. Now, we have an agreement with the municipality – at the end of each day, the women in the market will make sure that the premises are clean when they leave in the evening. The demolition squads continue to come once a month. And I believe that they should come. **They should**

come so that our women are kept in check, kept in check in terms of the amount of space they are occupying and in terms of the claims on the space they make from time to time. They should come, the municipality should come, *aana chahiye* [must come].

By Way of a Conclusion

The accounts narrated here provide some insights into the spectrums of security-insecurity which groups living in slums, squatter settlements and now in rehabilitation housing experience in their daily lives at various points of time. What becomes evident is that legal tools such as ownership documents, housing rights and property rights do not automatically (or necessarily) relieve poor groups of the insecurities and fears they face as they try to consolidate their (social, economic and political) positions in the city. At the same time, insecurity need not be a chronic and an absolute condition. Sometimes, insecurities and fear open up avenues of (material and symbolic) access for poor groups. Having said this, it must also be noted that it is not only poorer groups who experience security and insecurity of tenure in their daily lives in the city. Even propertied persons/groups are confronted with similar conditions, albeit on a much reduced scale, as mega infrastructure is being developed in Indian cities to turn them into so-called world-class habitats. Thus, propertied persons in Bangalore and Mumbai are fighting to secure their possessions which have been threatened by the onset of metro rail systems and through acts of widening roads, supposedly in order to ease traffic flows. We are, therefore, as the Chinese have famously said, "living in interesting times", where we are now confronted with new regimes, systems, processes and moments that challenge conventional legal and economic notions of property.

Fear, security-insecurity, threats, negotiations, contestations – such is life in a city... perpetually... There is no end... perhaps new beginnings... new understandings... new challenges... new opportunities...

Notes

1. The names of all places and persons have been changed to protect the identities of the people who talked to me during fieldwork.
2. Discounting the fact that legal ownership is only one form of ownership, and that there are many other forms – cultural, social and historical.
3. The view that titles allow poor people to obtain loans from banks has been challenged on account of the fact that banks may not value poor people's properties very highly, and hence poor people may not always receive loans, even when they possess titles (Shafi and Payne, 2007).
4. In this essay, poverty is not conceived of as a static economic condition. Rather, the experience of poverty changes from time to time as individuals and groups face different life events, and become part of and/or are excluded from various social, economic, political and cultural networks from time to time. Hence, the notion of poverty is rather fluid, and the understanding of it is derived from the individuals' and groups' current life experiences as well as historical trajectories.

5. During my later visits to Gate Number 8, I found people building houses with bamboo and tin on plots of land they had purchased through supposedly 'informal' dealings. Houses were built either overnight or within a span of two or three days. Thus, consolidation has once again begun at Gate Number 8 as people are navigating the fear of demolitions and are beginning to build their own hutments/houses.

6. During fieldwork in Johannesburg in November-December 2009, women from informal settlement townships explained that when they first came to reside in the townships, the earlier residents would try to frighten them away by saying that the area was haunted. This fieldwork was carried out with support from the Centre de Sciences Humaines (CSH), New Delhi, under the India-South Africa (ISA) project.

7. The 'sale' of the houses often happened through powers of attorney created in the names of the 'buyers'. Legally, those who were allotted houses under the R&R policy could not sell their houses for the first ten years of their tenure. Hence, instead of sale deeds, sellers and buyers entered into their transactions with the buyer naming the seller in the power of attorney as the legal 'caretaker' of his/her house. Currently, the prices and values of R&R houses are rising in Mumbai because water supply has been somewhat regularised in most housing colonies, transport infrastructure in terms of public buses and trains has been created for people living there, and other amenities have been established. It is likely that those who have 'purchased' the R&R houses through powers of attorney may be faced with negotiations, contestations and confrontations by the 'original sellers', who may want to come back to claim the benefits of the rising prices and the speculation around their houses. What this also suggests is that the act of allotting a house to a poor family does not automatically confer security on them. Instead, even under the so-called 'housing for the poor' schemes, people do face insecure conditions, and they have to consolidate their tenure over time.

References

- Benjamin, Solomon. "Touts, Pirates and Ghosts". In (eds.) Monica Narula, Shuddhabrata Sengupta et al., **Sarai Reader 05: Bare Acts** *(Sarai, the Centre for the Study of Developing Societies, 2005, Delhi), pp. 242-254. Available online at http://www.sarai.net/publications/readers/05-bare-acts/01_solly.pdf.*
- _____. "Occupancy Urbanism: Radicalizing Politics and Economy beyond Policy and Programs". In **International Journal of Urban and Regional Research** *32 (3), pp. 719-729 (September 2008).*
- Benjamin, Solomon and R. Bhuvaneswari. "Urban Futures of Poor Groups in Chennai and Bangalore: How These are Shaped by the Relationships between Parastatals and Local Bodies". In (eds.) Niraja Gopal Jayal, Amit Prakash and Pradeep Sharma, **Local Governance in India: Decentralization and Beyond** *(Oxford University Press, 2006, New Delhi).*
- Das, PK. "Manifesto of a Housing Activist". In (eds.) Sujata Patel and Alice Thorner, **Bombay: Metaphor for Modern India** *(Oxford University Press, 1995, New Delhi).*
- de Soto, Hernando. **The Other Path: The Economic Answer to Terrorism** *(Basic Books, 1989, New York).*
- de Soto, Hernando. **The Mystery of Capital: Why Capitalism Triumphs in the West and Fails Everywhere Else** *(Bantam Press, 2000, Great Britain).*
- de Souza, Flavio AM. "Land Tenure Security and Housing Improvements in Recife, Brazil". In **Habitat International** *23 (1), pp. 19-33 (1999).*
- _____. "Perceived Security of Land Tenure in Recife, Brazil". In **Habitat International** *25, pp. 175-190 (2001a).*
- _____. "The Future of Informal Settlements: Lessons in Legalization of Disputed Urban Land in Recife, Brazil". In **Geoforum** *32, pp. 483-492 (2001b).*
- Razzaz, Omar M. "Examining Property Rights and Investment in Informal Settlements: The Case of Jordan". In **Land Economics** *69 (4), pp. 341-355 (November 1993).*
- Shafi, Salma A. and Geoffrey Payne. "Land Tenure Security and Land Administration in Bangladesh". In **Local Partnerships for Urban Poverty Alleviation – Final Report.** *Submitted to LGED, UNDP and UN-Habitat, June 2007.*
- Shetty, Prasad. "Rethinking Real-Estate: A Cultural Perspective" *(Collective Research Initiatives Trust, 2007, Mumbai).*
- World Bank. "World Development Report – Housing: Enabling Markets to Work" *(The World Bank, 1993, Washington DC).*

The Cow Ate It Up

AMITABH KUMAR

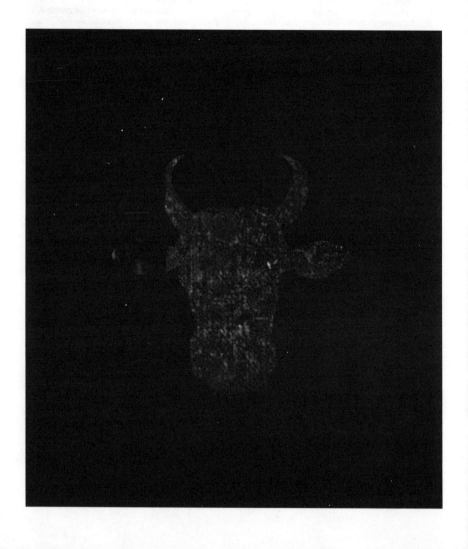

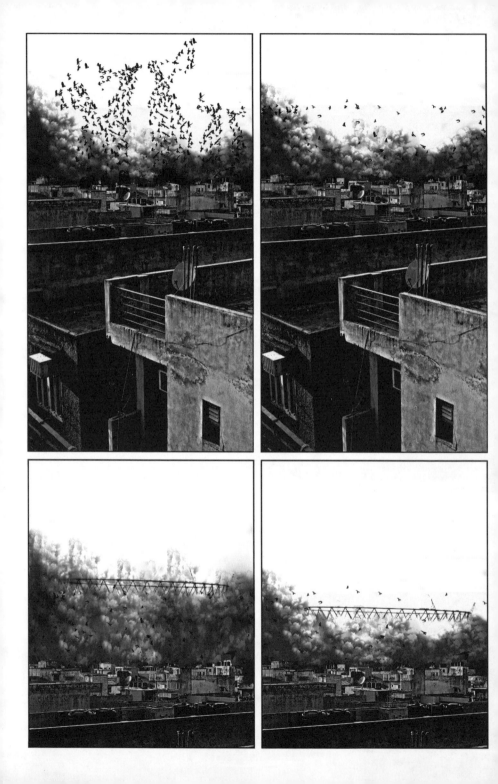

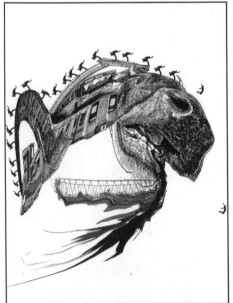

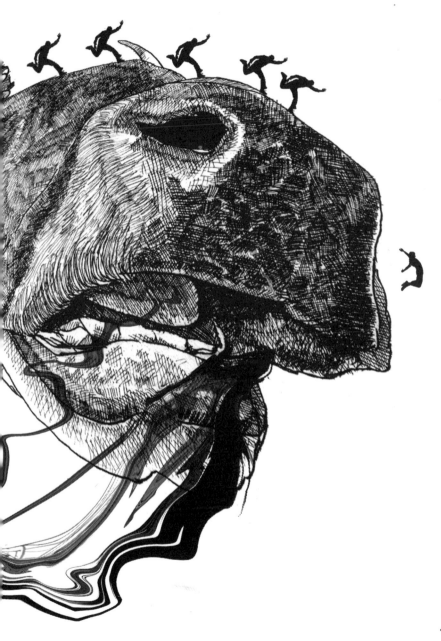

AFRAID ATLAS

Bethlehem

JONATHAN WATKINS

Since his death *c.* A.D. 33, countless millions have been taught to believe that Jesus Christ was born on 25 December Zero B.C. in Bethlehem. In that town, a church has been built over the X-marks-the-spot assumed to be the actual birthplace, the manger in the stable. Strangely, it is now a subterranean place, a grotto in a crypt, a pilgrimage destination that compels believers to kneel and count blessings, a place of spiritual intensity that inspires all kinds of weird behaviour. Touristic tendencies mix with a kind of self-induced autism whereby young priests pray fervently, oblivious to others in crowds milling around, also feeling the need to be there. Upstairs, candles and postcards are for sale, forcing the correspondence between religious relics and souvenirs.

On 4 January 1966, 1,965 years and 10 days after Christ is supposed to have been born, On Kawara started his *Today* series, an ongoing work comprising, to date, thousands of *Date Paintings*. They are paintings that are essentially inscriptions of the date of the day on which they were made – relics, souvenirs of a day that the artist lived through. White, standard, *sans serif* combinations of letters from the Roman alphabet and Arabic numerals – i.e. modern, Western-style – they comprise stark statements of units of time in the Christian calendar. This is a significant choice for a Japanese artist, brought up in the light of Shinto, Buddhist and Christian ideologies, whose formative years were lived through World War II.

On Kawara began *Date Paintings* shortly after arriving in New York, the welcoming city of the world power that dropped its atomic bombs on Hiroshima and Nagasaki. Japan? (Mexico? Paris?) The United States? The birthday of Christ? Thanksgiving? The birthday of the Emperor? New Year? Any place, any time… Post-war certainties were clearly arbitrary, symptoms of an all-too-human necessity, to an artist who is as intelligent as he is sensitive. The Christian calendar? Why not?

On 17 September 1998, seven *Date Paintings, 1-7 January 1997*, were installed in a kindergarten in Sydney's inner city, the day before the opening of the 11th Biennale of Sydney. This was the first manifestation of 'Pure Consciousness', an exhibition devised by the artist for children who are about six years old, beginning to learn to read and count, finding out that there are seven days in a week, that Tuesday follows Monday, Wednesday Thursday, etc. A wider world is being revealed to them. They are seeing countless things for the first time, with 'pure consciousness', a condition that On Kawara suggests as both sufficient and necessary for personal fulfilment. With the fresh pairs of eyes of the children involved, his paintings are apprehended simply, profoundly, in a particular kind of classroom; not to be used as 'artistic' teaching aids, but there to co-exist with young people, who live happily without a definition of art.

Since Sydney, the seven *Date Paintings*, in the same consecutive sequence, have been installed in kindergartens all over the world, from Istanbul to the Ivory Coast, from the Amazon to Avignon, from Shanghai to Toronto, from London to Lund. Clearly, the artist's proposition is as international as it is practically modest, reflecting his own identity as a peripatetic, unpresuming citizen of the world.

On Kawara was a schoolboy, an occupant of classrooms, when the Japanese holocaust occurred. He describes a radical scepticism that then coloured his everyday life, whereby he answered "I don't understand" to every question his teachers asked. Later, after the outbreak of the Korean War in 1950 and the American occupation, he started travelling globally, looking for an authentic way to express himself. He eventually found it in the cave paintings of Altamira, Spain, in 1963. The *Date Paintings* are a direct response to the beautiful pictures On Kawara saw on the walls of those prehistoric 'rooms', illuminations in darkness, pictures made long before anyone had learnt how to write and much longer before anyone had formulated even the vaguest definition of art.

Now, here we are in the kindergarten of Dar Al-Kalima College, Bethlehem, with On Kawara's *Date Paintings* hung on a wall that also provides the backdrop for good, clear didactic charts – numbers one to ten, alphabets, etc. – and a wide range of stationery, pencils, crayons, glue, scissors, paper, cards, filling shelves and cupboards. There is modelling clay and other art class material. Cheerful mobiles, assemblages made by the children who occupy this room every day, hang from the ceiling above a configuration of chairs and tables, organised into groups that suggest friendliness. This is a well-organised classroom, not the abject interior one might have expected to find somewhere in Palestine, resembling scenes broadcast on TV news.

The Dar Al-Kalima kindergarten is affiliated with the International Cultural Centre in Bethlehem, sponsored by the Lutheran church. There we had the privilege to meet Senior Pastor Mitri Raheb who, with good humour, suggested that even God had had enough of religion in Palestine/Israel. His argument essentially is that the Palestinians are engaged in a long war – much more than a battle – and that, for each Palestinian, an entire life of fighting simply is not fair. There must be places of refuge, where one can enjoy and/or imagine a peaceful, civilised existence as something normal. Otherwise, eventually, all hope will be lost.

Now, here we are again in this kindergarten, this time with the children. They are very welcoming, funny, as they try out their English. Hello. "Hello". In the playground, they are amused by our attempts to kick their footballs back into their games. They are confident-shy, like all kids of their age all over the world. They giggle together, hands over mouths, as they observe the behaviour of these aliens that have landed in their school. They couldn't be more curious and engaging. On the first evening after the *Date Paintings* were installed, we attended a meeting in the kindergarten with parents and children where all sorts of ideas about art and life were tested. It was one of the most stimulating symposiums that ever happened around an art event. Why were we here? Why On Kawara? Hiroshima/Palestine? And, oh yes, that's right, Jesus – the ultimate peacemaker – was born in Bethlehem…

We spent that night in Ramallah, having negotiated the Israeli check points that skirt around Jerusalem. The swagger of the young, 20-something Israeli soldiers with their machine guns, their enjoyment of power, their games of stop-and-search, could not have been more tedious, more insulting. In between the check points, we caught glimpses of the new wall, the wall that is choking the life out of Bethlehem, the wall that is separating innocent people from land that is rightfully theirs, the wall that is essentially counterproductive. It is a structure that continually reminds Palestinians from the occupied territories that they cannot move between their towns without Israeli permission, without the humiliating process of asking an aggressor – and one who has America's warm support – for a basic human right. Of all the places in the world destined to receive On Kawara's 'Pure Consciousness', this one could not be more poignant.

Otondro Prohori
Guarding Who? Against What?

NAEEM MOHAIEMEN

Of all the things written about the regime, put-downs were always in Bengali. English was for seminar talk.

A former writer, exiled in London, wrote in *Samakal*: "Alright then, let us accept the fiction of the Caretaker. So we have been gifted an army-civilian hybrid, calling itself a 'Caretaker Government'. But we always know a caretaker to be a *darwan*. But here you come back after an evening dinner to your own house, and your *darwan* won't let you in".

Later, after the military had left, really left, and not willingly, I looked back on those two years, 2006-07. It was easy to map so many of us, silenced so quickly. With a minimum of action, only a hint of menace.

At the beginning, it was probably quite confusing, right? For you? For me too. The army was feared, but the democracy that came before was chaos, battles, musical chairs. Maybe there was a secret sigh of relief at the disruption of politics.

Later, after the bloom wore off, by month three (it happened quickly), little fragments of dissent started trickling out. Essays, letters, rumours, *chika* slogans, whispers, rumblings.

In the Middle of Nowhere, Rumi Ahmed's blog, published "The Darkness". A squadron of police marching up the steps of the Public Library to enforce the new law requiring all lights to be out by 8 p.m. To save electricity. The Metallica song on my infernal soundtrack.

Proxy battles were staged, not against khaki but against perceived allies. Our laureate came to speak on campus and was met by groups of students blocking his entrance. How dare he throw his name into the election ring during an army-backed government? *Dalal*. Stooge. The noble Nobelist was in for a surprise. In Europe, he was on a panel with Bob Geldof, Angela Merkel, and here people were calling him *jolpai dalal*. *Jolpai*, the color of the uniform, swiped over him, his frame.

Dissent grew in gradual layers over the months and always with counter-reactions. Physics. A brutal grinding of links. The death of Choles Ritchil. The torture of journalist Akash.

The midnight arrest of CNN stringer Tasneem Khalil.

Zafar Sobhan came over to my house to talk face-to-face, to tell me Tasneem's body was black and blue. *He lifted his shirt to show me. You see why I'm not using the phone any more?*

Thanks a lot, Zafar, you also called me the night of his arrest. Woke my father up in the middle of the night. Hope they're not tapping your phone.

I had also 'seen' Tasneem, the morning after his arrest. Blogs were reposting urgent appeals, petitions were gearing up, Embassy Row was calling intelligence contacts. But wait, there was tasneem.k on my gchat window.

<Idle>, flashed his status. <Idle>.

Hey, are you out… where are you…, I typed.

A rather long silence. And then the chat window logged out.

Oh dear, who have I just written to?

Of course he had given up his password. You would do the same. Stupid to be brave.

Something about that arrest shook our micro circles. A chill of silence. Less and less texting, fewer phone calls, everything migrated to email. A professor called and asked me over one evening. Technical advice *lagbe re*. We discussed security measures. Making backups and deleting files. Renaming folders. Her partner had bought a fingerprint-activated pen drive. That was a bit much, I couldn't figure out how to make it work.

Tasneem's computer and laptop had been the torturer's honey pot, we all learnt a lesson.

The Caretaker Government took over Bangladesh from the politicians on January 11, 2007.

1/11. A nice, pithy, numerical tag for regime change.

Until August of that year, the silencing worked smoothly. Then, one afternoon, a fight broke out on the university campus. The army had requisitioned the university gym since January. One of the key flashpoints. Now three jawans were watching a football match. Someone's umbrella was blocking their view. A soldier shouted, *oi shora!* The umbrella would not move. Maybe it was his lover he was shielding from the sun.

The soldiers moved closer. Suddenly students also started paying attention. One or two of them stood up. Looking over, curious. Idle hands loosely out of pockets. *Thonga* of nuts dropped to the ground. Sandals back on feet. A push, a shove. *Tora janish amra ke*, do you know who we are? I heard the line repeated later. But who said it? Soldier or student?

The soldiers went back to find their comrades in the gym. The students went back as well. Between temporary barrack and dormitory, the numbers were suddenly against the army. By night, burning barrels littered the campus. Riot police spraying the air with gas and bullets. The soldiers barricaded inside the gym. At midnight, a senior officer went on television and said it was an "unfortunate incident".

Next day, the army withdrew from campus. The city smelt blood, riots flared on all campuses: Chittagong, Rajshahi and back to Dhaka. Fighting spread to the shops. The students were joined by urchins and flotsam. The invincible object meets the...

As groups gathered, courage was in numbers. Closed-off spaces opened wide. A quiet building to eat *muri chira* now hosted coded gestures. I was happy to plough through any newly open door. *Jodi laiga jai,* the lottery slogan for accidental connections.

A little bit of glasnost, but Allah and Army remain off-limits.

Recently, a newspaper editor told me: I need to put an affiliation in your byline.
– But I have no affiliation.
– I need to put an organisation.
– Why? This is my personal view, not from an organisation.
– Still needs an organisation.
– But then it will seem like an organisation is endorsing this.
– Are they?
– No. So why give it?
– Because, listen, if they call, I need to be able to identify the writer. And you need an affiliation for that.
– You would hand over author information like that?
– Ahha, why are you *gula*fying things together? No one is handing anything over. They will just want to reach you. To invite you over. For a cup of tea and a chat.

When the Parjatan office was boarded up, I didn't raise an eyebrow. Their slogan for useless decades: Visit Bangladesh before the Tourists Come. No big loss. After the shuttering, tractors moved in.

Then one day, the tarp came down, a new sign went up. Dhaka Cantonment Starts Here. Overnight, the khaki zone had extended from Old Airport all the way to Bijoy Sharani. The Cantonment now envelops and faces off against the prime minister's office. Right next to the baroque sculpture of the three oysters.

In 1975, tanks had to roll from the Cantonment to Dhanmondi. Now it would take minutes to form a pincer.

No wonder they were relaxed about giving elections.

The politicians also note the new geography. And 'behave'.

Ferdous was the first to tell me who the new CNG stations were going to. One franchise is with the main network of Army Welfare.

I thought of Kaa's song. *Trust in me, just in me. Shut your eyes and trust in me. You can sleep safe and sound. Knowing I am around. Slip into silent slumber. Sail on a silver mist. Slowly and surely your senses. Will cease to resist.*

Ekota. Unity. Until the Caretaker withdraws. And then it will be back to taking your eyes out at night, after the coloured panel wins against the bleached.

F. Rahman Hall. Student Union Chairman. Withdraw False Case.
A few months later, at dawn, the same hero would be caught in a bank robbery.
The getaway car hadn't been tuned, it stalled a mile away.

When no court stepped in to save the Rangs Building, we understood the army bulldozers were unstoppable. When the building suddenly collapsed, the workers' families started camping outside at the water fountain circle.

An old man from the villages who would not be bullied, cowed or threatened. Whose son was melting in the heat, between the girders of floors five and six.

He only said, I have come to bury my son. I won't ever leave.

I thought of panning up and taking in the construction sponsor. The Mobile Co. But it seemed pointless to take crowd-pleaser potshots at the expats. When everyone else is getting in line for a share, it's too easy to lob at MNCs.

The digging outside my house, for a mystery cable line and a 'mega' (pronounced 'myaga') hub, is by a new company called Emoh. After I asked for their permission documents, they handed over a folded, photocopied letter from the Dhaka City Corporation. At the top is the operations manager's name, another retired officer. The expats have only quarterly report goals, that's almost easier to size up.

Back to elections. Back to democracy. The new normal. Mission accomplished.

But the residues are still here.

A temporary camp for highway construction.
Phantom investor.
New chairman.
List of approved guests.

Shadow falls. A theorist talks about the architecture of occupation, hollow land. But security presence in Asia is subtle. Suit-tie-coat-*bideshi*-degree. Think tanks, seminars, conferences, talk shows, newspapers. Everyone has an opinion on the century's obsession. War against an invisible enemy.

They tell us, we know all the answers. How to catch them, inside and outside borders. How to keep them out. Facial hair, surname, skin hue, city of birth, passport – the full spectrum domination of motivation recognition. It's not who you are, it's who we say you are.

Dhaka is now inside a security-zone bubble. Will democracy remove the steel wire barricades and midnight checks on Dhanmondi Bridge? On the day after the state of Emergency was lifted, I saw a homeless woman drying her family's clothes on that same wire barricade. A sweet, fleeting moment.

But a few days later, the barricades were back in action. The demand for ID, the sudden stop-and-search, the rummaging inside your camera bag, the interrogation.

Eto raat e beriyechen keno? Janen na din-kal kharap? These bad times keep good people home. Only thugs and drunks out at the witching hour.

I feel a searing nostalgia for open space, a time before these 'temporary' structures. Temporary camps that never leave. It's all to make you safe and secure. Safe from what?

A long pause.

Yourself, your weaker side, your politics, your affiliations, your nightmares, your ideology, your rights, your friends and neighbours.

Your dreams.

Conversation on Locating Conflict

NANNA HEIDENREICH + NICOLE WOLF

Where is this place?*

Happy to report that Iran is still going strong, regardless of my updating or not.

She, who writes from Iran, tells me she experiences the question of emotions, the emotional illiteracy/literacy divide, as a major obstacle in the process of translation between here and there. I understand what she is talking about as I am on the 'there' side of this divide and am concerned about it, about the divide: what ways of relating can we come up with to negotiate it, to bridge this divide?

I am usually very wary of pathos, for instance of the use of affect and emotion in political cinema, even though I am intensely critical of a mere 'contentism'. The lack of emotional language in my politics is, of course, specific for a time and place, it entails specific details that make up the grid of my place of 'enunciation', and it is this specificity that makes it difficult for the images and accounts to travel from here to there, from them to me. But I do tend to have a thing for polemics. Since polemics only work in a very limited space and time, they can shed light on those limits. He, who delivered a great translation of an email sent from an art magazine to her using polemics as a tool, he agrees with her – the two write with so much

Where is this place? Where is this city, His City?

...I don't know what it might have been like in the early 90s, when there was widespread state brutality in Kashmir, for this old man to sit here in his shop.
Hansa Thapliyal

I got involved in somebody else's practice of relation. I was mesmerised by somebody else's strategy to try and take appropriate account of a context overwhelmed with daily violence and the instrumentalisation of the politics of fear.

Which place do you go if to be protected from violence by the nation-state is to be exposed to the violence wielded by the nation-state, and thus to rely on the nation-state for protection from violence is precisely to exchange one potential violence for another? (Butler, 2009: 26)

From Iran to Kashmir – another casualty in the stream of global unrest? Or invisibilities of different kinds? Who speaks what from there, and how do I listen?

In one documentary account, I see people running, running for their lives.

NANNA

NICOLE

*All writings in italics are quotes, from written texts and videos circulating on the Internet as well as personal communication and email

poignancy, it should make tears well up in your eyes (laughter and pathos both) – that urgency, involvement, makes the art magazine's request to her unbearable (I will tell you about it in a moment).

He, she, others writing from and to Iran, involved, glued to the Internet for hours, for good reasons – the Internet linked closely to all those microdissidences – organised a talk/screening/discussion later that year in Berlin. They decided to show a video that used much of the material that the *citizen journalists*, as she calls the bloggers, spread, but to not show the material itself, unmediated – for example, one of the beautiful and strong Rooftop poems, "Where Is This Place?" (see below). It would have made them cry, she says, and it would have silenced those attending, both because they do not feel the same, quite likely, they come from a distance, but they would also, quite likely, have been completely incapable of handling the emotions.

Some Questions

Whose involvement is sincere, who appropriates? When is it actually involvement, and when should one rather remain quiet? How do we negotiate the borders of the national, what are the outlines of an internationalism (today?), how do we negotiate our location and where we speak from, and how do we link that to where others speak from, or other locations and their politics? Where am I political and where appropriating?

If one central entry node for accountability, for entering the sphere of recognition, is the acknowledgment of the right to fear, the question can also be asked like this: *how do we, as any spectator suppos-*

The mainstream media reporter is usually shown as standing heroically in the midst of situations like this, fearless, to bring us the immediacy and the news. Where do I stand when I look? When I watch the news, when I watch a documentary introducing people running, scared faces – a sign of uttermost precarity. And, where do I stand when I attempt to follow the choices of the Kashmiri photographer, Syed Muzafar, for framing daily experiences in Srinagar, and the choices of Hansa Thapliyal to work with his images, initially shot for the daily Urdu newspaper *Afaque* for her installation *His City*?[1]

Yellow and blue trees are not a metaphor here either but a strategy to engage. Something is returned which was destroyed or faded from within the image frame. Something is added through a craft, like a gift.

Art Spaces

The installation: walls made of cotton fabric and light metal pipes create a small space within the larger exhibition building, the fabric hanging in a manner that reminded me of clothes drying racks. Longish pieces of textile in different light colours and variant width with black-and-white photographs printed on the mostly coarse cotton material. The images spread unevenly over the textile panels. Looking at the stills I took of the installation, I at times wonder whether they appear like flags – but whom, which place or what sentiment, do they represent, celebrate or commemorate? There were certainly no symbols, icons or stripes.

No written text accompanied the images, but different narratives unfolded when I attended to the varied arrangements of the images. Images of movement, traffic,

NANNA

NICOLE

edly not involved in or merely not injured by a suffering he or she looks at, apprehend the other's suffering – and fear? This was the question we started off with.

Now I would like to add: how do I not only apprehend; how, where and in what form do I get involved? What and where is the place of the political, my politics, my place of politics?

Let me get to this specific place, to the writings from/on Iran, to her writing, his translation, the art magazine.

Blogging is an alternative sphere of communication. It is a place for the other voice, in many ways taking over what could be considered the tasks of journalism and its media, but also immediate or, to use another word (and not use 'authentic' or 'real'... too troublesome), direct. In Iran, following the election fraud in June 2009, blogs have been a source of communication for the protests, both for the protestors themselves but also to let the world out there know what is happening, since the regular media channels are all censored and/or controlled, and journalists are either in jail or no longer in the country. Many blogs provide detailed information on the protests, what happens where, giving translations of the speeches of the Iranian 'government', as well as interpretations of actions and tactics. They also collect and list the names of those who are imprisoned and publish accounts of torture. They write, as does she, who is gifted with the talent for the right words and the right questions, as *citizen journalists*. The writing is part of the protest, not only its mirror: *they are making use of everything they have at hand and turning it into a powerful tool in the cause. From slogans from the Revolu-*

urban activity, of crowds of people gathering, sitting or standing in public spaces, listening to a speech, of houses and roads affected by explosions or fire, of soldiers, people parading in front of army tanks, people pointing.

Some prints had small additions through embroidery, crafted with light-coloured thread, subtle but clear: the outline of a house half in ruins or of a door sill, a sparrow next to a shrine, the contours of a child's head, maybe bandaged, a blue and a yellow tree growing from behind a house, the facial outline of a baby on the lap of a woman who might be its mother, a fish in a bag carried over a bridge, two forearms and hands, one gripping the shirt of a man and pulling it over his head, the other hand reaching towards the shoulder of what could possibly be another soldier. Both hands were also extracted from the image where they appeared first. Seeing them separate, the human physique traced and sketched with a pencil, one becoming a fist, the other attaining a gesture of care, or maybe merely lifted to reach out, both attain a sense of fragility common to any human body lacking a nurturing context.

> *To be a body is to be exposed to social crafting and form, and that is what makes the ontology of the body a social ontology.*
> (Butler, 2009: 3)

There was also the portrait of a man, reappearing twice in the installation. Once next to a group of women, possibly protesting; once printed on a small piece of cloth like a handkerchief, with flowers embroidered next to the still of the face. A reference to

NANNA

NICOLE

tion that they subvert and poetically appropriate and set free of a fixed meaning to consumer technology that they use to communicate directly and unhierarchically to the world about their situation as citizen journalists, changing the landscape of journalism forever.

Hamid Dabashi, in his angry response in *Al-Ahram Weekly Online* (Issue 956, pp. 16-22, July 2009) to Slavoj Žižek's "Berlusconi in Tehran" text, published in *The London Review of Books* (Vol. 31, No. 14, 23 July 2009), writes that *for people like Žižek, social upheavals in what they call the Third World are a matter of theoretical entertainment.* He wants him to shut up and learn first. He also criticises the writer of the *Angry Arab* website, Asad Abu Khalil, for ignoring the voices of the protest and only focusing on the official media (CNN, who also know shit, or who rather prefer to know nothing). *We need to bypass intellectual couch potatoes and catch up with our people. Millions of people, young and old, lower and middle class, men and women, have poured in their masses of millions into the streets, launched their Intifada, demanding their constitutional rights and civil liberties. Who are these people? What language do they speak, what songs do they sing, what slogans do they chant, to what music do they sing and dance, what sacrifices have they made, what dungeons have they crowded, what epic poetry are they citing, what philosophers, theologians, jurists, poets, novelists, singers, song writers, musicians, webloggers soar in their souls, and for what ideals have their hearts and minds ached for generations and centuries?*

[W]ebloggers who soar in the souls of 'these people', Dabashi writes – immediately,

photographs which families keep for many years of the ones who disappeared and might already be dead but are still waited for. This gesture seemed special, to me less for the personification or personalisation of the conflict through a face but by being a respectful act of repetition of a practice of mourning.

Those documents – of which some had appeared once in an Urdu Kashmiri newspaper, others might have never been utilised to report and all of which were eventually stored in a plastic bag in Syed Muzafar's office, initially with no further intention to use them – were thus displaced, taken out of their production context, given another life.[2]

My response to seeing them in *His City* was affective, I would even say emotional on a certain level. I felt deeply moved and went back several times to look at them. I felt addressed, and now I am wondering about those sentiments. We often talk about closure through emotion, about art appropriating politics for a nice digestible story. Did the installation create a comfort zone for me, a soft encounter with a conflict zone? Allowing me a bit of participation by deciphering the images? Or, what can be thought and done with an affective response to all the possible stories a document might entail?

Working in Srinagar, I found a place of rest, and a place to learn something about colour. Hansa joined a former government worker who had left his government job during the early 90s to run a small tailoring shop in Srinagar where he embroiders – he makes a step aside. Learning his craft of embroidery becomes, as I understood, another side-stepping, the other voice: the people, actually *these people*, as he puts it: he wants it to be specific, the knowledge, and thus those who speak.

She, who writes from Tehran about the various forms the protest takes, the nightly soundscapes, the daily demonstrations, the gatherings, the street fights, the communication which finds all kinds of channels even when phone calls, cell phones and email are no option, the camouflage, the struggle with fear, the fearlessness of the struggle, she then got an email, from this art magazine which sits elsewhere (sits: thinks, operates, markets, works, acts), they loved the melon juice, it became a metaphor for why they publish an art magazine at all. Their email was baffling. He, who is witty and fearless too, rewrote that email, no, he translated it. They write, he writes, this: *We really want to exploit the work that you are still in a process of understanding which you happened to have 'produced' in Iran (I suppose I'm being too 'productivist' in my understanding of your activities as an 'artist', no?)... We have a few design obstructions because actually we think your blog would be more interesting if it becomes more catchy-to-the-eye... you have to understand most of our 'readers' just skim through the mag, so we have to make it visually appealing. Therefore we would like to disregard the content and focus on the form. But it's up to you in the end, your experiences are important, and I think it's great how you only talk about your direct experiences (vocab of the day, dramatically omit – as if it's possible to include anything else in such a moment). But do you actually believe in 'authentic experience'? Isn't that also a bit outdated*

now by the filmmaker/artist/storyteller feeling paralysed before starting her work towards a collaborative documentary film project which asked for moving from encounters with images to encounters with people.[3] How to address one's fear of not being equipped to address people with experience of daily violence, of not knowing how to approach the situation and how to speak of it? And – how to not be affected by the pervading atmosphere of fear, paranoia and suspicion, or move and think along its parameters?

Crossing the bridge daily and looking at the city from the tailor's shop became a momentary interruption of seeking access through talking, understanding through gathering information, opinions and narrated experiences, a stepping outside of a zone of paranoia. Precisely this suspension and interruption of the given 'logic of the action', in terms of the politics of the place and in terms of producing a response to a place of conflict, provided the knowledge of a craft that was later translated into a gift towards Muzafar's images, and which I experienced as yet another gift, another invitation to look at images from Kashmir and what they might tell. The conversation between the photographs, the cloth and the carefully chosen parts drawn out or imaginary details added through thread seemed to act like folds, layers of stories and relations.

What can be produced if nothing is assumed yet? Where is the place of the political if no definite language is forthcoming yet? The blogs on Iran also allowed me to follow somebody searching for a language to think and tell what he/she experienced.

NANNA

NICOLE

these days? You tell me – what was the real political potential of the event (I need some conversation material, please)?

For some, blogging is the voice of the people; for some, it provides metaphors for art – ice-cream and melon juice as edible, consumable metaphors.

Dabashi bashed Žižek because, he says, he writes when he knows nothing. Is he right about that? How political can you be, if you consider your voice to be only 'specific'? Should you wait, no, learn for years before you raise your voice, or, rather, your published voice? Or is Dabashi's argument not also one about the capitalising on politics, on atrocities, on fear, on resistance, within the spheres of art, academia, critique, theory, thinking, which get paid for? This is, of course, always linked to the question of who gets heard, who surfaces within the sphere of recognition ('recognition' being another word for the geopolitical design of 'the world').

What an amazing people, *these people* – yes, Dabashi is right here in this wording, *these people*, he writes. We have to acknowledge the specific time and place of a struggle, account for those who stand up against the violence, who raise their voices against the call of fear. *The emphatic unity of the people, their creative self-organisation and improvised forms of protest, the unique mixture of spontaneity and discipline*, Žižek writes. They are fearless also because they are capable of a collective empathy – what happens to one of us happens to all of us – shaping an incredible and insistently continuing protest, from which, indeed, we need to learn.

More Questions

Whose task is it to make things heard?

Hansa shares a conversation with Syed Muzafar where he tells her that after some time he started getting his adrenaline going when taking images of violence, of wounded bodies, and that a new fear towards images of beauty developed for him. The thrill and yet routine of capturing particular signs of what makes a place a conflict zone is a recurring theme, a distancing device for the maker and the viewer of those images. Every documentary filmmaker knows it's often very easy to make images of the horrific – and consequently knows about the exploitation that is entailed hereby and by the casting of people and places as victims and subjecting them to being looked at. At the same time, the divide that happens between the onlooker, seemingly safe, and a place or a people suffering might cause distress in the viewer because the act of looking is painful for myself while I look. Do I critique those images also because I don't want to feel that pain and the fear of experiencing it? Or is it actually harder to relate otherwise?

Looking for a Language of Empathy

What I most strongly experienced in *His City* was permeability. A permeability of sincere attempts to relate, of ways of looking at a daily context that is saturated with violence, which is self-evidently there as a constant layer of daily experiences, and at photographs taken of this context and transported to Mumbai, and thus a collaboration of practices and responses to Kashmir. There were fragilities that I sensed in the nevertheless decisive choices of photographic framing and in choices to carefully work upon partly faded and torn photographs through cloth and embroidery. Being sus-

NANNA

NICOLE

(Of course, always also linked to the fundamentals: who speaks, who listens?). Can Žižek only write, as Dabashi states, entirely impressionistically? Where is this place called 'involvement'? When does an account of something get accounted for, and when does it become regarded as mere 'form'? What if art hijacks politics? What if politics become the mere input for the acquisition of cultural capital?

Sources

http://weekly.ahram.org.eg/2009/956/op5.htm (accessed 15 November 2009).
http://www.lrb.co.uk/v31/n14/slavoj-zizek/berlus-coni-in-tehran (accessed 15 November 2009).
https://un.poivron.org/~tasche/ (accessed 15 November 2009).
http://www.sidewalklyrics.com/ (accessed 15 November 2009).
http://iranfacts.blogspot.com/ (accessed 15 November 2009).
http://www.mightierthan.com/2009/07/rooftop (accessed 15 November 2009).

pended and experiencing those choices felt precious and put me in a particular place from where I now look at the many other accounts of Kashmir.

I wonder – can artistic and poetic strategies be in dialogue with a theoretical proposal of *a politics toward a consideration of precarity as an existing and promising site for coalitional exchange* so as to understand precariousness as a shared condition, and precarity as the politically induced condition that would deny equal exposure through the radically unequal distribution of wealth and the differential ways of exposing a certain population, racially and nationally conceptualized, to greater violence? (Butler, 2009: 28)

Refrences

Budak, Adam, Anselm Franke, Hila Peleg, Raqs Media Collective. **Manifesta 7: Index** (Silvana Editoriale, 2008, Milan).
Butler, Judith. **Frames of War: When Is Life Grievable** (Verso, 2009, London/ New York).

NANNA

NICOLE

Poem for the Rooftops of Iran: "Where Is This Place?"

Friday the 19th of June 2009 / Tomorrow, Saturday / Tomorrow is a day of destiny
Tonight, the cries of Allah-o Akbar are heard louder and louder than the nights before
Where is this place? / Where is this place where every door is closed?
Where is this place where people are simply calling God?
Where is this place where the sound of Allah-o Akbar gets louder and louder?
I wait every night to see if the sounds will get louder and whether the number increases
It shakes me / I wonder if God is shaken
Where is this place where so many innocent people are entrapped?
Where is this place where no one comes to our aid?
Where is this place where only with our silence are we sending our voices to the world?
Where is this place where the young shed blood and then people go and pray?
Standing on that same blood and pray
Where is this place where the citizens are called vagrants?
Where is this place? You want me to tell you?
This place is Iran.
The home place of you and me.
This place is Iran.
http://www.youtube.com/watch?v=pKUZuv6_bus&feature=player_embedded

Notes

1. The multi-media installation, **His City,** *was commissioned by Raqs Media Collective for 'The Rest of Now', the exhibition they curated for The European Biennial Manifesta 7. Direct quotations from Hansa Thapliyal can be found in Adam Budak, Anselm Franke, Hila Peleg, Raqs Media Collective,* **Manifesta 7: Index** *(Silvana Editoriale, 2008, Milan), p.105.*

2. The images are now also part of **Godaam: The Digital Image Archive,** *kept at Majlis (a "centre for rights discourse and inter-disciplinary arts initiatives"). They were initially collected by Hansa Thapliyal and made accessible through Majlis. The politics of working with an archive of that kind, for cultural and pedagogical purposes, was discussed at a workshop held in Pondicherry in February 2008; cf. http://www.majlisbombay.org/godaam_kashmir.htm (accessed 15 November 2009).*

3. **Yi As Akh Padshah Bai** *(There Was a Queen..., 2007), dirs. Kavita Pai and Hansa Thapliyal.*

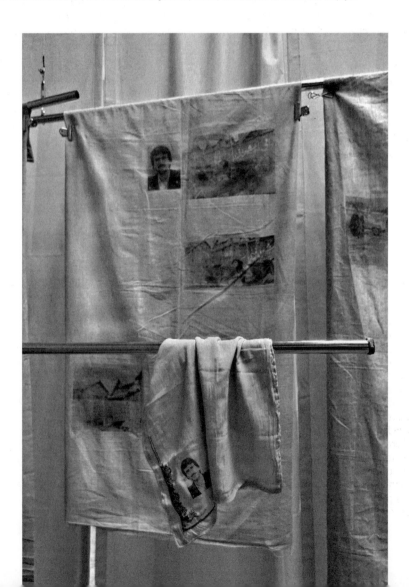

Dirt and Dust
A Lover's Letter

F. ZAHIR MIBINEH

This piece is part of a collective memory. I am quite fond of the elasticity of this term, 'collective memory': for one, this text draws upon, recalls and comprises a memory that I alone do not possess. At the same time, 'our collective memory' is a much larger project, one I take part in constructing with friends and strangers. Memory, for us, is not the ability to tap into a past impression. It is, instead, a faculty of the present moment, for each time we remember, something more current enters the picture. Thus, our memory is always changing its form, tone and colour. The content remains similar throughout – this past May, my partner and I travelled to Iran. We quickly found ourselves confronted with an urgent question: when did 'I' turn into 'we'? Much of this text has its origins in reports I wrote, attempting to understand what was taking place in Iran after the June 2009 presidential elections. I have realised that these reports no longer serve a purpose as static bookmarks of a time many of us have come to know only through media coverage. For us, whether in Iran or not, whether Iranian or not (and the definition of this particular identity can arguably be applied as a metaphor to anyone today who finds him or herself in love), to speak (and, by extension, write) about what 'happened' misses the mark: we should ask ourselves, 'what is happening'? The amorous convergence of me, my partner, my friends and those strangers amongst whom I silently marched, flashing victory signs in the air until our arms became sore, can only be described as an encounter of the people. It is not my role to depict the horrors of politically-sanctioned violence and torture, nor is it my place to imaginatively embrace a romantic notion of uprising and revolution. My romance continues elsewhere, with the everyday development of our collective memory, which in itself is our greatest treasure. I write to you, oh lover, as an 'I', with the desire that you begin to notice in every 'I' a 'we'. The Greek chorus, after all, brought with it a 'time outside time' – alongside the linear, accumulative narrative of the tragedy, the chorus staged the de-temporalised anxieties, fears and political realities of the time in its collectively subjective goat-song. Their response to the disaster? To sing and dance.

30 December 2009

Shall I talk about the weather?

The weather – the times – the winds of change, the breeze of forgetfulness, the breath of life, the gusts of chaos. Or a weather, *ein Gewitter* – "a tempest of dirt and dust has driven half of the nation to a standstill".[1]

What happens when the tempest clears?

> *The hazy dirt and dust set, and from behind the mountains the sun rises, and with it reality's bounty of autoresemblant greys which, only until a few hours ago, were so entangled that it appeared fast impossible to distinguish 'right' from 'wrong', 'oppressor' from 'oppressed' or 'pure' from 'sullied'. Lo! Now the hour arrives to cut the Moirean thread apportioning the good and the bad of our times. Yet, if you look closer, you can still recognise a trace of white in every black, there lies a bit of grey in every white, and the greens, pale to deep, are inextricable from one another. However, it appears that, regardless of what happens, our tomorrow bears no resemblance to yesterday. In comparing today to 30 or even a thousand-three-hundred years ago, those who attempt to seek the path leading to tomorrow in yesterday are deeply misguided: this river will not repeat itself.[2]*

I am afraid. First, I am afraid that my words will hurt, confuse or displease you; for some reason, I am negative about all of this. You've always said that what may be my biggest strength, and yet also my biggest weakness, is that I am too quick to find words to describe something which has not been fully digested. My mind races when I experience something inspiring – and there are far too many inspirations in this world. And so, I develop ways and expressions to recount this experience, but my weakness, as you point out, is that then I take the additional step of formulating a position from what I have said. All of this implies a certain propensity to speak without fully thinking about the entire picture. I become obsessed with small fragments. And so, I am afraid that this attempt to write will alienate you once again, as I have done before. But I am trying, trying to not take a position, to leave my obsessive fragments open to interpretation. Most importantly, you should understand that my position is not stationary – in fact, it may be non-existent. It is aligned with many different strains of thought, at times it is idiosyncratically abstruse, other times it gives away its affinities readily. This is where my anxiety is most clear. As you are unsure, I am not sure.

I fear also that I cannot, as I have been demanded to do by others (and, at times, myself), try and show 'how it really was' or what 'the people' are seeing, saying and experiencing. My intimacy with 'the people' only remains through you. You and I are the people. I am afraid for us and, by extension, for the people. What was a combination of a beautiful sense of return to a land and an inclusion in its transformation has now become far more complicated. Not only have we been confronted by violence – not to say that we weren't before – but this violence has shown itself amongst us. It is *my* land, it is *your* fault, it is *my* right, it is *your* tyranny. I obsess over the memory of us standing at the corner of Valiasr Street (the

Messiah) and Enghelab Street (the Revolution), afraid of what we would see once we joined the masses marching past us, and also afraid of ourselves, of what violence we hold in our thoughts and speech. We both asked one another: why are you here? What do you want? Why do you take pictures? Why do you write reports? We both answered: I'm not sure. We then both declared that we were searching for a non-violent language, a way of relating, describing and translating our experience together into something that moves beyond the rhetoric of conflict, strays away from injecting messianic blindness into any notion of a 'revolution' we may be holding on to. The waters continue to flow past our cold feet: the river has changed since we last stepped into it. What I am afraid of is our future – and keep in mind that fear, in the sense of *trembling before God*, is not solely negative. It can mean that I respect the future. What I mean to say is that now, after violence proved inevitable, is it possible to work towards a future in which such violence doesn't have to repeat itself? A future in which we will not say "that was a time, which promised us heaven, but created a hell on earth"?[3]

I am looking for the 'right word' to use at the 'right time' to unlock the poetry held in the prose: precisely that split-second before the arrow, *zärtlich gezielt*, pierces the surface. I'm afraid I have to piece together fragments of material I've written, reread and rewritten, like shards of sky and cloud put back together to recreate the storm. The puzzle, however, is not so easy to finish. Each time I visit these fragments, I obsessively move them around, break them apart, re-order them, like a witch doctor who hopes that with the proper rhythm of his invocative movements, the parched sky will finally open up to unleash the torrential, long-overdue rain. Everything I've been writing and will write about, that is, all that concerns our shared relationship to this land, is a love letter. Fragments of a love letter in a state of continuous composition. Although the amorous procedure with which we engage with one another (through which we engage with the land as we come to knowledge of our surroundings through the impossible encounter of you and me saying 'I love you') assumes that we are one and one and not two. The work we do together occurs on multiple levels. Our roles are constantly shifting. The perilous voyage through the situation repeats itself upon return. In the meantime, we are immobile, protecting ourselves either through distance, circumnavigation or an affair with our everyday lives, all of which ensure that the situation does not cause us to collapse fully and lose our respective positions. We tell stories to each other, stories which provoke us to wander again, to retrace our steps and to take new ones, allowing our 'knowledge' of the situation to develop in time. Yet, as we narrate, we also demand, an imperative voice that calls into the void. This demand only occurs when we find ourselves apart, confronted by the unknown absence of the other – and, in this case, the other may be you or it may be the land, as both have become indiscernible. I'm not sure.

Silence is betrayed by rumour; protest by violence.

In any case, I can say that where I am now, I can only see the surface. But that is the arrow's goal, after all, to graze against the surface ever so slightly.

You are rabble / you are dirt and dust / you are the black halo, you suppress and are blind / I am the courageous hero, and this land is mine![4]

5 July 2009

Around noontime, a slowly simmering, sulfurous haze settled onto the Tehran skyline, approaching the city with an invisible stealth until it had fully infested the streets and alleyways of the capital. This strange air appeared to envelop Tehran in a suffocating embrace, radiating through the sky like steam in a sauna. Later I found out that this tempest of dirt and dust had arrived from Baghdad.

Only the previous day had the same air blown through the Western regions of Iran, crossing several mountain ranges until it encountered Tehran's formidable pollution. The wall-like Alborz mountain range, sheltering Tehran from the North and acting as a geo-meteorological separation barrier from the sub-tropical Caspian region only 60 kilometres over *hill and dale*, functioned like a terminus for the malarial Baghdadi air. Although Tehran may have been spared the intensity endured by the plague's initial contacts, the remaining wind blowing through from Iraq would slowly trickle its way to Tehran and stop flat-on-its-face before the height of the Alborz, forecasting a much longer period of suppression as the city became the weather's metaphorical garbage dump, or, more appropriately, the *event horizon* of a black hole.

6 December 2009

What happens when an outsider encounters an incomprehensible event?

I am not who you think I am. I am *neither East nor West*, I am simply elsewhere. What I am trying to say is that I am the non-unique product of a shared history of Diaspora that in my particular context can be described as 'Iranian', and which, of course, is related to specific circumstances that have historically shaped Iran and determined the movements of its people, but which is not especially noteworthy in relation to other Diasporic communities and their self-understanding. My self-understanding as an 'Iranian' or an 'American' (given the supposed multiculturalism of the United States, a hyphenated identity can flourish with ease – one would think!) was complicated by the fact that I felt myself scattered around the world; in thought and interest drawn specifically to the 'Middle East', but clearly conditioned by my own process of self-identification within the terms I picked up in a 'Western' social and educational context. It was perhaps later, maybe now, that I could begin to articulate the non-negative sense of displacement I had felt all along as I grew up, whether that immediately had to do with being 'different' (culturally, physically, sexually, etc.), or whether it pertained, in general, more to a feeling of dissatisfaction and scepticism whenever I encountered individuals completely sure of their identities as singular, dual or plural. To be sure, I have promised myself to not make a muddle out of identity, but to instead try and focus on themes and issues that the experience of being *here and elsewhere* brings to the table, if anything then as an attempt to envision how my own subjectivity, as a constant outsider (perhaps 'stranger-friend' is most appropriate), relates to events as I encounter them and try to comprehend.

15 December 2009
The sea today is boisterous, windy; white-tipped waves like dolphin fins pierce its slate surface and move along the water in a northerly direction. The weather here in Beirut is still gentle, even if it may be a bit chilly as a semblance of winter encroaches, not comparable (I am sure) to what you are experiencing. We have been separated by the challenge of time that will characterise the upcoming months as I try and stay here and you return there, where our love began.

11 November 2009
The sea is old. The sea carries away. I imagine how easy it is to venture 'across the sea'.

There was one, there wasn't one, except for someone there was no one. A man stood here a long time ago, when the beach was rocky and covered in dry grass, when cactus paths grew their way towards the shore, when aloe and herbs imbued the humid air with a warm fragrance. A man looked out onto the sea and felt guilty every day for not paying more attention to it. His friends and family would catch him straying from work, distracted, lost in contemplation. One day, the man disappeared. He had built a small ship overnight and at sunrise set out across the sea, content to spend the remainder of his days alone with the water. No one heard from him again – they lamented his loss. Over time, his story grew to myth – the disappearance became important, necessary, perhaps destined, not a tragic loss but a renewal of some sort of contract with nature. When will he ever return again?

The man disappeared to those who knew him but appeared, over the course of time, as the current pushed him across the sea and the wind blew him in spirals to somewhere else. Thirsty, hungry, sunburned, salt-wounded, he landed on an island. How far away from where he came, he did not know.

To those living on this island, the arrival of this man was a foundational event. Someone, the first one, a man, a god, a hero, a ghost, appears from the sea, what was thought to be a border of the end of the world for the island itself. Until that day, the islanders conceived of their world as a cloud floating on a flat table of water, the centre of creation, the only place under the sun where men and women lived. Above, below and around were the borders set by the gods and the creatures of the known world. And so, on this day, a creature that bore resemblance to them appeared from an *Other* world. He allowed them to imagine *somewhere else*.

The man's disappearance *across* and appearance *from* the sea allows for imagination to produce legend. It is a story of a primal encounter. His departure and arrival allow for others to come and go; he breaks the barriers that had kept the imaginative coordinates of reality, of here and there, of what is and what is not, stable and fixed.

6 July 2009

I'm beginning to find that the events of the day are less important than what that day offers to thought through its sensory phenomena: ah, the weather, which has so gracefully aligned itself to developments in the complex situation here ever since I arrived – as if Nature, whose 'side' remains ambiguous, were attempting to express its prophetic foreshadowing of human events. Perhaps, as if the distinction between the collected sum of strained mental and physical activity here has created some material rupture in the laws of physics, atomic particles were being realigned to create terrifying natural occurrences. For example, the torrential winds of the pre-election period; the thunder and lightning boiling in the sky as fights broke out in the city post-election; the quiet, amnesiac sun of the second week when hope seemed to diminish; the second coming of something unknown and unclear in the Baghdadi winds of the third week that demanded *disappearance*.

28 December 2009

I've started a good routine of reading 15 pages of a book everyday. Psychologically, this very manageable amount of pages comforts me and also instills in me a peaked enthusiasm for more. So when I finish 15 pages of one book and still feel the urge to read on, I visit another book and continue on the same process. This helps me juggle ideas, as I am prone to do, and to cross over thoughts I've grasped in my short-term memory in a productive way. D. bought me a copy of *A Lover's Discourse* by Roland Barthes for Christmas. I've been browsing through it the past days. One of the fragmentary entries in this book is on The Absent One, comparing the absence of the beloved to the anxiety of losing one's mother, to the encroachment of death, to the fumbling attempts of making meaning out of silence through language. I will share with you a quote:

> Sometimes I have no difficulty enduring absence. Then I am 'normal': I fall in with the way 'everyone' endures the departure of a 'beloved person'... This endured absence is nothing more or less than forgetfulness. I am, intermittently, unfaithful. This is the condition of my survival; for if I did not forget, I should die. The lover who doesn't forget *sometimes* dies of excess, exhaustion, and tension of memory.[5]

10 September 2009

I had a very uncomfortable dream. I think it may have been lucid. I did not sense myself asleep, yet I was no longer aware of what was happening in the bedroom around me. It was more a feeling of hovering over my own body. More specifically, it felt as if my body were hovering in darkness, although the sun was shining brightly through the window and onto my white sheets.

I don't remember the full dream. I awoke with an atmospheric sense of confusion, but a concrete moment lingered. You are talking. You are sitting in front of me wearing your grey and blue checked jumper, the one that I've always thought was too big for you. You were clearly excited, recounting a story whose details I do not recall anymore. Afterwards, to my exhaustion, you began posing many questions to me: "Do you remember when…?" "You read that article, didn't you?" "Remember that day when we…?" These questions asked more from me than their immediate concerns. They depended on me. They depended on my memory of our shared experiences. They stressed a common bond between us. But there I stay, staring at you blankly: I didn't know what you were talking about! I couldn't remember anything you were referring to! I was overtaken by a sense of panic. Then, trying to cover up my discomfort, I forced a smile and a nod, pretending to remember. I knew immediately that you had figured me out. You looked me in the eyes, seeing they were empty and elsewhere. I wrenched in pain, struggling to remember, hoping you wouldn't perceive my agony. You didn't say a word. Instead, you laughed. I felt you move a far, far distance away, retreating in self-protection against a dangerous amnesia that had stripped me clean.

My eyes flashed open. D. was no longer home, he had left hours ago. Silence; only the gurgling of the Buddhist fountain in the neighbour's backyard crept in through the window. I confess to losing my memory.

"But you were there? You were there! Don't you remember?"

29 June 2009
A collective memory is being created.
I have decided to capture the moment.

What would I do if I were not Iranian?
Are my judgements of the current situation in Iran misguided?

My dreams do not narrate anything any more.

I have decided to collect 'our' dreams.

Our dreams articulate themselves as questions.
I have decided to collect our questions.
Our questions manifest as images.

What if these images are just fragments?

Our questions become images.

These images narrate the processes that build up our memories.
Our collective memory.

Finally, I fell sleep.[6]

24 November 2009

The sea is so close, a street away. It spreads itself across my line of sight, at a gentle angle from where I sit on my balcony. I keep thinking about last week, when you and I were in the South. The twilight hour we spent in Tyre together lingers deliciously in my memory. There – after the sun had set but before the darkness had fully crept in – sitting in the ruined amphitheatre of the agora, we were surrounded by a grounded silence that rooted our bodies into the stone. I felt that my legs were much longer than they actually were; as they dangled over the bleacher-style steps of the amphitheatre, my feet melted into the darkness emanating from the earthy grotto underneath. It was as if they were planted into the rich, black soil like arcane mandrake roots, suspiciously human. We were alone at the archaeological site. We didn't speak to one another; we sat next to each other. The sea and the cicadas were the only sounds that could be heard. There, unlike Beirut, where, ironically, the sea is so close yet so silent, we could hear the water as its waves broke rhythmically against the shore, sending the smooth smell of salt and plastic bottles into the air. The dull hum of its incessant movement, its laps back and forth, gave the sensation of a crisply cool blanket on a fresh bed, waiting for a sleeper to dive in, wrap himself inside, shiver in anticipation of the contradictory coming warmth.

Here, no sea-voice and no cicada-song. The twilight hour after sunset and before sunrise finds a peak in the cacophonous traffic, cars either coming home from work (on weekends, going out) or going to work (perhaps 'work' is not accurate in this city, let's just say these are the hours in which cars come and go, from and to places). This must be the *hour of the wolf*, as it is said, 'the hour when most men die and most children are born'. I can imagine such an hour when I remember that prolonged, grounded moment, sitting with you in the blue-dark, feet rooted into the black, embraced by the beckoning caress of the sea and the star-sparkle-welcome of the cicadas' sonic twinkles. Here I could die, here I can see inside me and around! You said to me: "I see history, I understand what it means to love a country, why men and women have fought and died to protect home, how they have suffered in exile, what distance means". What continues to live on, life itself, presents itself, unchanged in form. In content, however, life reveals itself as an irrational set of deviations, contortions and mutations. But when I wake up before sunrise to the honks and screeches, the sea cast invisible by the movement of the traffic (a blue, solid extension of the sky, the city becomes a highway floating on clouds), I cannot, in this moment of living bodies inside machines, confronting one another through will, metal and pitch, imagine that this dark hour exists as the threshold between this life and another-to-be. The hour of the wolf, in the city, is perhaps more the hour of hot coffee, alarm clocks, grumpy beginnings and elephantine thuds: *an elephant in the room* is a saying that means the truth is monstrously present although everyone attempts (and, arguably, fails) to ignore it.

28 December 2009

I am afraid of forgetting. I've been struggling with this fear ever since we left Iran in August. I have periods of time in which I am 'normal' – I find ways to reconnect with what is taking place there, where I can tap into the reservoir of my memory and make sense of the picture that develops in relation to my present distance. Yet, other times, the fear of forgetting gives me a sharp, pyramid-pointed headache, numbing me with its taunting persistence. It speaks to me, reminds me of one thing: without being there, I can not be a part of what is going on. I resist. As I've engaged with this fear, I have begun to understand the need for repetition. Why do people commemorate events yearly, repeat the narratives of a particular day, recite the same slogans or chants, perform the same gestures? Because they are afraid of forgetting. Or is it a greater fear – the fear of the ultimate forgetting, death, the still-mind state of cold, incommunicable otherness? The rest of the year, the symbolic moment of repeating what is on the brink of being forgotten fades away into the ordinary routine, making room for our everyday survival to continue on as it did. That's when we become unfaithful to one another: once we step outside of suspended reality and engage in an affair with life. What to do then? I'm thinking that once the commemorating event has come and passed, once we've come to terms with the day after, when the administration of things seems inevitable, we should recite poetry. It's like the 15 pages of a book a day – a poem a day – or, even more, it helps repeat, microscopically, the transient presence, that *thing* which risks slipping away from the hand that attempts to administer it. The poem makes sense as a tool, helping me at least to not forget. Its lines, rhythmically patterned, are meant to elevate language a step above, to make words hold more weight, if only by imposing a repetitive arrangement upon them. I will repeat myself, repeat many things – either I am writing a poem to you now or I am commemorating an event. Is there a difference? In any case, I repeat in order to join you in your fight against forgetfulness: against forgetting what our love means, what we shared, how we have been treated, how the news has passed us over to the periphery of its gaze in the past months, how the tyrants feel that if they ignore us, we will fade away. I repeat to assure myself that despite distance, comfort and distraction, I am an individual being-with, becoming-butterfly, intoxicated in you. Of course, I mean to say 'you' in the plural.

14 June 2009

They have guns. They pointed them at us. They are not afraid to shoot. They took down house numbers. For now, we are safe. But we can't be sure. There are four of us here: two filmmakers, an artist and a writer. We are not alone, but there are many of them and they are ready for violence. This is a coup d'état, and, if things get worse, there will be a crackdown. If that is the case, they may come back, and we may be arrested, questioned, put in jail, who knows? Let the world know our situation.

10 November 2009

There was and there wasn't...

Meaning: everything existed and nothing existed. How can there be nothing from every-thing? How does everything co-exist with nothing? What time or tense is taking place in this statement?

There was one and there wasn't one...

Now this statement is quite different. A subject has been introduced into the everything/ nothing duality, meaning 'someone existed and no one existed'. But whether someone or no one, the subject, or its lack, occupies a general existence, not a nothingness of any sort. Either one is on scene, in the event, part of a becoming, or no one is there, no one has (yet) arrived, no one is participating. Somehow, this statement anticipates action – the one who was, is, but hasn't yet begun to do something, to articulate its being; the one who wasn't has yet to be, but may perhaps come later and take part. Therefore, in this statement, there are ***two***, a pair, a conversation or dialogue – not a one and its lack, rather a double of the one who is (the double – perhaps death? the constant risk of disappearance? the Messiah: one who was [is] and the one who wasn't [isn't] *at the same time?*).

21 December 2009

I read the following in an article by Farnaz Fassihi entitled "The Doctor Who Defied Tehran":

> Mothers of individuals killed in Iran's anti-government protests this year have formed a support group, Grieving Mothers, who march silently Sunday afternoons at Laleh Park in Tehran holding pictures of their dead children. This month, security officials arrested 15 members. They were freed a few days later when crowds gathered near the jail, demanding their release.[7]

I don't want to make any spectacular comparisons, but so much of what's going on there takes on, for me, the quality of Greek tragedy. I know you and I have talked about this extensively, the night you were at my apartment in Beirut; we sat on the balcony and ate custard apples together. That night, I fell silent while listening to your eloquence. I didn't feel as though I could respond to your sensitive thoughts, gracefully adorned with hesitation. I mentioned that I had been thinking about Greek tragedy, specifically the role that the chorus played, as representatives of the 'people', a form of running commentary with multiple perspectives, or a super-ego voice-in-the-head that appears onstage, collecting the voice of those who comprise, for lack of a better word, the 'common'. Later that night, after you had left, I received an email from you, apologising for your lack of clarity, saying that you felt as though you were quite inarticulate and that you were sorry if that had left me with a feeling of frustration. Ironic that it was exactly the opposite! In any case, did I ever tell you I was in a college experimental production of Euripides' *The Suppliants* (alright, it was more a multimedia theatre piece, a collage of *The Suppliants* with two short Beckett plays)? I was in the chorus of suppliant women, grieving Argive mothers who journey to Athens in order to beg Theseus to recover the bodies of their dead sons who had fallen at the hands of

Thebes' invading army. These mothers are driven by the belief that all Greeks, regardless of their sins, deserve burial. We had to say our lines in ancient Greek, quite an exhilarating challenge: a Classics professor and a dance choreographer taught us how to combine the tonal pronunciation with the rhythm and metre of the verse itself into a complete movement, uniting voice and body. We, the Grieving Mothers, may as well have been silent; delivering our lines in Greek emphasised the emotive and sonic qualities of our body-song, rather than fixating on the audience comprehending the 'meaning' of our lines. Indeed, *The Suppliants* is unique amongst Euripides' tragedies in that the chorus arrives on stage in silence, and remains silent for a significant duration of the play.

Why are they so afraid of the dead? When the Baghdadi winds shut down half the country this past July, the first thought that sprung into my head was that the ghosts of the Iran-Iraq War were invading. An army of blind ghosts, their vengeance turned foul air. Such an army would consist of not only Iraqis, but of all the weary souls who-do-not-lie-in-peace, foremost the Iranian child-soldiers used as 'human shields' in the final years of the Holy Defence, sent in waves to first clear the battlefield of mines and then as 'living grenades' thrown underneath invading tanks. Despite the elaborate martyrology that emerges from their little-known biographies and the ceremonies established by the Islamic Republic to honour them, such as the archival footage of the Iran-Iraq War shown daily on state-run television before the news begins, I have little faith that these souls have managed to cross the threshold from this world to the next. Instead, they are trapped in-between.

Could these Grieving Mothers be accompanied by the hundreds of thousands of those other grieving mothers who still bear the memory of their martyred sons and husbands? They both would gather to demand that their children be able to rest in peace, free from the propaganda that uses and abuses their memory – one group sees their children continuously tarnished as terrorists, rogues, vandals, criminals, who deserved to die and who do not merit a proper funeral or even a mourning ceremony; the other group does not cease to encounter their children lauded as heroes of the Revolution, painted effigies of their rosy-cheeked faces dotting murals across the country, their sacrificial actions praised repeatedly at yearly commemorations remembering those who fell during the war. In the combined supplication of the Grieving Mothers, similar issues at stake in *The Suppliants* come to the table. Some of these mothers are told their children are "dirt and dust". Other mothers are supposedly comforted by an empty insistence – your children gave up their lives for the Land! Whether dirt, dust or the motherland, these dead children have not yet been given up to the earth. They hover and whisper, words are spoken about them, tears are shed for them. The earth is the source of both life and death. It is and should be life's final resting place. It is, however, also the ground upon which politics is played, wars raged, revolutions unleashed. Maybe then, they are afraid of the dead, because they know they have depended on them for too long. Because they are guilty of that tragic sin, to not allow the dead to be buried: "The only writer of history with the gift of setting alight the sparks of hope in the past, is the one who is convinced of this: that not even the dead will be safe from the enemy, if he is victorious. And this enemy has not ceased to be victorious".[8]

7 July 2009

A few nights ago, I was having a late conversation with R. He, in passing, briefly mentioned that one particular aspect of Shi'ite Islam is the capacity to imagine, as a constructive tool to deal with what is denied-as-disaster, and, in turn, claimed as 'disappearance'. According to him, unlike other religious traditions which claim distinction through what is witnessed, such as the revelation of the Ten Commandments to Moses on Mount Sinai or the Resurrection of Jesus Christ, Shi'ite Islam is, in terms of events, impoverished by its *lack* of witnessing, or, rather, it is afflicted by a series of losses: Ali's arbitration at Siffin giving Mu'awiyah the upper hand; Hossein's martyrdom at Karbala, leaving the Prophet's family scattered and hunted; the 12th Imam's mysterious Occultation, his resolve to be in this world without being noticed. The absence of visible 'results' in the development of a Shi'a 'consciousness' has, in turn, led theologians to rely heavily on the esoteric, intrinsic nature of God's revelation, a practice that colours the reading of the Qur'an as well as any approach to theological matters. A precarious balance between the visible and the invisible arises. I am reminded of Borges' Hakim, the Veiled Prophet:

> First there came a trembling. The promised face of the Apostle, the face which had journeyed to the heavens, was indeed white, but it was white with the whiteness of leprosy. It was so swollen (or so incredible) that it seemed to be a mask. It had no eyebrows; the lower eyelid of the right eye dropped upon the senile cheek; a dangling cluster of nodular growths was eating away its lips; the flat and inhuman nose resembled that of a lion. Hakim's voice attempted one final deception: *Thy abominable sins forbid thee to look upon my radiance...,* he began. No one was listening; he was riddled with spears.[9]

During the course of Hakim's ministry, an insistence on the sacrosanct invisibility of his face kept him in a position of power – as long as his followers believed that to see would mean to no longer be able to see, Hakim remained in control. What I suspect was Hakim's greatest downfall was his inability to distinguish the balance between seeing and not seeing: he did not present *himself* as holy, only his *face*. Through this, he exposed the sight of his other-than-face to the knowledge engendered and demanded by vision. His only option, in my opinion, would have been to *disappear* at the moment that his followers acknowledged his holiness. Then, he would truly venture into the realm of *effect*, that is, the invisible, where he could continue his ministry undercover, perhaps to the point of success. Of course, such a move may have meant that he, sooner or later, would be superseded by another who would claim the *effect* of his holiness. This claim would have to be negotiated between the usurper and the occulted. Such a negotiation, concerned over a conflicting will-to-power, could only take place within the realm of the *alam al-khiyal,* the world of imagination, and not in the world of men. The veil passes from one face to another. It acts, somehow, as a screen upon which the imagination of its effect is projected. All that remains for a Shi'a subjectivity, if there is one, is to imagine. If this imagination is compromised by time, that is if a believer is given the right opportunity to actually see and to gather knowledge from that act of such seeing, the illusion of the disappeared, the ghostly, the occulted and, ultimately, the Messianic *effect*, is shattered: Hakim's leprous face reveals itself.

27 December 2009

Today is 'Ashura. The day here began sunny and clear; outside, the usual congested traffic was noticeably absent. My ears were perked to attention. They were awaiting a signal from outside, confirming that today is the day that it is. I heard music from across the street, although I could not pinpoint from where it was playing. It was a dull chant, open to interpretation: was it a mourning-song in commemoration of the day, a prayer being broadcast or a melancholic tune, devoid of that symbolic reference I was seeking? My thoughts were with you, knowing you were already awake and, perhaps, out on the streets.

I didn't want to see blood. Knowing that in Beirut, the traditional bloodshed accompanying 'Ashura processions is banned, I had decided for some time now to go to Dahiyya, the Shi'a neighbourhood in the south of the city, to witness what today would offer. I felt nostalgia for those inconvenient summer visits to Tehran as a child (somehow, our trip always coincided in those years with the months of mourning). I remember when I was ten years old and had just been circumcised, my aunt took me to a gathering on the night before 'Ashura. That awkward image of me in a pink skirt (pink, by an amusing coincidence; a skirt, to avoid any uncomfortable pressure on my wounded-still, healing private parts), sitting in a sea of wailing women-in-black, bored and hungry, belonged to a register of impressions fuelling my expectations for the day. No, not that I imagined today would see me cross-dressing, nor that I would be, by virtue of a long-gone pre-pubescence, able to blend in once again amongst weeping women. Rather, I expected that same mixture of the awkward and the sensory, that banality of boredom and hunger tense in confrontation with the special otherworldliness of this day's accompanying rites and rituals. I sought to transpose my presence in Beirut, so distant from you, through imagining that today, in Dahiyya, I would encounter a tear in the fabric of space-time: upon entering the frenzy of the masses here, I could then join myself with you there. As you moved among the masses there, fighting to be with one another, I would throw myself here into the sea of black-clad bodies, hungry for rights and recognition.

What I found in Dahiyya was, literally, dirt and dust. The sun was bright and hot and the crowds were already dispersing, going home for lunch or picking up snacks on the street. As I imagined, everyone was in black. Groups of young men with green headbands walked barefoot while girls flirted from the sidelines. I think I arrived too late. The frenzy I sought after proved anticlimactic: the scene bore more of a resemblance to an eerie monochrome street carnival, complete with roadside trinkets, souvenirs and grilled hamburgers. I wandered around for half an hour and decided it was time to head back home. On my way back to the bus stop, I was attacked by harsh winds, clouds of dirt arising from the ruined houses left over from recent conflicts, accompanied by the fresh dust of concrete-laden construction sites.

29 December 2009

I've been following what took place in Tehran on 'Ashura. I can imagine the media's excitement about the day – *what a good story! This is gonna be great!* Isn't it amusing that the media coverage after the June elections stopped once Michael Jackson died? I suppose, in a post-spectacular landscape, whatever event ceases to serve as the basis for a Hollywood screenplay is simply dropped, another one offering itself almost immediately. Well, this isn't a *good story*. It's not a *story*. The danger of 'Ashura is that Hossein's murder at Karbala by Yazid is, after all, a *story*. Whether there was one or there was no one doesn't really matter – a story risks replacing our real and true witness to *life*. We tell each other stories late at night, to quell our fears from the dark figures and strange sounds creeping into the room. These stories help us to fall asleep.

> *Fear succeeds by monopolising ambiguity; it casts its shadow on our capability to assess our time and condition. If we continuously remind ourselves of this, then we no longer have a reason to be afraid.*[10]

What is our time and condition now? Not what was our time and condition in some 'once upon a time', but where am I, where are you, right now? What do you want from this life? The story can be listened to before bedtime, but it shouldn't fill our waking days with its dreamy narrative. It seems the repetitions I've been employing in order to stave off the spectre of forgetfulness are no longer necessary. Somehow, I had become religious – my gestures of remembrance were similar to the neurotic fingering of prayer beads accompanied by an inner running monologue addressed to a fearsome god. I don't think we should pray any more. We won't forget, of this I am sure. I will continue writing to you, sensing your presence near, but this time I will focus on staying awake and clear-sighted. I will abandon my commemoration of the past, what I suppose has been keeping me distant from you. I will instead hold your hand firmly and walk with you into the day. Whether they beat us, arrest us or kill us, we have one another, and, as you are all I can truly know, that means we have the people. The people, whether dead or alive, remain: we march through a forest of stars, we blow in with the wind, we are made from dirt and dust and to that we will return, but, for now, we can only be the courageous heroes.

Notes
1. Headline from an article published in the Iranian newspaper, Etelaat, July 2009.
2. This is a quote from the introduction to an article written by Ebrahim Nabavi, "The Hour of the Wolf and the Lamb", Rah-e-Sabz website, 29 December 2009. Available at: http://www.rahesabz.net/story/6579/ (accessed 30 December 2009). The last sentence in Farsi reads differently, translating literally to 'this river will not repeat itself'. The expression reminded me of the fragment from Heraclitus, normally translated as 'you cannot step twice into the same river'.

3. *Akbar Ganji talking to Afshin Molavi.* The Soul of Iran *(Norton, 2005, New York).*

4. *Chorus from the song, "Khak-o-Khashak", by the band, The Abjeez.*

5. *Roland Barthes.* A Lover's Discourse *(Vintage Books, 2002, London).*

6. *Extract from the video,* The Epic of the Lovers: God, the Mafia and the Citizens, *by Azin Feizabadi and Ida Momennejad, June 2009.*

7. *Farnaz Fassihi. "The Doctor Who Defied Tehran". In* The Wall Street Journal, *21 December 2009. Available at: http://online.wsj.com/article/SB126118381849697953.html#articleTabs%3Darticle (accessed 30 December 2009).*

8. *Walter Benjamin [1940]. "On the Concept of History". Available at: http://www.efn.org/~dredmond/ThesesonHistory.html (accessed 30 December 2009).*

9. *Jorge Luis Borges. "Hakim, the Masked Dyer of Merv". In* Collected Fictions, *(trans.) Andrew Hurley (Penguin, 1998, London), pp. 40-44.*

10. *Ebrahim Navabi. Available at: http://www.rahesabz.net/story/6579/ (accessed 30 December 2009).*

Within the Circle of Fear
Field Notes from Iraqi Kurdistan

FRANCESCA RECCHIA

Living in northern Iraq makes fear a close acquaintance. Expressions such as 'post-conflict contexts' or 'countries in transition to democracy' are part of daily conversations and evoke a sense of instability, a fragile equilibrium that can crumble at any point. A country that has undergone years of war has to take into account long trails of clearing mine fields, digging mass graves, dealing with trauma, restoring a sense of accountability and allowing processes of reconciliation. The line between success and failure is very fine, the fear of collapse a haunting ghost. Yet the pervasiveness and omnipresence of such a fear transforms it into white noise, and it fades into the background.

In the northwest corner of Kurdistan, in the middle of a ploughed field, lies the oldest intact aqueduct in the world, dating from 700 B.C. With cuneiform writings carved into its stones, the aqueduct at Jerwan is a remarkable piece of human history that both men and boys use today as a hangout spot. They meet there to drink and spray-paint their own version of 'when a man loves a woman' on the ancient stones. Still, the place preserves a timeless atmosphere: something eerie, yet peaceful. On the other side of the aqueduct, only a few metres away, lies an empty field where red triangular warning signs indicate the presence of land mines. Neither the drinkers nor the graffiti artists take notice and would surely laugh at anyone's shock or fear. Like the acrobat who walks on a suspended rope, those who have lived on the verge of a constant disaster assess risk – and consequently fear – on a different scale.

The Federal Region of Kurdistan occupies the strategic area in the north of Iraq; it borders Iran, Turkey and Syria, and possesses one of the largest unexploited oil reservoirs in the world. The Region has had an autonomous government since 1991 and is undergoing a steady process of social, political and economic development. At first glance, the area is safe and politically stable. A closer look reveals a more complex and articulated situation.

As is the case with many developing countries, the dichotomy between rural and urban areas in Kurdistan is dramatic. The global trend of the growing economic divide between the cities and the countryside is accentuated here by the consequences of specific political history. During the 1980s, Saddam Hussein's attacks mainly targeted villages in the mountains; within a decade, the Ba'ath regime destroyed more than 4,000 of them with the explicit intention of annihilating logistic support to the *peshmerga* (the Kurdish irregular army). These destructions have displaced thousands of people and seriously disrupted the economy. Since 1991, the Kurdish Regional Government, in collaboration with UN agencies and NGOs, has rebuilt more than 2,000 villages. Yet living conditions there are harsh. Many settlements still lack services, infrastructure and access to resources. Since 2005, both droughts and aggressive water pumping have depleted ancient aquifers, forcing more than 100,000 people to leave their villages.[1]

Furthermore, the majority of these settlements are located in the mountains that mark the borders of Kurdistan and Iraq with neighbouring countries, and are constantly exposed to the uncertainties of regional diplomatic relations. Iran has been shelling the Iraqi mountains since the 1980s. Tensions between the Turkish government and the Kurdish Workers Party (PKK) mount by the hour, despite official political statements that declare otherwise. Diplomatic relations between Syria and Iraq came to a sudden halt during the summer of 2009 and were never completely restored. The southern border of Kurdistan with the rest of Iraq is a combination of disputed areas (Khanaqin, Kirkuk and Mosul being the main cities), potentially explosive ethnic tensions as well as extensive and unexploited oil fields. If we were to consider Kurdistan as a set of concentric circles, the outermost of them would be a conundrum that defeats any logical argument for a simple solution. From the inner side of the circle, though, the situation appears to be quite different.

The recent access to oil revenue has radically changed the face of Kurdistan. Thousands of Kurds are returning from Europe and the United States, enticed by the economic opportunities in their homeland. The coalition between the two main parties (the Kurdistan Democratic Party and the Patriotic Union of Kurdistan) after years of tension and a civil war (1994-96) guarantees a (convenient) balance and provides political stability. Within the space of two decades, the region has changed from a mainly rural to a fully urbanised one. More than half the four million Kurds currently living in the Federal Region of Kurdistan are distributed among the three main cities (Erbil, Dohuk and Sulemaniya); the capital, Erbil, has a population of 1.3 million.

In 1928, Archibald Hamilton – the engineer who under the British Mandate built the spectacular road that climbs into the mountains to connect Iraq and Iran – described Erbil thus: "Arbil by day towers as a mountain and a landmark, by night its lights shine as a beacon for many miles" (Hamilton, 2004: 49). Eighty years later, Erbil, the Arbela of Alexander the Great, known also as Hawler, still fits Hamilton's depiction both in physical and symbolic terms.

Erbil is promoting its role as capital city through the construction of a multi-faceted identity: it is a goldmine for business people and foreign investors and a safe haven for refugees and internally displaced persons; it is leading the way through massive economic investment in urban development while also betting on its ancient history. Building its present on a combination of mythical past and projection towards the future, Erbil has managed an acrobatic leap to shove both the memories of recent traumas and the discourse of fear to its margins. On the one hand, the city – in collaboration with UNESCO – is trying to have its

Citadel included in the list of World Heritage Sites, it being one of the oldest continuously inhabited cities in the world. On the other hand, it is shaping its present (but hopefully not its future, considering the recent financial blows) as a possible next Dubai.[2] Nihad Qoja, the mayor of Erbil, has often referred to the Emirates city as both an emblem of progress and an example to emulate.

This Dubai-dreaming frenzy has now assumed an ironic twist, taking into account the fate of the city itself after the financial and real estate crisis. Still, the parallel is both revealing of the general mood and useful as a tool to analyse the present situation. Oil, real estate speculation, tax free investment and tourism are the magic phrases of the alchemy of the present. The pace of transformation is so fast that it becomes difficult to keep up with what is new. The thirst for opportunity and the excitement of new possibilities mix to produce an intoxicating cocktail.[3]

Marco Polo travelled through Kurdistan in the 12th century and took note of the perennial fire in the oilfields of Kirkuk. Italo Calvino, in a wonderful contemporary rendition of Polo's travels, has the explorer describing Octavia, one of Calvino's *Invisible Cities*, to Kublai Khan thus:

> If you chose to believe me, good. Now I will tell you how Octavia, the spider-web city is made. There is a precipice between two steep mountains: the city is over the void. [...] Suspended over the abyss, the life of Octavia's inhabitants is less uncertain than in other cities. They know the net will last only so long. (Calvino, 1997: 67)

Following years of violence and instability, the present wave of wealth and urban growth in Kurdistan is a vertiginous experience of hopes and promises. Erbil, as the spider-web city over the abyss, prospers and grows in a desperate attempt to turn the future into the present. There is no certainty about tomorrow, as there has never been for the Kurds through decades of war. The scars of Saddam Hussein's 1988 genocide campaign have still not healed; Al-Anfal and Halabja remain a constitutive part of Kurdish identity.[4] The heaviness of the past increases expectations from the current phase of stability: only the present is present. The mask of possibility hides the fear of loss; uncertainty about tomorrow becomes the impetus for a shiny today.

In his essay "Geology of New Fears", Lieven de Cauter introduces his discussion on contemporary (Western) fears by defining fear itself as one of the primordial human drives connected to the survival instinct. He argues that "[w]hen one is constantly able to perceive all possibilities and impossibilities, all dangers and risks, one is likely to become nervous, timorous or just plain scared" (de Cauter, 2004: 117). The likelihood of such an occurrence seems to me contextually specific. Looking at it from Kurdistan, the constant exposure to the fear of all "possibilities and impossibilities" morphs itself into a kind of immunity. Some say that the more you suffer, the more your ability to bear pain grows. Fear possibly works along similar lines. Being aware of all dangers might increase the threshold of what is to be feared.

de Cauter constructs his essay around a list of new fears – Demographic Fear, Economic Fear, Xenophobia, Agoraphobia or Political Fear, Fear of Terrorism. While this catalogue seems to make perfect sense within a Western framework, it loses strength when analysed against the situation in Kurdistan. One of the main differences lies in the discrepancy between abstract collective paranoia and actual physical risk. The leap beyond fear is conceivable when the possibility of danger is so pervasive that it is removed from the picture. Take the Fear of Terrorism, for example. The West hides terror attacks behind discussions of media manipulation, protection of soft targets and color-coded terror alerts. In Kurdistan, the government openly and proudly admits that it's been three years since the last attack. In the West, that would be terrifying information, but here it's comforting.

From the peripheral stand point of this essay, what is at stake is an interesting political counter-strategy. In the West, the public discourse of fear is more and more used as a political device to deploy control and justify the restriction of civil rights and freedoms. Kurdistan shows an opposite trend. It is, in fact, the removal and repression of the discourse of fear from the public domain that becomes the tool to gain political consensus, instill trust and confidence, and attract increasing flows of capital and investment. Following such a shift in geopolitical perspective, it seems to me that it is not quite anger – as de Cauter claims[5] – that emancipates men from fear. Rather, the awareness that the spider-web that holds the city *can only last so long* generates a new conceptualisation. It is not that people are not afraid anymore or that fear has been eliminated. When fear has been so historically engraved in the collective consciousness of a people, it seems to me that its existence is the main reason for its very disappearance.

Notes

1. I owe Sebastian Meyer this information; Sebastian Meyer, "Kurdistan Karez", http://www.photoshelter.com/c/sebmeyer/gallery/Kurdistan-Karez/G0000bJBztyjW7ZQ/ (accessed 14 December 2009)
2. Ahmed S. Wali. "Erbil: The Next Dubai". In **Hawler Tribune**, *9 April 2009.*
3. Ibid. Wali, writing of the year 2008, states, "The cabinet of the Kurdistan Regional Government has approved a supplementary budget of $161 million for Erbil, bringing the total for the province's budget to nearly 322 million dollars next year".
4. The 1986-89 military campaign that Saddam led against the Kurds is known as Al-Anfal, which literally means 'the spoils of war'. The name is taken from the eighth Sura of the Qu'ran, and refers to the trophy that the Muslims gained against the 'infidels' in 642 in the Battle of Badr. The Anfal operation lasted three years and culminated with the chemical attacks on Halabja that killed about 4,000 people within a few hours.
5. "He who is angry is no longer afraid" (de Cauter, 2004).

References

- *Calvino, Italo.* **Invisible Cities.** *(Trans.) William Weaver (Vintage Books, 1997, London).*
- *de Cauter, Lieven. "Geology of New Fears". In* **The Capsular Civilization: On the City in the Age of Fear** *(NAi Publishers, 2004, Rotterdam).*
- *Hamilton, Archibald Milne [1937].* **Road through Kurdistan: Travels in Northern Iraq** *(Tauris Parke Paperbacks, 2004, London).*

Fear Yourself More than the Other

AGON HAMZA

1.

One of Karl Marx's main theses is realised: capitalism is a global system. It has established its form of production and circulation at the global level, and, as Alain Badiou claims, it prides itself on its global nature.[1] The world of capitalism defines itself as based on democracy/democratisation, human rights, ecology and the free circulation of capital.

The capitalist-democratic regimes have presented themselves after the fall of the Berlin Wall as a universal value, as the only possible political system. This system, this mode of production with its political coordinates, was portrayed as the one most fit to human nature, the one humanity had longed for throughout history. In the 1990s, the decade of the realisation of the liberal dream, democracy was the prerequisite for capitalism; as Badiou often repeats, our problem is not so much capitalism as democracy.

2.

Another thesis has been proposed recently by Rastko Močnik, who says that capitalism does not need democracy; on the contrary, it is authoritarian regimes that suit capitalism better.[2] According to Močnik, democracy is the precise ideological condition injected into countries in conflict or internal tension (translation mine). That is to say, democracy is *le passé* in order to maintain capitalist order. If democracy was a political necessity for the utopian 1990s, the first decade of our century has everywhere seen the appearance of authoritarian regimes. This is what is happening across Europe, with Italy's Silvio Berlusconi and Russia's Vladimir Putin as the sublime exemplars of this political proposition.

The fall of the Berlin Wall inaugurated the precise ideological configuration for the 'new' to take place. Politicians, financial speculators, mainstream thinkers and academics tell us that the fall of Berlin Wall marked the beginning of new possibilities. It meant that the ideological struggle was over, that liberal capitalism had triumphed over 20th century ideological platforms and their perverted forms (the totalitarianisms: Nazism, Fascism and Stalinism), and that now we could peacefully rest in our unique liberal capitalism with democracy as its consummate political form of organisation. Francis Fukuyama announced the end of utopian visions with his thesis of "the end of history", and the beginning of the new, liberal-democratic utopia.

3.

Liberal democracy stands for 'the dream realised' in a precise sense: in psychoanalysis, 'the dream realised' has a name. It's called horror. In his recent book, *First as Tragedy, Then as Farce*,[3] Slavoj Žižek recognises "the happy Clintonite era" of the 1990s as a purely utopian era that had to come to an end. The book's title draws on Marx's observation in *The 18th Brumaire of Louis Napoleon*: "Hegel remarks somewhere that all great world-historic facts and personages appear, so to speak, twice. He forgot to add: the first time as tragedy, the second time as farce". Žižek applies this formula to the opening years of the 21st century. Utopia is over: first with the tragedy of September 11, 2001, then with the farce of the ongoing financial meltdown at the close of the century's first decade, as what Lacan would have called the Real of liberal democracy.

4.

How do we grasp the ideological propositions of our era? The fall of the Berlin Wall did not mark the end of all walls. The fear generated by 'ideological struggles' is now transposed into fear of worker immigrants, of new fundamentalisms (religious, ethnic), of new forms of sexism, and so on. New walls are popping up – not only physically (Palestine, the US-Mexico border, also recall the proposal of the mayor of one Italian city to build a wall through the city as a division of the poor from the rich), but also in the form of 'administrative' walls, such as visa regimes. Liberal capitalism in its ideological-political configuration is unable to resolve the problems it generates. In order to maintain its ideological body, it has to invent new forms of fear – fear of the toxic Other.

5.

The Society for the Protection of Animals Abroad (SPANA) is a British charity that works in some of the poorest countries of the world. Its aim is to protect animals. As the short description provided on their webpage states, they are "not an ordinary animal charity – we know that working animals ensure that families can make a living".[4] SPANA is well aware of the crucial importance of animals in the lives of poor families in underdeveloped countries. They're also very precise: "When a working animal falls sick or becomes injured, there rarely is a qualified vet nearby. If there is one, most people cannot afford the treatment. So, while the animal remains sick and untreated, it won't be earning any money for the family. They will be going to bed hungry every night".[5] SPANA sent a veterinary team to Kosovo shortly after British troops arrived in the capital, Prishtina, in 1999. Its activists also worked with schools to encourage children to respect and care for animals that have been neglected. In one report in *The Times* in July 1999, SPANA claims its experts came to Kosovo "to bring crucial help to war-traumatized animals".[6]

6.

In the Republic of Kosovo, KFOR (the acronym for the NATO forces in Kosovo) cannot dominate and rule by means of force alone. In Kosovo, we all witness KFOR's systematic violence every day. Leave aside the regular patrols we daily see, concentrate only on the ideological campaign, and the result is not very different. Billboards and advertisements in each and every newspaper, on all national television channels, over each and every radio station and also TV and Radio KFOR[7]: they are nothing but a brutal demonstration of their force.

Apart from its function as a Repressive Apparatus, KFOR has also decided that it has a mission as an ideological agent: it bombards us with campaigns expressing the need for more tolerance, love, respect, etc. This campaign that started in June 1999 continues today. In the latest billboards to appear along the roads of Kosovo, we see a dog and a cat embracing one another. The slogan reads, "They can. Why can't you?" This is meant to imply multi-ethnic tolerance, coexistence, etc. But the effect of this 'anti-racist' campaign is that KFOR itself slides into racism. The paradox is that the literal content of the billboards is the Real of liberal European multi-ethnicity as a concept: European multi-ethnicity (in its liberal configuration) is as possible as the coexistence of a dog with a cat.

KFOR does indeed function *predominantly* by repression, but its 'educational campaign' is just as massive (perhaps Gramsci is right when he wrote on the state as an educator). Along with other colonial structures (mostly European Union missions in Kosovo), KFOR tells us that they are in Kosovo for our own benefit and good. Their charity has no limits.

7.

Benevolent charity claims that Kosovo citizens are traumatised subjects. This is what they care for and that's all that interests them. They're kind-hearted, and all their activities look noble. But what these colonial structures mean is that Kosovars are incapable subjects, or desubstancialised subjects. Therefore, we have to be under 'international supervision'; we have to be under their paternal care, so to speak, because we are not responsible for our acts, gestures and so forth. EU representatives in Kosovo often repeat that they are here to help Kosovar institutions due to their limited capacities. Thus does colonisation take on the political face of charity.

8.

"Colonized society is not merely portrayed as a society without values. The colonist is not content with stating that the colonized world has lost its values or worse never possessed any. The 'Native' is declared impervious to ethics, representing not only the absence of values but also the negation of values", says Frantz Fanon.[8] Our colonisers are here to teach us what democracy, tolerance and human rights are as the highest human political and cultural values. Following the same line of argumentation (and taking SPANA into account), one cannot but say that White European liberalism/freedom not only contains further inhibitions, but their (political) *whiteness* is constituted on the perpetual fear of the toxic Other. One has only to look at migrant workers (*immigrants without residence papers*). If they stay where they are (in their Third World countries), they are perceived as terrorists, fundamentalists, radicals, etc., whereas if they move abroad (to the First, capitalist, World), they become toxic subjects. Somehow they're good if they stay 'there' where they are, if they remain in their own folkloric and cultural exoticism. They're good if they remain as subjects-to-be-exploited.

The same happens in the Republic of Kosovo. We're constantly told that the EU, NATO, the UN and other missions are here for our own good. The main paradigms of their administration (or "supervision", as they like to put it) are: stability, multi-ethnicity, tolerance and other ultimately racist concepts. Each of them should be briefly examined.

9.

Kosovo political and social activist Albin Kurti writes that "EULEX [the European Union Rule of Law Mission in Kosovo] defines itself as a 'crisis management operation', as if the crisis is here to stay and merely has to be managed. '(Re)solution', the traditional vocabulary of international missions, has been replaced by 'management'. 'Crisis management' means the prevention of the explosion of a crisis, not the elimination of the crisis or its causes".[9]

10.

The European liberal conception of multiethnicity is the ultimate racist concept, turned into one of the main premises of the international administration in Kosovo. This is not to be read as an opposition to different cultures living together, or as a claim that all forms of multiethnicity are disguised racism – on the contrary. But, far from bringing people together, liberal European 'multiethnicity' necessarily leads to partition, to keeping the 'other' as far away as possible. While in classic colonialism, the colonised were called tribes, in our postmodern forms of colonisation, we're recognised as 'ethnicities'. 'Ethnicity' is another form of censorship, as Žižek said in the lecture he gave in Prishtina in May 2009. Therefore, we are not allowed to have a fully sovereign state.

Kosovo is perceived as a society that needs to be supervised. Pathological societies are those whose 'healthy' existence is dependent on a Master, a supervisor. In the eyes of Brussels, Washington, New York, etc., we are seen as a pathological society. As wars exploded in the beginning of the 1990s in the former Yugoslavia, Slovenian philosopher Mladen Dolar said, "The European unconscious is structured like the Balkans". That is to say, European political 'perversion' was so strongly repressed that it had to be projected somewhere else. The other place is, of course, the Balkans.

Notes

1. Alain Badiou. **The Meaning of Sarkozy** *(Verso, 2008, London/New York).*

2. Rastko Močnik. "Kapitalizam ne treba demokraciju". Interview for **Slobodna Dalmatija**. *Available at: http:// www.slobodnadalmacija.hr/Hrvatska/tabid/66/articleType/ArticleView/articleId/55876/Default.aspx (accessed 5 November 2009).*

3. Slavoj Žižek. **First as Tragedy, Then as Farce** *(Verso, 2009, London/New York).*

4. http://www.spana.org/about-us/index.html (accessed 5 November 2009).

5. http://www.spana.org/the-big-picture/families-rely-on-animals.html (accessed 5 November 2009).

6.Vanessa Pupovac."Therapeutising Refugees, Pathologising Populations: International Psycho-Social Programmes in Kosovo". Available at: http://reliefweb.int/rw/lib.nsf/db900sid/LGEL-5FDDDM/$file/hcr-therapeurising-aug02.pdf?openelement (accessed 5 November 2009).

7. It is very important to emphasise that KFOR is perhaps the only army (and that, supranational) I know of which has its own television and radio stations.

8. Frantz Fanon. **The Wretched of the Earth** *(Grove Press, 2004, New York), p. 6.*

9. Albin Kurti. "Causing Damage in Kosovo". Available at: http://euobserver.com/7/28602 (accessed 5 November 2009).

On Idealists and Realists
A Memory of Fear, Silence and the 1990s Yugoslav Wars
MAJA PETROVIĆ-ŠTEGER

In contemporary Serbia, human and other remains of the 1990s wars, besides being understood as mythological, religious and political, are acquiring a new quality. Post-conflict forensic intervention into the landscapes of the Yugoslav mass graves had offered a new, DNA-based evaluation of dead bodies and other remnants. It is no longer possible to sustain the claim that traditional private (and public) treatment of the remains represents an index of backwardness, political propaganda and atavism, as was maintained in the early 1990s. On the contrary, foreign agencies today see the active involvement of locals in questions of the remains and their commemoration as progressive, liberal and moral.

But how do Serbs see morality and the memories of the 1990s wars, and how do they experience post-conflict time? In an anthropological monograph, provisionally entitled *Human Remains, Postconflict Spirits: An Anthropology of Redress in Contemporary Serbia and Tasmania*, I attempt to fathom and answer these questions.[1] While focusing on specific political practices around the dead body, the book draws particular attention to an increasingly important supranational language and code of practice in claiming to right past wrongs, as rectification takes human remains as its assumed evidence and their management as its central mode.

What follows is an excerpt from a fieldwork interview from 2003. It is a portrait of an ex-soldier talking about fear, silence and memories of the war.

Srđan's Story

After a number of afternoons spent with Mrs Krušić in her apartment and her office, she asked me one day if I would like to meet her cousin, the husband of her late sister's daughter. In her words, he was a young, silent man, who "foolishly spends all his time in practicing martial arts and Capoeira", but as he had some war experience, she thought he might prove interesting to me.

When I met Srđan, I was immediately struck by his extremely erect posture, which turned out to match the linearity of the story he told. Unlike most of my respondents, who would jump around in their recollections much as they would restlessly get up and walk about the room, Srđan inclined on a wooden chair whilst offering me his confidences. His tale began in 1991 when, in order to do his obligatory military service, he spent nine months in the bat-tlefields on the borders of Serbia and Croatia. He was only 20 years old at the time, a young and successful freeclimber and speleologist. In his memory, it was a snowless but very long and cold winter. The fields cracked under the thick mist and ice and the weight of people and cattle running away, trying to find shelter.

> The story is very simple. There is no mystery about it whatsoever. I started as a Yugoslav army soldier but very soon became a member of a paramilitary unit, part of its diversion squad. [...] When we were away from the frontline, we used to live in a motel. The people, I mean the locals, accepted us quickly. The food was fine as there were plenty of potatoes and vagrant cattle that nobody had wanted to take along. [...] We were a small division of just 12 people, but on manoeuvres, we would move only in groups of four. That was the best number. The most efficient, for sure. There we would often bump into the old hunters, people who just rambled around, or into the army units, which did not know who they were meant to fight and who they were meant to protect. It was a mess. A real mess, I'm telling you. [...] Although I had trained at shooting as a sport even before the war, it took me a while to get used to 65 percent of the weaponry used. And I had no time to lose. I had to be sober and quick in working out and anticipating what would happen, if I was to survive. I had to move. You had to move. To keep moving all the time. If you stopped moving, you would die. [...] Nobody died in my unit though. We were very organised, and protected each other at all times. The rule was that either all of us would fall or none. One couldn't carry on, alive or dead, once others had died. That was the ultimate rule.

When I asked what he would have done had somebody died, and whether he had seen any burials whilst in the war, he answered:

> Whenever we came across the dead, they would be transported into the back-ground. The villagers usually did the burying of the locals. Professional soldiers were transported back to their homes through army channels. The same system that provided us with food was used as a channel for transporting the dead. The army worked very well. But that is not the important thing... since nobody died in my squad.

Although I had not expected an emotional account of his wartime experience, I felt slightly uncomfortable listening to Srđan's detailed spatial and technical rendition. His calm, practically forensic characterisations of the scene brought to my mind texts of military literature in which the narratives are fully ordered and defined, bulked out with the imagery of knights-errant. The only thing betraying his nervousness was the odour of the sweat in the dim room full of children's toys and sports equipment. While talking to me, Srđan would stand up only to fetch food or tea for Tara, his two-year-old daughter. Although they agreed that she should stay with her grandmother in the other room, the girl kept coming in for a hug or a cuddle with her father. Their fragility and tenderness contrasted strongly with the ambience otherwise and with the room's walls being completely covered in medals, escutcheons, bows, spears, pistols and paintings of forests.

Srđan confessed he was unsettled on his return to Belgrade. Everybody expected he would be happy to be home, but he felt nervous, tense and unfocused, and was unable to gather his resources for a long time.

> In the squad, I was active, and my instincts were on full alert. I was alive even though I was surrounded with the dead. But back home, in Belgrade, I became a dead person. Although this [Belgrade] is a super-fast environment, really charged with life, I felt really disturbed… distracted so to speak. There were too many sounds, too much light, too many people and too much information all of a sudden… I felt hugely uncomfortable. I simply could not pull myself together. I felt as if I was under attack. Certainly much more so than I felt while on the battlefields. It sounds stupid, I know. I craved for the silence and the sound of the wind. Back there, I felt oddly calm and somehow natural. I felt as if I was developing new senses and instincts in the forest. But here, in town… it was just too much.

"It should have been easy", he said, "to go out and find people to talk about it, as many wanted to compete with their fictitious warfare achievements or to moralise about the cruelties of war, even though they did not get off their backsides and leave Mummy's warm home". But he could not talk to anyone. The only person with whom he was at peace was his grandfather. I asked if he could tell more about what he said to him. Instead of answering me, he turned his head away. His voice became slightly more upset and almost imperceptibly angrier than before.

> I never wanted to say anything back then. You know, it was very popular for a while to talk about your war experiences. And then, just as it had been popular, it became very unpopular all of a sudden. People started to treat me as a criminal, as an abnormal person, as somebody who obviously suffered from 'Vietnam Syndrome' or something like that. This entire story about Vietnam Syndrome is fundamentally idiotic anyway because if we follow that logic, then all the people who live in the Balkans are completely crazy. Everybody here was in the war or at least has someone that fought at some time in the past. Just count the wars: the revolutions against the Turks, the First World War, the Thesaloniki war, the Second World War, the Partisans' and the Četniks' war… we fought so much that we must then all be mad.

He went on:

> The story about the war is so dependent on politics, so exploited by it, full of it, that it really irritates me. And the story that's doing the rounds now, the story of truth, accountability and reconciliation, well, that's just the most insulting story I've heard for a long time. It's just being used as a political front and nothing else. I don't know anyone who's really been reconciled through this programme. This is why I don't want to discuss it. Our politicians want to appear democratic all of a sudden, and this stuff just furthers their ambitions. These bastards aren't any better than the war profiteers were. They are peace profiteers [*mirnodopski profiteri*], nothing else. [...] Come on, we live in Serbia. We can't be citizens of the world and Europeans all of a sudden. I can't stand these stories. This is also why I never go to Croatia, to the seaside, although we have a house there. I'd go to Slovenia, Greece, to Montenegro, wherever, but I couldn't go to Croatia anymore... Because I know, I know there are going to be more problems in the future. Things can't be resolved or forgotten so quickly. In my family, we used to say, if you put rotten meat into a fridge, you see how much it stinks only when it begins to melt! And this is what is happening today.

Stroking his daughter's head in his lap, he concluded: "I cannot let myself be scarred again. I simply can't".

It took many more interviews and detailed family histories for me to understand that his last sentence referred less to the physical wounds he got in the war than his profound fear of subsequent emotional injury. With time, I learned that Srđan's family, although ethnically Serbian, had been settled in Croatia for as long as they could remember. Both his mother and father came from villages that were geographically very close to the place where he spent the winter of 1991. As he assured me, he could not have known that he would be posted to the region at the time of his mobilisation into the army. His aunt, whom I met on a couple of occasions, explained to me that during 1943 and 1944, the greater part of their family was slaughtered by the Ustaša while the other part perished from tuberculosis.[2] Her father, Srđan's grandfather, was captured and imprisoned, but once the war was over, he returned to his native village, close to Slavonska Požega. She remembers that, as a child, Srđan used to spend all his summer vacations with his grandparents, playing in the woods, helping them look after cattle or manure the fields. After implying that I had heard bits and pieces of his grandfather's life, Srđan told me his grandfather, then a retired schoolteacher, had taught his grandson many things and had discussed the Second World War with him. Even as a small child, Srđan was able to distinguish indigenous inhabitants from newcomers in the village. Many ritual practices of village life were also impressed upon him. He remembers what flowers to plant by the family vault – sage was supposedly particularly good for the ancestors' spirits – and he still remembers how he was told off whenever he climbed the apple tree that grew by the tomb.

Although they had a huge, marble family vault in the village, old Ilija, my grandfather, decided to move to Serbia the moment the last war broke out, back in 1991. Within a couple of months, he managed to swap his household with a Croat who lived in Serbia and wanted to join his family in Croatia. They bartered the land and the house, and, as Ilija said, everything went through properly, in a neat and legal fashion. The Croatian guy was a very nice man, and both of them were happy with the deal. The man even helped him once, when he brought the remains of his wife and family to the new place. [...] You see, I remember all these details. I rarely dream, but if I do, I often dream about that apple tree. It's nothing special, I know, but I feel sort of impaired and somehow... cheated. I don't want to attach myself emotionally to the people there anymore because... that's just not good for me. I know I will lose them again. This is why I will not let my daughter be taken to the Croatian seaside. The experiences I lived through have altered my criteria. I want to distance myself. Not to feel hatred or contempt – I do not want to feel anything, actually... I just want to be free.

Srđan struck me as harsh in his assertions of the cyclical logic and the unbreakability of the historical hatreds of the former Yugoslavia. This wasn't so much because of the conventionality of his argument, which would be accepted by many (or at least would have been back in early 2000), but because of how comfortably he seemed able to state his position, which came over as less an attempt to rationalise his own experience and more as something imputed as a form of embodied knowledge to his family background. It wasn't so much that he sensed or feared that ethnic conflict might eventually flare up again as that he had gained access to the 'knowledge' that it would – if ever he failed to take sufficient care. He spoke of his war experiences not as a source of warrior pride or as a disease, but rather as the basis for a survival manual.

At this moment, Slađana, Srđan's wife, came back from work and broke into our discussion. I had met Slađana before, and I knew how devoted she was to her husband. I also knew that despite the depth of their relationship, she had found it hard for a long time to reconcile herself to the fact that he had been an actual combatant in the war. Frequently describing him as the most dignified, tender and chivalrous man she had ever met, she confided to me that it was still a problem to her to accept how deep the martial strain in his family ran. While he was still in the room, she said:

I had a different childhood, you know. My parents raised me and my brother in the spirit of Tito, of a united Yugoslavia. I believed that the Yugoslav army was supposed to protect all of us and not side with some against the others. My grandmother was a well-respected professor of Law and Socialism at the University. I was taught to love differences and to... eh... But what am I talking for? I don't know. Maybe he is right when he says Tara can't be taught in this way. He says she must learn to be a realist and not an empty idealist. [Slađana looked at Srđan as she said this, somewhat questioningly.] He wants to take her to the villages to see how cattle are killed so she can know what she eats, where food comes from. And that frightens me. It really does. So much, actually. I don't want my child to become squeamish, but I fear for her.

Srđan shook his head and went to the kitchen. It was more than obvious that he wanted to change the subject. Looking at the sports medals that hung on the walls, I asked him if he kept up his conditioning for anything but freeclimbing. "Yes, I was a passionate speleologist and studied geology. I always dreamt of travelling to Africa and the East. I wanted to go to the border of Chad and Libya and draw geo-charts there. But that doesn't make sense anymore. I have a private business now and work with satellite communications". In a very business-like, technical manner, he turned to the laptop, wanting to show me his webpage and portfolio, but at that very moment, the electricity switched off. When we realised that all other windows in the block were brightly lit but ours, Slađana started yelling at Srđan. I finished the interview, excused myself and left. But on the way home, Slađana's screamed reproaches kept coming back to me:

Couldn't you pay the bills for God's sake?! I put out the money and the bill. Do you always have to forget such essential things? It's always the same with you. Always. Don't you ever dare accuse me again of being an idealist. You think you are a real-ist or what? If it weren't for me, I don't know how we would manage this house at all! It is you who can't even get on top of the simplest thing like bills!

Postscriptum

The narrative I have illustrated above, one of very many collected in the book, runs a gamut of emotions associated with experiences of fear, loss and personal insecurity in the former Yugoslavia. The account is neither self-contained nor self-evident as to its import. The people I spoke with have chosen to tell me stories about the relations they were willing to expose, objects they found important, or activities, dreams and memories that continued to haunt their everyday lives. The stories show the tellers riveted and undone by these very relations, by the objects and memories that still exercise them. Although many accounts had a firm narrative dimension, the stories were not always chronologically ordered: often they began with their end, or sought to shed light on what was their temporal middle, moving back and forth in time to describe the respondents' childhood or to outline their possible futures. In analysing their narratives, I have appropriated this storytelling rhythm as a method in itself. By mimicking their narrational movements, my parsing has also gone backwards and forwards in trying to understand the burden of their words. In so doing, I was interested in the manner in which these interrelated stories, beliefs and activities help maintain, regulate and transmit sentiments out of which ideas about past conflict and human remains are constituted. Cautioned that "the situation of discourse is not the same as what is said or, indeed, what is sayable" (Butler, 2004: 139), I treated the narrative not only as rhetoric but as enunciation, linking people with their imagined and experienced histories, and structuring their future expectations.

My intention in recalling these ethnographic moments is to point to the various ways in which history, war and ideas about the future may be constituted. These are produced, maintained and transmitted not only in stories but also in objects, in people's activities, or in their reluctance to perform them, in their opinions (about reconciliation, and NGOs, for example), in their experiences of travelling and of places. In their fears. They thus form the techniques and technologies of accounting for time, change, affliction and emotions in post-conflict Serbia.

In exploring the ongoing promotion of images of and practices relating to human and other remains, the rehearsed stories of a conflictual past and of shattered families were constructive also in permitting the enumeration and organisation of my respondents' family histories. As Sladana said to me on one occasion:

I have never thought as much and as deeply of my family as I did in the last couple of years. I have such a deep urge now to learn everything, to write down every single memory from our family history, and to talk about it with my daughter when she grows up. [...] The problem is, I still have to decide which history I will tell her. Mine or my husband's.

Notes

1. In its comparative analysis of the trajectories taken by dead bodies in the post-conflict scenarios of Serbia and Tasmania, **Human Remains, Postconflict Spirit** (forthcoming) investigates the treatment of human remains, and the conceptualisation, evaluation and numbering of dead bodies by legal and technoscientific apparatuses as they imaginatively project body parts into novel configurations of what it is to be human. The book asks in what ways does DNA identification of missing persons' body parts inform collective political, legal and moral understandings of justice and reconciliation? What counts as, and what gauges the value of, a dead body in a post-conflict society? How many pieces of human remains constitute a person worth claiming for repatriation in a time of bioscientific and technological advances?

2. During the later part of the Second World War, in which Yugoslavia fought against German occupation, along with the war atrocities, mass slaughters also occurred among Yugoslavs themselves. More than a million Yugoslavs died in the war, mostly at the hands of other Yugoslavs. Committed by numerous groups, and on all sides (the perpetrators being Partisans against those perceived as fascists; Croatian fascists, known as Ustaša, against Serbs, Jews and Gypsies; Serbian royalists, known as Četniks, against Partisans, Muslims and other Croats, etc.), these multiple massacres, mention of which was silenced and suppressed during Tito's regime, became the object of revisionist histories, usually political and nationalistic, in the late 1980s.

Reference

• Butler, Judith. **Precarious Life: The Powers of Mourning and Violence** (Verso, 2004, London/ New York).

Graves: Buried Evidence from Kashmir[1]

ANGANA P. CHATTERJI, PARVEZ IMROZ, GAUTAM NAVLAKHA,
ZAHIR-UD-DIN, MIHIR DESAI, KHURRAM PARVEZ

The songs I sing are songs of death.

Woman mourning her son, Kupwara[2]

My son was killed in a 'fake encounter'. Buried by the police as a 'Pakistani terror-ist'. We want justice. We want his name restored. We want his memory healed.

Community elder, Srinagar[3]

Regipora Village, Kupwara District

The Indian state's governance of Indian-administered Kashmir requires the use of *discipline* and *death* as techniques of social control. The structure of governance affiliated with militarisation in Kashmir necessitates dispersed and intense forms of psychosocial regulation.[4] As an established nation-state, India's objective has been to discipline and assimilate Kashmir into its territory.[5] To do so has required the domestication of Kashmiri peoples through the selective use of discipline and death as regulatory mechanisms.[6] Discipline is affected through military presence, surveillance, punishment and fear. Death is disbursed through 'extrajudicial' means and those authorised by law. Psychosocial control is exercised through the use of death and deception to discipline the living.[7] Discipline rewards forgetting, isolation and depoliticisation.[8]

Between 1989-2009, the actions of India's military and paramilitary forces in Kashmir have resulted in 8,000+ enforced and involuntary disappearances and 70,000+ deaths, including through extrajudicial or 'fake encounter' executions, custodial brutality and other means.[9] Lawyers have reportedly filed 15,000 petitions since 1990, inquiring, largely unsuccessfully, into the location and health of detainees and the charges against them.[10]

Mourning the dead is a habitual practice of dissent amid Kashmir civil society. The conventional and recognised cemeteries that hold Kashmir's dead are maintained and cared for by local people and organisations. Alongside these cemeteries are other clandestine graveyards, often unnamed, unmarked, undecorated. They exist amid habitations, next to schools and homes, by the roadside and town square, in prayer grounds and forests, at the edges of fields and community cemeteries across rural and urban space.

This research into unknown, unmarked and mass graves was conducted by the International People's Tribunal on Human Rights and Justice in Indian-administered Kashmir (IPTK) between November 2006 and November 2009. The graveyards we investigated entomb bodies of those murdered in encounter and fake encounter killings between 1990 and 2009.[11]

Between November 2006 and January 2008, prior to the formal constitution of IPTK, the Association of Parents of Disappeared Persons, a member of the Jammu and Kashmir Coalition of Civil Society which instituted IPTK, conducted initial research and released a document in April 2008 with details of certain graves in Baramulla district. Following the constitution of IPTK, the Tribunal scrutinised and re-verified this information between April 2008 and November 2009, and conducted further and extensive research in the border districts of Bandipora, Baramulla and Kupwara in northwestern Kashmir.[12]

The graves, their creation and effect, belong to the present history of Kashmir, to a continuing chronicle of violence and violation. The graves are hyper-present in the local imaginary but rarely spoken of in public. These 'secrets' are hidden from/through speech. As a gravedigger in a rural town stated: "They [graves] are there to be noticed and to make us fear them [security personnel]. We all know what they are, where they are, but we cannot say so. To speak of them is treasonous".[13]

Based on our investigations, we note the following:

District	Graves documented by IPTK	Unnamed graves[14] (of those documented)	Graves with two bodies	Graves with more than two bodies
Baramulla 33 villages investigated	1,122 w. 1,321 bodies[15]	1,013 90.3 percent	140	17 [Total 76+ bodies]
Kupwara 14 villages investigated	1,453 w. 1487 bodies	1,278 87.9 percent	8	4 [Total 30 bodies]
Bandipora 8 villages investigated	125 w. 135 bodies	82 65.6 percent	6	2 [Total 6 bodies]
Total 3 districts 55 villages	Total 2,700 w. 2,943+ bodies	Total 2,373 87.9 percent	Total 154 w. 308 bodies	Total 23 w. 112+ bodies

Next-of-kin, community and collective testimony and archival research evidences that most of the bodies in the graves recorded above were of men. In Baramulla, of the 1,122 graves, approximately 99 percent of those buried were men. Gravediggers and caretakers were unable to give an exact count, given the extent of defacement of some of the bodies. In Kupwara, of the 1,453 graves, 1,451 were of men and two of women. In Bandipora, all 125 graves were of men. The context of killings in Kashmir has engendered a landscape where the death of men has rendered vulnerable the living, especially women, children and other gender identified groups.

Next-of-kin, community and collective testimony and archival research evidences that, in various instances, 'encounter' killings across Kashmir have, in fact, been authenticated as 'fake encounter' killings. Post-death, the bodies of these victims were routinely handled by military and paramilitary personnel, including the local police. The bodies were then brought to the 'secret graveyards', primarily by personnel of the Jammu and Kashmir Police. In one instance, we learned that the body had been buried on the premises of a police station. In another instance, local communities buried cadavers that had been thrown into a ditch by security forces.[16] There are serious allegations that, in particular instances, security personnel have been involved in accepting bribes and smuggling narcotics.[17]

We have been reliably informed that, prior to the delivery of bodies to the 'secret grave-yards', security forces personnel selected local male residents or professional gravediggers, usually those respected within the local community, and asked that graves be prepared to bury the dead. The graveyards were prevalently constructed on local religious or community owned and/or used land, and dug by local residents at the coercion of security personnel. The persons preparing the graves were usually informed in advance of the number of bodies to be buried. Professional gravediggers and local residents who were forced to become gravediggers and caretakers were directed to dig the graves but were largely not supervised by security personnel during the process of digging or burial. In the process of soliciting their labour, gravediggers and caretakers were routinely intimidated and not remunerated for their services.[18]

In the Islamic religious ethos and the Shari'at,[19] death, and care of the dead, is interpreted as a directive to the living, linked to atonement and forgiveness. Gravediggers and caretak-ers attempted burial of the corpses in accordance with such tradition. Local community members and gravediggers that prepared the graves routinely constructed one grave per body. When permissible, they offered *Salat* (prayer) prior to burial. At times, they planted flowers on the graves. For gravediggers and caretakers, the requirement of burial of the dead was prioritised over *whose* body was being inhumed and its possible identity and politi-cal affiliation or non-affiliation.

In instances where the number of bodies brought by security personnel exceeded the initial injunction given by the security personnel regarding the number of graves to be prepared, more than one body was buried in each grave. Further, when the killings took place in certain conditions, the bodies involved were buried together, as noted below. In the 2,700 graves we investigated, the body count was 2,943+. Within the 2,700 graves, 154 graves contained two bodies each and 23 graves contained more than two cadavers. Within these 23 graves, the number of bodies ranged from three to 17, including:

Hathlonga village, Baramulla district	1 grave. Containing 8 bodies, torched to death in a hut. Security personnel claimed all to be militants. The incident occurred in August-September 1995 between Hathlonga and Nambla village in the Uri area. Security personnel used explosive substances to blast a hutment with 8 persons inside.
Nullah Nigley,[20] Leyan Marg, Gulmarg, Baramulla district	1 grave. Containing 12 bodies buried in the early 1990s.

Gharkote village, Baramulla district	1 grave. Containing 16 bodies, torched to death. Security personnel claimed all to be militants killed in the early 1990s. The persons died in mortar shelling on a hut in which they were staying, undertaken by security forces.
Army Brigade Headquarters, Rampur, Uri, Baramulla district	1 grave. The grave contained numerous bodies. The bodies were entombed in a ditch, reportedly 7.62 metres deep, inside the army camp. The bodies had been deposited in the ditch between 1991-2003. No outside person is permitted to visit the camp.[21]
Wilgam Martyrs' Graveyard, Kupwara district	1 grave. Containing 5 skulls. Police claimed that all 5 belonged to unidentified foreign militants killed in an encounter with security forces in the Bangas area of Kupwara in 1999. Only the skulls, all extensively damaged, were handed to the locals for burial, who determined to bury them collectively.
Kalarus Main (Martyrs') Graveyard, Kupwara district	1 grave. Containing 5 bodies. Kalarus Police handed the skeletal remains (bones) belonging to 5 bodies to local community members. These human skeletons had been located by a Gujjar livestock herder, from the mountains between Kalarus and Machil, who informed the police about them.[22] Then, in November or December of 2007, the police handed over all 5 damaged skeletons in a sack to local residents, who buried the bones in one grave to conserve space in the graveyard.
Kanenar Kalarus Graveyard, Kupwara district	1 grave. Containing 17 bodies. All torched to death in December 1990 by mortar shelling on huts located in the vicinity of this grave. All bodies were extensively damaged and buried per the directions of security personnel.

The bodies buried in the 2,700 graves investigated by IPTK were routinely delivered at night, some bearing marks of torture and burns. Photographs of the dead have been reportedly documented by local police stations, even as they are not rendered into the public domain.[23] Systems of identification were developed by gravediggers and caretakers in tagging the bodies prior to burial. Gravediggers and caretakers devised systems through which the bodies were identified and kept identifiable for next-of-kin. Identification occurred through clothing, distinguishing characteristics and marks and/or numbering. The process of identification, dependent on literacy, threat, fear and other factors, was usually orally recorded and remembered, or recorded in writing.

In instances where, post-burial, bodies have been identified, two methods have prevalently been used. These are: 1. exhumation, and 2. identification through the use of photographs. In instances where photographs have been

Hamam Markote, Baramulla District

used to identify the body, the family/next-of-kin of the deceased has been able to identify the body from the photographs maintained by the police. Following which, graveyard identification records have been able to match the photograph of the deceased with the grave in which the body was buried. On occasion, these graves have been exhumed and the bodies transported and re-buried by next-of-kin at the place of residence or family burial grounds of the deceased.

In the discourse of the Indian Armed Forces and the Jammu and Kashmir Police, the dead buried in unknown and unmarked graves are uniformly stated to be "foreign militants/terrorists". Security forces claim that the dead were unidentified foreign or Kashmiri militants, killed while infiltrating across the border areas into Kashmir or travelling from Kashmir into Pakistan to seek arms training.[24]

Exhumation and identification have not occurred in sizeable cases. Where exhumations have been undertaken or the bodies in unknown graves have been identified through other means, in numerous instances, as detailed below, records indicate the dead to be local people, non-militant or militant, killed in fake encounters.[25]

Our investigations included, and extended beyond, villages and districts in Bandipora, Baramulla, and Kupwara.[26] From our research into the 2,700 graves in Bandipora, Baramulla, and Kupwara, and from additional inquiry into other areas, we note the following:

Of 49 bodies buried + 1 body drowned

[Whose cases were available for study]
[These bodies were from, and had been killed
and buried in, numerous districts]

[49 were recorded as militants or foreign
insurgents by security forces]

Following investigations:
47 were killed in fake encounters
41 were identified to be local civilians
1 was identified as a local militant
7 remain unidentified
None were identified as foreign insurgents

All those identified were male
39 were of Muslim descent; 4 were of Hindu
descent; 7 were not determined

Of these 50 bodies

30 bodies were exhumed
1 was recovered from a lake

All 31 were identified as male
All 31 were of Muslim descent

Post-exhumation:
30 were identified as local civilians
1 was identified as a local militant
None were identified as foreign
insurgents[27]

In certain occurrences of fake encounter killings, where the bodies of victims have been identified, it was found that civilians resident in one geographic area in Kashmir were killed in another area.[28] At times, these bodies were transferred to yet another area, then buried.[29] In one instance, we learned that the killings took place outside Kashmir, for example, in the state of Gujarat in India.[30]

In instances of 'encounter' killings, which have later been verified as 'fake' encounter deaths, security forces have manufactured the identities of victims, and entered into record a list of arms and ammunition being carried by them. On 29 April 2007, for example, armed forces claimed the killing of four militants of the Lashkar-e-Toiba.[31] Three of the four male bodies were buried in Sedarpora village in Kandi area, Kupwara district. The bodies were brought to local community members by the police, and local community members were required by the police to bury them.

The First Information Report (No. 101/07, dated 29 April 2007)[32] filed by the police stated that the deceased were "four Pakistani terrorists identified as 1. Abu-Safayan, 2. Abu-Hafiz, 3. Abu-Sadiq, 4. Abu-Ashraf". The First Information Report (FIR) also stated that "the following war-like stores were recovered... A. AK-47 = 4; B. Amm[unition] AK-47 = 170 rounds; C. Magazine AK-47 = 11;... E. Grenade = 4..."[33]

The bodies of three of the four persons named above were later identified as having been residents of Kashmir killed in fake encounters. Their names were identified as Reyaz Ahmad Bhat, Manzoor Ahmad Wagay and Sartaj Ahmad Ganai. The identity of the fourth body has not been ascertained. Sartaj Ahmad Ganai was identified as a local militant who had joined the militancy on 1 April 2007. Reyaz Ahmad Bhat and Manzoor Ahmad Wagay were identified as ordinary civilians.

Next-of-kin stated that, in interactions with police and armed forces personnel, those disappeared and/or killed in fake encounters were routinely and uniformly presented as "violent" and "anti-social" without corroboration and as objects of danger to their families and society. Through organising deception, Kashmiri Muslim men are posed as agents in cross-border armed militant negotiations, as harbingers of violence to Kashmiri Muslim women *and* the Indian nation.

In another instance, Ali Mohammad Padder was killed in a fake encounter in Ganderbal district on 7 March 2006. Security officials reported Padder to be a foreign militant, named Shaheen Bhai, from Pakistan. Security officials claimed to have recovered an AK-56 rifle.[34]

Chewah Graveyard, Safapora, Bandipora District

Investigations revealed otherwise. The body was exhumed on 3 February 2007 and identified to be that of Ali Mohammad Padder, a junior employee of the Rural Development Depart-ment and a Kashmiri. A civilian involved in Padder's burial stated: "The left side of his face was mutilated. I suppose they had fired bullets in his head. His shirt was burnt, his eyes had been gouged out and many parts of his body bore injury marks as if he had been hit by explosives".[35]

In claiming these bodies as uniformly "foreign militants/terrorists", state discourse ex-aggerates the presence of external groups and cross-border infiltration. State discourse positions cross-border infiltration as critical to mobilising and sustaining local struggles for territorial and political self-determination.[36] This refutes the contention of Kashmiris that their struggles for self-determination have, through history and the present, been local and endemic.[37]

Local community members have also testified that, in addition to the burials, bodies of persons killed by security forces have been disposed of in the Chenab and Jhelum rivers of Kashmir. Local community members testified that, for example, on 1 January 1996, four persons were cast into the Chenab river in Doda district. Of them, one person survived. According to a statement made by Talib Hussain, the survivor: "On the evening of 1 January 1996, Mohammad Hussain, Fazal Hussain, Faried Ahmad and I were picked up from the home by members of the Village Defence Committee (VDC)".[38]

VDCs are made operational by security forces and supported by the state. VDC members are recruited by Hindu nationalist/militant groups and are organised as civilian 'self-defence' campaigns and militias. In the understanding of local communities, these campaigns are staged as retribution for anti-national activities. A network of VDC's has been instituted throughout the Jammu region and in certain parts of Kashmir. VDC personnel are predomi-nantly of Hindu and Sikh descent, and in some instances include Muslim villagers deemed "trustworthy" by VDC personnel.

The testimony continued: "After finishing our daily work from a brick kiln, I was having food at my house with Mohammad Hussain, a colleague and friend of mine, and there was a sudden noise from the outside. We came out of the house and spotted five VDC members in khaki dress armed with 303 rifles.[39] Mohammad Hussain was taken away and so was I. They took us to the truck. I thought they would take us for interrogation. I was asked how many children I had. I replied, four, and he said that it was enough. They blindfolded me... I was asked to get out. Then they pushed me toward the Chenab [river]. I was forced to jump, and due to swimming, I survived. I caught hold of a rock. They fired at me. After they left, I climbed up to the shore and managed to reach the road and hitch a ride to Kishtwar where I offered prayers. The whereabouts of the other three were not ascertained and their dead bodies were not recovered".

It appears that diverse techniques of rule used by the military and paramilitary in Kashmir generate and circulate death and the fear of death. These techniques of rule are used to kill and create fear, not just of death but of murder. Across Bandipora, Baramulla, and Kupwara, the people who were forced to bury the dead in the unmarked and unknown graves attest to the detrimental psychosocial and physical health impacts they suffered. These graveyards have been placed next to schools and homes, and their affect on women and children is daunting. Massified testaments of state power, these unknown, unmarked and mass graves seek to produce social death and proscribe remembrance. Acknowledgement and articulation of events that precipitate these deaths are forbidden. Internalisation of loss and horror is intended to produce fear and isolation. Keeping alive memory, local communities state, is resistance.[40]

Atta Mohammad, 68 years of age, gravedigger and caretaker at Chehal Bimyar in Baramulla district, testified to burying 203 bodies on a hillside adjacent to the Jhelum river between 2002 and 2006. These bodies were delivered to him by the police, primarily after dark. In November and December of 2008, while he was away from his village, two other cadavers were buried in Chehal, one whose right leg was fractured.

Atta Mohammad stated that the bodies he has buried appear in his nightmares, each in graphic, gruesome detail. "I have been terrorised by this task that was forced upon me. My nights are tormented and I cannot sleep, the bodies and graves appear and reappear in my dreams. My heart is weak from this labour. I have tried to remember all this... the sound of the earth as I covered the graves... bodies and faces that were mutilated... mothers who would never find their sons. My memory is an obligation. My memory is my contribution. I am tired, I am so very tired".[41]

Kanenar Kalarus Grave, Kupwara District
Grave with 17 bodies

Notes

1. "Graves: Buried Evidence in Kashmir" is reproduced with permission from the first chapter of a report titled "Graves", in Buried Evidence: Unknown, Unmarked and Mass Graves in Indian-administered Kashmir; A Preliminary Report, published by the International People's Tribunal on Human Rights and Justice in Indian-administered Kashmir (IPTK). The complete report can be accessed at http://www.kashmirprocess.org/ .

2. Personal communication, IPTK, 2008. As appropriate, quotations are anonymous, or pseudonyms or aliases have been used, and identities of persons and place names have been listed or omitted respecting and adhering to issues of confidentiality and security. Insertion(s) within [ ] in the quotations are ours. Where names have been used, we do so with informed consent and with the hope that noting them will render these names further in the public domain and, in so doing, afford concern and safeguard.

3. Personal communication, IPTK, 2009. Srinagar is the capital city of Kashmir.

4. Indian-administered Kashmir includes Kashmir, Jammu and the Ladakh region.

5. Unless otherwise specified, 'Kashmir' refers to Indian-administered Kashmir.

6. Note: The population of Kashmir was recorded at approximately 69,00,000 in 2008, with Muslims, approximately 80 percent of Sufi heritage, constituting approximately 95 percent of the population. Across Jammu and Kashmir, approximately 67 percent of the population was recorded as being of Muslim descent. See Office of the Registrar General and Census Commissioner, India, "Census 2001: State-wise Population by Religion" (Government of India, 2001, New Delhi). The Census Commission projected the population of Jammu and Kashmir to be 11.4 million in 2008, see Office of the Registrar General and Census Commissioner, India, "Projected Total Population by Sex as on 1st March 2001-2026: India, States and Union Territories" (Government of India, 2001, New Delhi); British Broadcasting Corporation, "The Future of Kashmir?", June 2003, date noted in Kanishkan Sathasivam, **Uneasy Neighbours: India, Pakistan and US Foreign Policy** (Ashgate, 2005, Burlington), p. 45.

7. Deception operates through systematically distorted communication as the ordering principle in regular interactions between state-legitimated authorities and civilian populations.

8. We draw on the work of Michel Foucault, **Discipline and Punish: The Birth of the Prison** (Pantheon Press, 1979, New York); **Power/Knowledge** (Pantheon Press, 1980, New York); "Governmentality" in (ed.) James Faubion, **Power: Essential Works of Foucault 1954-1984**, Vol. 3, (The New Press, 2000, New York), pp. 201-22; **Security, Territory, Population: Lectures at the Collège De France 1977-1978**, (trans.) Graham Burchell (Palgrave Macmillan, 2007, New York).

9. Including, during 2008, when 151 civilians were reportedly killed. See Angana Chatterji, "Letter of Appeal to the UN Re. Cases of Security Forces Killing and Injuring Civilians in Kashmir (September 11)", 2008; Gautam Navlakha, "India in Kashmir: Winning a Battle Only to Lose a War?" in **Economic and Political Weekly**, 43 (45), pp. 43-49 (8 November 2008); Public Commission on Human Rights, "State of Human Rights in Jammu and Kashmir" (Coalition of Civil Society, 2006, Srinagar). For context and history, see Human Rights Watch, "India's Secret Army in Kashmir" (Human Rights Watch, 1996, New York) and Michael Kolodner, "Violence as Policy in the Occupations of Palestine, Kashmir and Northern Ireland" (Master's Thesis, 1996, Amherst College).

10. They have been supported by approximately 2,00,000 family members of the disappeared seeking restitution, according to the Association of Parents of Disappeared Persons (APDP).

11. 'We' refers to the authors of the report and IPTK staff, unless otherwise noted. Encounter killing: killing of civilians alleged to be involved in armed confrontation with state forces. Fake encounter killing: extrajudicial killing of civilians, often while they are in the custody of state forces, recorded by officials as resulting from an armed confrontation with state forces instigated by the recently deceased. See Human Rights Watch, "India: Overhaul Abusive, Failing Police System" (Human Rights Watch, New York, 2009).

12. These districts in Indian-held Kashmir border Pakistan-held Azad Kashmir and the Northern Areas. (**azad**: free, Urdu.) Traditionally, Bandipora and Kupwara were part of Baramulla district. There are 22 administrative districts in Indian-administered Jammu and Kashmir, with ten districts in Kashmir. The Siachen glacier is under the control of the Indian armed forces and not under the administration of Jammu and Kashmir.

13. Personal communication, IPTK, 2008.

14. Unnamed at/during the time of our investigations.

15. w.: with. For district and village details, see section entitled "'Exhumed Truths': Kupwara, Baramulla, and Bandipora Districts" in **Buried Evidence: Unknown, Unmarked, and Mass Graves in Indian-administered Kashmir**, available at: http://www.kashmirprocess.org/reports/graves/05Pages3948.html#ExhumedTruths.

16. We learned this through our investigations, ibid.

17. We learned this through our investigations, see section entitled "'Encounter'/Fake Encounter: An Index" in **Buried Evidence: Unknown, Unmarked, and Mass Graves in Indian-administered Kashmir**, available at: http://www.kashmirprocess.org/reports/graves/08Pages6978.html#Encounter.

18. Gravediggers: we refer to professional gravediggers; caretakers: we refer to those who were forced into grave digging.

19. Shari'at, Shari'a: Islamic law.

20. **Nullah**: tributary of a stream.

21. The IPTK spoke with persons who had travelled inside the camp for reasons of work.

22. Gujjar: tribal group; here, prevalently identified as Muslim. Some Gujjar groups can be migratory.

23. Per the police manual, all dead bodies must be photographed.

24. While some persons did travel to Pakistan to seek training, such activity was largely confined to the early days of the armed militancy, circa the late 1980s through the early to mid-1990s. The graves of such persons killed by the Indian armed forces are usually located on the border, in mountainous terrain far away from villages and towns, as, for example, in Gali Nullah, Gulmarg, in Baramulla district, where there exists one grave containing 12 bodies. All were claimed to be militants in the Muslim Janbaz Force (MJF), a Kashmiri organisation, and were killed by security forces in May-June 1991 in an ambush attack in the Gali area, situated between the Tosmaidaan and Afarvat hills. There were 15 members of MJF present, and one survived.

25. For details, see Buried Evidence: Unknown, Unmarked, and Mass Graves in Indian-administered Kashmir, available at: http://www.kashmirprocess.org/reports/graves/. In Kashmir, local resistance groups distinguish themselves as "militants" and/or "freedom fighters", and further distinguish themselves as "armed militants" or "nonviolent militants". Struggle, armed and nonviolent, is discoursed by dominant India as "terrorism"/"anti-nationalism". Post-2001, as Robert Wirsing states: "the Kashmiri freedom struggle was being increasingly conflated with... terrorism", see Kashmir in the Shadow of Rivalries in a Nuclear Age *(M.E. Sharpe, 2003, New York), p. 118; also Talal Asad,* On Suicide Bombing *(Columbia University Press, 2007, New York); Olivier Roy,* Globalized Islam: The Search for a New Ummah *[community of the faithful] (Columbia University Press, 2004, New York).*

26. For details, see sub-section, 'Methodology' in the section entitled "Context" in the original report. Available at: http://www.kashmirprocess.org/reports/graves/05Pages3948.html.

27. For details, see section entitled "'Encounter'/Fake Encounter: An Index", op. cit.

28. We learned this through our investigations, see section entitled "'Encounter'/Fake Encounter: An Index", ibid.

29. We learned this through our investigations, ibid.

30. We learned this through our investigations, ibid.

31. Lashkar-e-Toiba: Islamist militant organisation, founded in Afghanistan, banned as a terrorist organisation by Australia, India, Pakistan, Russia, the United Kingdom and the United States.

32. No.: number.

33. AK-47, also Avtomat (automatic) Kalashnikov (name of designer), an assault rifle initially developed in the former Soviet Union in 1947.

34. An assault rifle developed in 1956, the AK-56 is a Chinese version of the AK-47.

35. Personal communication, IPTK, 2008-2009.

36. Self-determination: in this context, the ability of a people to determine their political or national status and future without coercion. Legal and political processes through which the legitimacy of any claims to self-determination may be resolved, or a 'people' may define themselves as such, are inconsistent. The Atlantic Charter of 1941 accepts the principles of self-determination as does the United Nations Charter of 1945, which situated the right to self-determination within international law and diplomacy. Article 1 of the International Covenant on Civil and Political Rights (ICCPR) and the International Covenant on Economic, Social and Cultural Rights (ICESCR) states that: "All peoples have the right of self-determination. By virtue of that right they freely determine their political status and freely pursue their economic, social and cultural development". Article 15 of the United Nations Universal Declaration of Human Rights endorses the right of individuals to a nationality and the right to change one's nationality. See Allen Buchanan, Justice, Legitimacy and Self-Determination: Moral Foundations for International Law *(Oxford University Press, 2007, New York); (ed.) Wolfgang F. Danspeckgruber,* The Self-Determination of Peoples: Community, Nation, and State in an Interdependent World *(Lynne Rienner Publishers, 2002, Boulder); Martin Griffiths, "Self-determination, International Society and World Order" in* Macquarie University Law Journal, *1 (2003); Hurst Hannum,* Autonomy, Sovereignty, and Self-Determination: The Accommodation of Conflicting Rights *(University of Pennsylvania Press,1996, Philadelphia); Percy Lehning,* Theories of Secession *(Routledge, 1998, New York); Aleksandar Pavkovic and Peter Radan, "In Pursuit of Sovereignty and Self-determination: Peoples, States and Secession in the International Order" in* Macquarie University Law Journal, *1 (2003).*

37. Even when external solidarities were cultivated by militant groups, as in the early 1990s.

38. Personal communication, IPTK, 2008-2009. The witness has spoken on public record.

39. Khaki: beige coloured garment used by Hindu militants/nationalists. A .303 is a British-developed (initially, in the 1880s) .311-inch calibre rifle.

40. We draw on Abdul R. JanMohamed, The Death-Bound-Subject: Richard Wright's Archaeology of Death *(Duke University Press, 2005, Durham); also Veena Das, "The Act of Witnessing: Violence, Poisonous Knowledge and Subjectivity", in (eds.) Veena Das, Arthur Kleinman, Mamphela Ramphele and Pamela Reynolds,* Violence and Subjectivity *(University of California Press, 2002, Berkeley), pp. 205-25.*

41. Personal communication, IPTK, 2008-2009. Atta Mohammad has spoken on public record before the State Human Rights Commission in Srinagar and to members of the local and international press corps.

Fear, Sexuality and the Future
Thinking Sex (Panic), Monstrosity and Prostitution

SVATI P. SHAH

In order to fight this monster, we must know more about it. Lack of information, statistical and otherwise, have left us looking at footprints of a creature whose shape, size and ferocity we can only guess. It lurks in the shadows. The profiles of its cronies and their networks are sketchy. Its victims are too afraid to run away and speak up, their number unknown. The monster takes different shapes, depending on the culture, time and the context, in collusion with other unlawful undertakings: illegal migration, forced labour, paedophilia, child exploitation, civil conflicts and coerced prostitution. This monster is hard to detect because it defies categorization. Although the UN Protocol's definition of "trafficking in persons" is detailed, in popular parlance, the emphasis is placed on the acts of buying and selling victims, rather than their exploitation. And then there are misconceptions: our girls are beautiful… it's only prostitution, *high ranking officials have told me. Ladies and gentlemen, let's call it what it is: modern slavery.*
Opening Statement by UN Office on Drugs and Crime (UNODC) Executive Director Antonio Maria at the 2008 Vienna Forum to Fight Human Trafficking[1]

This UNODC statement on human trafficking and monstrosity evokes what has become the dominant international discourse on prostitution. Maria's statement covers the gamut of issues that have been critiqued by activists and scholars critical of the criminalisation of sexual commerce – migration, prostitution and "modern slavery". The wide range of perspectives, research and writing on sexual commerce notwithstanding, many governments have adopted laws and policies that conflate prostitution and human trafficking, and emphasise the criminalisation of migrants, a move that has been the subject of a fierce and well-documented set of debates. While the matter is far from settled, the criminalisation of sexual commerce seems to be gaining traction, aided by a public discourse in which prostitution and harm are becoming interchangeable and a visible, state-centred response is the foregone recourse. The influence of the abolitionist ideal that all prostitution be eradicated is clear, in funding streams for abolitionist anti-trafficking groups, in the heightened interest in training police to do anti-prostitution work and in recent, failed efforts to amend India's law on prostitution such that prostitution would have been further criminalised. This essay explores the ways in which fear contributes toward producing the criminalisation of prostitution as common sense, by rendering sex workers themselves monstrously un-human. I suggest that fear sustains the notion of the sex worker monster, a "beast who is all body and no soul".[2] Read through Foucauldian abnormality and Mbembe's necropower, monstrosity is a critical trope for sex work, a lens through which we may explore the ways in which fear produces marginality and, among other things, juridical exceptionalism for urban, brothel-based sex work. Normativising fears of sex work ultimately require monstrosity as a structuring parameter for the contemporary representation and regulation of prostitution in India. While the Indian context is not unique in its response to prostitution in recent years, the intersections of international neoliberal development agendas and national debates on prostitution and sexual autonomy have found unique purchase in both India and, more generally, South Asia. Here, I understand monstrosity as key to producing an ambiguous set of marginalities within normative power.

Fear and the History of Risk

Fear has had a long career in organising the biopolitical regulation of sex workers in Indian urban centres, although India has tended, until relatively recently, to focus on containment[3] rather than elimination. The 'civilising' project of the colonial government treated prostitution as inevitable, something to be managed through a moral geography manifested in urban space. The new, neoliberal civilising project, like the old, includes the protection of women's honour as a core value, but it aims to build women's 'equality' and 'dignity' in the Global South by eliminating trafficking and prostitution, while ignoring male and trans-sex workers in the process. The thread linking the old and new is the risk of sexually transmitted disease; in the colonial and contemporary contexts, sex workers themselves embody 'risk', and are both feared and desired within the discourse of risk.

Since the beginning of the HIV/AIDS epidemic in the 1980s, epidemiological 'risk', in India, has been categorically ascribed to sex workers, who were written into the discourse on AIDS as vectors of HIV transmission and as inherently risky subjects. The conflation of sex work and human trafficking has added the ostensible 'risk' ascribed to migration to the 'risk' of prostitution as well. The notion of migrants inhabiting the category of epidemiological or criminal 'risk' is nothing new. The relationship between risk and migrancy has been elaborated, for example, within critiques of neoliberalism, and in scholarship that addresses increased international border surveillance and state-sponsored regulation of poor migrants from countries in the Global South, even as barriers to the migration of capital continue to be systematically decreased.[4] The familiar terrain of epidemiological risk is framed by the broader rubric of fear and the social and political marginality it produces.

This marginality has had far-reaching effects, including the lack of recourse to legal protections for sex workers, who are figured as subjects transgressing the law rather than ever being seen as legitimate objects of legal transgression. The fear that has kept this marginality in place becomes the basis for rationalising exceptional state-sponsored regulation of red light areas and sex worker subjects, as well as providing a staging ground for producing sex work as spectacle through new technologies of surveillance deployed by public health interventions and the media. Fear ultimately becomes the first note in a clarion call against sexual commerce in all its forms, where sex work signifies dangerously marked bodies, spaces, and the immanent possibility of realising a whorish, dystopic future. Figuring prostitution as degenerative is key to stipulating this possibility, a possibility that is enabled between prostitution and fear, and articulated as the conflation of sex work and trafficking. Fear mobilises this vision, conceptually binding prostitution and violence. The consequences of allowing prostitution to continue to exist in the world unabated are primarily articulated through the language of the risk of disease and the degradation of 'humanity'; fears that are initially attached to paid sex, then to sex workers themselves, with the gaping possibility that eventually, *inevitably*, all sex will be thus degraded. In this dystopic vision, the commoditisation of sex devolves to normative, non-sex worker subjects as well, even as love and sex become permanently estranged, and women, whose iconicity as sellers of sex is paramount, are divested of 'honour', where honour is read through the category of humanity. Without honour, monsters remain.

Sex Panics and 'Modern-day Slavery'

The fears that produce the contemporary moral panic over prostitution are institutionalised within the dominant anti-trafficking framework, and are often articulated through the familiar abolitionist argument that prostitution constitutes 'modern-day slavery'. Critics of abolitionism have pointed out that prostitution and chattel slavery are necessarily distinct, and that evoking 'slavery' in the contemporary context of sexual commerce recapitulates Victorian-era fears of 'White slavery'.[5] But what does invoking slavery mean in this context? If we take the rhetorical evocation of slavery to its logical conclusion via the necropolitical, it means that sex work is figured as death in the dominant anti-trafficking framework.

> As an instrument of labor, the slave has a price. As a property, he or she has a value. His or her labor is needed and used. The slave is therefore kept alive but in a *state of injury*, in a phantomlike world of horrors and intense cruelty and profanity. The violent tenor of the slave's life is manifested through the overseer's disposition to behave in a cruel and intemperate manner and *in the spectacle of pain inflicted on the slave's body... Slave life, in many ways, is a form of death-in-life.*[6] (Mbembe, 2003, emphasis added)

If sex workers are cast as 'modern slaves', as "instrument[s] of labor", then sex workers are also kept alive but in "a state of injury". The abolitionist contention is that prostitution is the ultimate injury to body and idealised humanity. Pushing the use of 'slavery' toward the limits of its implications for sex work, then, sex workers as slaves are interpolated as dead-in-life. They exist in half-life, written into the anti-trafficking framework as the living dead, as it were, (infectious) zombie-like monsters needing to be rescued back into non-sex worker 'alive-in-life' humanity.

Reading monstrosity through Foucault's theory of the 'abnormals', I am suggesting that fear envisions monstrously embodied prostitution, and that this buttresses both a regulatory regime that has deepened the criminality of sex workers over the past decade, and a discursive regime that spectacularises prostitution. The spectacle of prostitution has placed an added focus on the regulation of urban sexual commerce through brothel raids and extrajudicial detention and violence by a host of state and non-state actors. Raids have always been a staple of regulating urban prostitution, though they now have the weight of being an important rescue strategy for victims of trafficking in anti-trafficking efforts as well. Raids, brothel demolitions and brothel lock-outs have been stepped up as efforts are made by abolitionist groups to shift the primary object of the fear of prostitution from female sex workers, who are now constructed as victims to be rescued, to madams, pimps and 'traffickers', whose monstrosity is ostensibly superlative because it adheres to sex (as opposed to managers in other industries, whose abusiveness is not a given and whose exploitative practices, if they occur, are understood within discourses of class and addressed through organising strategies associated with workplace exploitation). 'Traffickers', pimps, and madams are the new objects of terror from whom sex workers must be rescued, by any means necessary. However, the shift from fearing sex workers to fearing their ostensible exploiters is fragmentary, as any adult involved in sexual commerce is bundled into an economy of fear and state-sponsored regulation, and targeted by the same range of extrajudicial regulatory measures.

Following on this reading of the enslaved un-humanity of sex worker subjects, a Foucauldian reading of monstrosity becomes not only possible, but necessary. Foucauldian monstrosity belongs to

> the juridico-biological domain. The figures of the half-human, half-animal being… of double individualities… What makes a human monster a monster is not just its exceptionality relative to the species form; it is the disturbance it brings to juridical regularities (whether it is a question of marriage laws, canons of baptism, or rules of inheritance). The human monster combines the impossible and the forbidden…[7]

In their 2002 article, "Monster, Terrorist, Fag",[8] Jasbir Puar and Amit Rai review Michel Foucault's explication of human monstrosity and abnormality. In producing their analysis of the ways in which the discourse on the American war against 'terrorism' is also a discourse on the sexuality and masculinity of a mythologised enemy, Puar and Rai argue that "…the absolute power that produces and quarantines the monster finds its dispersal in techniques of normalization and discipline. What Foucault does, we believe, is enable an analysis of monstrosity within a broader history of sexuality". An analysis of monstrosity within the broader history of sexuality, in this context, raises the question of monstrosity's effectuation of "disturbance" to "juridical regularities", such as they are, for sex work.

Elsewhere,[9] I have argued that the spectacle of disreputable prostitution in Mumbai, embodied in the most visible of all red light districts in the city, Kamathipura, is defined and produced against the trope of non-sex worker subjectivity located in the 'respectable' districts of the city, which are necessarily situated outside this disreputable zone. Within the zone of disrepute, a juridico-legal state of exception operates, one in which the ends of reducing the criminal and health menace of prostitution justify the means of brothel raids and heightened surveillance. The ultimate effect of this state of exception is articulated in Mbembe's formulation of slavery and the necropolitical – the right to kill the monster, in this case, by any means necessary, in the service of protecting the non-sex worker public against it. The necropolitical management of brothel-based sex workers is undertaken in at least two ways. First, the quarantine (in remand homes) and criminalisation of sex workers done under the rubric of preventing their transmitting HIV, a rubric that is deployed in a discursive context that primarily defines sex workers as un-human vectors of disease. Second, the dispersal of sex workers, an effect of brothel raids and heightened surveillance in the era of HIV, thus interrupting their primary source of income and making survival, and life, much more tenuous – and ultimately untenable. Writing on juridical exceptionalism as "the normative basis of the right to kill", Mbembe observes:

> In such instances [of exceptionalism], power (and not necessarily state power) continuously refers and appeals to exception, emergency, and a fictionalized notion of the enemy. It also labors to produce that same exception, emergency, and fictionalized enemy. In other words, the question is: What is the relationship between politics and death in those systems that can function only in a state of emergency?[10]

Where exceptionalism is the primary mode of regulating prostitution, the relationship between politics and death is fear – specifically, the fear of monstrous sex worker-others. This fear ultimately structures a racialised other, one that is essentially different from the normative body politic and at the same time desired by it.

A Note on Prostitution, Fear and Racialisation
Thus far, I have suggested that fear produces sex worker monstrosity in the abolitionist discourse on sexual commerce, and that the excision of the monstrous is framed as a service to a greater common good: that of maintaining normative sexuality, defined against the sexual excess of prostitution. While this monstrosity is managed through necropower – the right to kill – the marginal social location that this monstrosity inhabits is not diametrically opposed to a normative centre. Rather, following on Clare Hemmings' essay on affect, this marginality may be understood as ambivalent, and not simply oppositional.

> To be 'other' is not only to be the object of another's gaze within the dominant; it also precipitates community that is historically resonant, that draws on and creates alternative signification of the same actions and events. Thus, social difference is not only opposite, but knowing and inflecting, and the social world is always crosscut with fissures that have a social and political history that signifies otherwise.[11]

Hemmings qualifies this ambiguity in a number of ways, as for example by her discussion of subjects who are "over-associated with affect", including sex worker subjects.[12] This over-association has a number of effects, including the "affective racialization" of over-associated subjects.

> ...[F]ollowing Frantz Fanon's (1952) insistence that social relations at both the macro and the micro level are based on unreasonable ties, critical race theorists argue that affect plays a role in both cementing sexed and raced relations of domination, and in providing the local investments necessary to counter those relations...[13]

I raise the question of racialisation here both as a provocation and as a means of bringing Mbembe and Hemmings together in this essay, within the postcolonial regulatory context of Mumbai's brothel-based sex industries. Racialisation has been central to critical work on prostitution, having been understood as a mode of articulating civilisational power against colonised subjects read through tropes of sexual excess. I evoke racialisation here in order to evoke the construction of biologically coded, immutable moral characteristics, rather than to advocate for a 'theory of races' in red light areas, although racialisation is an open question within the context of the large numbers of dalit women, men and *hijras* who live and work in India's sex sectors. Reading Mbembe and Hemmings through the lens of an ever-shifting yet seemingly intractable racialised matrix, the juridical exceptionalism that operates within the red light area could scarcely be mobilised without the unifying ideology of racialisation, if not 'race' per se, in which sex workers are inherently inferiorised, backward and in need of social rehabilitation.

Conclusion

In this essay, I have offered a schematic argument that calls for further attention to fear in critical studies of prostitution in India. I have argued that examining fear in the light of recent work on the politics of affect and postcolonialism can offer insight on the durability of the dominant anti-trafficking framework, despite a large body of work that has shown the framework's assumptions to be critically flawed. An analysis of the construction of monstrosity, as produced by the fear of excessive, unregulated sexuality, shows that monstrosity is central to rationalising criminalisation as the regulatory mode of choice in controlling, and potentially eradicating, sex work in India. I ultimately suggest that non-normative, other, amoral sexuality in the dominant anti-trafficking discourse is produced through fear in relation to both space and time – in space, through the construction of a dangerous urban zone, and in time, through visions of ignoble, decadent pre-colonial pasts and an abject, hyper-sexed, dystopic future. Flipping the frame, the fear of the sex worker-other may be read against exceedingly unexceptional fears among sex workers, and the other objects of exceptional regulation, of the arbitrary and violent tactics used against them by state and non-state actors, coupled with fears of failing to economically survive. These fears are evidenced in numerous accounts of sex workers who have faced extrajudicial detention, displacement from their homes and repeated arrests.

While a proper exploration of racialisation and caste in context of brothel-based sex work is beyond the scope of this essay, my discussion of affect, biopower and necropower raises the question of the intersections between racialisation, desire and monstrous embodiment in prostitution. This monstrosity must be read multiply. While I have focused on monstrosity as an abject category, used as a rationale by normative discourses for deploying biopower, racialised monstrosity also evokes surrealist readings of monstrosity, such as those mobilised, for example, by Negritude and other anti-colonial movements of the 20th century. Anti-colonial readings of surrealism allowed for figuring monstrosity as marvellous, fantastical and possible in the racialised postcolony.[14] While this evocation runs the risk of being taken up within the contemporary liberal individualist rhetoric of sex workers exercising 'choice' (an argument designed to counter abolitionist assertions that sex work is always already forced), I end with the notion of the fantastical as a gesture toward the possibility of alternate visions of the future, and of the present.

Notes

1. UN Office on Drugs and Crime. "Tracking a Monster". Available at: http://www.unodc.org/unodc/en/frontpage/tracking-a-monster.html (accessed 16 November 2009).
2. Judith Halberstam. Skin Shows: Gothic Horror and the Technology of Monsters (Duke University Press, 1995, Durham), p. 1.
3. This has been demonstrated by numerous feminist scholars writing on urban, brothel-based sex work, including, for example, Ratna Kapur, Prabha Kotiswaran, and Ashwini Tambe.
4. Saskia Sassen. Mobility of Labor and Capital: A Study in International Investment and Labor Flow (Cambridge University Press, 1988, Cambridge/New York).
5. Ashwini Tambe, Codes of Misconduct: The Regulation of Prostitution in Colonial Bombay (University of Minnesota Press, 2009, Minnesota); Philipa Levine, Prostitution, Race and Politics: Policing Venereal Disease in the British Empire (Routledge, 2003, New York).
6. Achille Mbembe. "Necropolitics". In Public Culture 1 (2003), p. 21.
7. Michel Foucault. "The Abnormals". In ed. Paul Rabinow, Ethics: Subjectivity and Truth, (trans.) Robert Hurley (New Press, 1997, New York), pp. 51-52, quoted in Puar and Rai, pp.118-119.
8. Jasbir K. Puar and Amit S. Rai. "Monster, Terrorist, Fag: The War on Terrorism and the Production of Docile Patriots". In Social Text 72 (2002).
9. Svati P. Shah. "Producing the Spectacle of Kamathipura: The Politics of Red Light Visibility in Mumbai". In Cultural Dynamics 18 (2006).
10. Mbembe, op.cit., p. 16.
11. Clare Hemmings, "Invoking Affect: Cultural Theory and the Ontological Turn", in Cultural Studies 5 (2005), p. 558; Homi K. Bhabha, The Location of Culture (Routledge, 1994, London); Frantz Fanon, Black Skins, White Masks (Pluto Press, 1952, London); Denize Kandyoti, "Identity and Its Discontents: Women and the Nation", in (eds.) P. Williams and L. Chrisman, Colonial Discourse and Postcolonial Theory: A Reader (Columbia University Press, 1994, New York), pp. 376-391; Edward Said, Orientalism (Random House, 1979, New York); Gayatri Spivak, A Critique of Postcolonial Reason: Toward a History of the Vanishing Present (Harvard University Press, 1999, Cambridge, MA).
12. Hemmings, ibid., p. 561.
13. Hemmings, ibid., p. 550.
14. Jeremy Biles, Ecce Monstrum: Georges Bataille and the Sacrifice of Form (Fordham University Press, 2007, New York); Aimé Césaire, Discourse on Colonialism (Monthly Review Press, 2000, New York).

Police States, Anthropology and Human Rights

NANDINI SUNDAR

3 January 2010

Ujjwal Kumar Singh, Professor of Political Science, Delhi University, and I have just returned (1 January 2010) from a visit to the police state of Chhattisgarh. Ujjwal had gone for research, and I had gone for a combination of research and verification purposes to assess the livelihood situation of villagers for our case before the Supreme Court,[1] both entirely legitimate activities. Indeed, to restrain a petitioner or witness from ensuring compliance with the Court's orders amounts to contempt of court. In Dantewada, we had checked into Hotel Madhuban on 29 December at around 2 p.m. without any problems, only to be told later that night that the management required the entire hotel to be instantly emptied because they were doing some *puja* (prayer ceremony) to mark the death anniversary of the hotel owner. We refused to leave at night, and were told we would have to leave at 6 a.m. instead because the rooms had to be cleaned. As expected, other guests checked in the next morning, *puja* notwithstanding.

At Sukma, we were detained by the police and Special Police Officers (SPOs) at the entrance to the town from about 7.30 till 10 p.m., with no explanation for why they had stopped us, and no questions as to why we were there or what our plans were. We were denied lodging – all the hotel owners had been told to claim they were full and refuse us rooms, and the Forest and Public Works departments had been advised not to make their guesthouses available, since 'Naxalites' were coming to stay. Indeed, the police told us that these days Naxalites had become so confident that they roamed around in jeeps on the highways. Since everything was mysteriously full in a small town like Sukma, the police advised us to leave that very night for Jagdalpur, the Bastar district headquarters, some 100 kilometres away. We decided instead to spend the night in the jeep, since we did not want to jeopardise friends by staying in their homes. Later, we contacted friends and they arranged for us to stay in the college boys' hostel, since students were away on vacation.

At midnight on the 30th, six to seven armed SPOs burst into our room at the college hostel, guns cocked, and then spent the night patrolling the grounds. Evidently, the SPOs have seen many films and know precisely how to achieve dramatic effect. They were also trying to open our jeep, presumably to plant something. We spent the night wondering whether they were going to take us to the *thana* (police station) the next morning and texting friends: "FYI: we are surrounded by SPOs". It wasn't clear what the proper etiquette was in such situations – were we sounding unnecessarily alarmist or was this what such police behaviour required of us?

The next morning, we were followed by seven armed SPOs with AK-47s from Sukma in an unmarked white car; this was replaced at Tongpal by 12 SPOs, in two jeeps. None of the SPOs had any name plates. Two women SPOs had been deputed especially for me. The SPOs also intimidated our jeep drivers by photographing them and the vehicle, and since very few people are willing to drive into the badlands of Dantewada in the first place, this is an effective way of ensuring we get no private transport in the future.

At Tongpal, I could see people I knew staring at the spectacle of my little police procession, but what could I say to them? Given that we could have had no normal conversation with anyone, we decided to do all the things one normally postpones. In 20 years of visiting Bastar, for example, I have never seen the Kutumbsar caves. Everywhere we went, including the *haat* (farmers' market) at Tongpal, the Tirathgarh waterfall and the Kutumbsar caves, as well as shops in Jagdalpur, the SPOs followed us, one pace behind, with their guns poised at the ready. In Kutumbsar, four of them stood in line behind us, patient but determined. Strange that at that moment, I was more worried about the fall-out of a stampede down the narrow steps caused by squawking children and eager tourists, than the fact of the police following us. There was even a brief moment of camaraderie with the cops, as we emerged silently from the cave, tourist sight unseen. They were disappointed that we did not go in – after all, how often do you get to go touristing with 'Naxalites' – but also perhaps bewildered, 'Surely Naxalites are made of sterner stuff'.

The state Director General of Police, Vishwa Ranjan, claimed over the phone that it was for our 'protection' that we were being given this treatment since there was news of Naxalite troop movement; he went on to tell *The Indian Express* (3 January 2010), "Anything can happen. Maoists can attack the activists to put the blame on the police. We will deploy a few companies of security forces for the security of the activists".

Clearly all the other tourists in Tirathgarh and Kutumbsar were under no threat from the Maoists – only we, who have been repeatedly accused in print and in court of being Naxalite supporters, were likely targets. As for the police ensuring that we got no accommodation and trying to send us from Sukma to Jagdalpur in the middle of the night, such pure concern for our welfare is touching. The Dantewada Superintendent of Police (SP), Amaresh Misra, was somewhat more honest when he said he had instructions from above to 'escort' out 'visiting dignitaries'. The Additional SP shouted at us for not being more 'constructive' – not surprisingly, though, with 12 swaggering SPOs snapping at one's heels, one is not always at one's constructive best. Indeed, I later regretted not turning the moment to ethnographic advantage by interviewing the SPOs about their lives.

The SPOs in their jeeps followed us some way from Jagdalpur to Raipur, the state capital, even when we were on the bus. In addition, two armed constables and a sub-inspector (SI) were sent on the bus to ensure we got to Raipur. We overheard the SI telling the armed constables to "take them down at Dhamtari", but fortunately this plan was abandoned. This sounded so preposterous that we naïvely believed he could not be referring to us, and looked around the bus for the 'real' Naxalites they meant to 'take out', casting suspicious eyes in particular at a hapless passenger in the seat next to us, who spoke with what seemed to us was a Telugu accent. (In the local version of profiling, vehicles with Andhra Pradesh number plates and speakers of Telegu, the language of the state, have had a particular problem with the police in Chhattisgarh since 2005, when the Salwa Judum started.) Such is the atmosphere of terror that a police state creates that even those who know better become complicit in its demonic fears. The poor SI narrowly missed getting a medal for bravery. As the good DGP tells the readers of the *Indian Express*, it would have been passed off as a Naxalite attack. On reaching Raipur, the SI was confused. Shouting loudly and forgetting himself, as bad cell phone connections are wont to make us all do, he said, "The IG [inspector-general] and SP had told me to follow them, but now what do I do with them?" The voice on the other end told him to go home. We flew out of Raipur the next morning. In real terms, this was a rather pointless exercise for the Chhattisgarh government, since we were scheduled to come home the following day anyway, bound by the inexorable timetable of the university and classes. But, symbolically, it allowed the SPOs to gloat that they had driven us out.

The Chhattisgarh government obviously wants to ensure that no news on their offensive or even on the everyday trauma of villagers reaches outside. Many villages have been depopulated in the south, both due to the immense fear created by Operation Green Hunt and the failure of the monsoons this year. All able-bodied adults are migrating to Andhra Pradesh for coolie work, leaving only children and the elderly in the villages. There are sporadic encounters – the day we were in Dantewada (29 December 2009), two 'Naxalites' were killed in the jungles of Vechapal and three arrested. A week before, seven people had been killed in Gumiapal. Who is getting killed and how is anyone's guess. Combing operations have intensified and 'Cobra' battalions have been flown in. A month ago, people were rushing to get identity cards made to show their bona fides, spending a scarce Rs. 100 on getting their photographs taken, before the police decided this was an avenue the Naxalites could misuse, and stopped it. People are confused – should one run or not? If you run, you will get shot. The Central Reserve Police Force (CRPF) deployed in the area repeatedly asked us, "Why is it that people run when they see us, and don't run when they see you? It must be because they are guilty" Or, they conclude from this, we are escorted in by the Naxalites. The simple fact that our being unarmed is the reason people talk to us, escapes them. But equally, if people stay in the village, there is no safety in numbers or public presence. A toddler in Gompad has lost his fingers, following a combing operation. There is compete terror, fear and hunger throughout the district. On the other side, the Maoists are killing 'informers' and mobilising villagers to 'defend' their areas with trees and trenches. Young men from newer areas are going off to get arms training. The college students we stayed with said a whole generation had missed out on coming to college because of the displacement and death caused by the Salwa Judum since 2005. Even those who graduated earlier have no future – there are no jobs. A student in our department lost his brother-in-law in a landmine blast – he was working with the Central Industrial Security Force at Bailadilla. His sister is bereft. The war is coming closer – it is no longer something out there in some 'field site', it is around me.

While the Chhattisgarh government is busy providing us 'protection', it has refused to restore the armed guard taken away from Communist Party of India (CPI) leader Manish Kunjam. He has had credible reports that his life is under threat, and he may face a replay of the Niyogi murder,[2] because of his opposition both to forcible and fraudulent land acquisition by multinationals like Tata and Essar, and to the Salwa Judum and Operation Green Hunt. Manish Kunjam is the single most important mass leader in the area who has been independent of both the state and the Maoists, and has taken a stand on various issues. Despite Chhattisgarh Chief Minister Raman Singh assuring the CPI leadership that he would be protected, the DGP has refused to act. I have known Manish for many years now – he is brave about himself in a way that I cannot be about him.

It is also remarkable that a government which can waste so many armed SPOs for an entire day and night on two people who do nothing more dangerous than teach and write, has been unable to catch the SPOs responsible for raping six young women, who have later moved court against them. Despite the trial court finding the SPOs and Salwa Judum leaders *prima facie* guilty of rape and issuing a standing warrant for their arrest on 30 October 2009, they are still 'absconding' two months later. Some of them actively and openly participate in *dharnas* (protest demonstrations) to block visiting activists, but they are invisible to the police. Earlier in June 2009, the Dantewada SP told the Supreme Court that he could not find one of the victims, even though she had deposed in the trial court the day before. Therefore, he said, he had asked the accused for an explanation, and they had assured him there was no basis to the charge and the women were only trying to malign them in their brave fight against Naxalism. In December, when local activist Himanshu Kumar, who was instrumental in helping the women come to court, reported that the rape victims were detained without cause for three or four days in Dornapal *thana* and generally terrorised, the chief secretary's response was to accuse him of running an "ugly motivated campaign". All good men these, good fathers, good husbands, good citizens. Unfortunately for these adivasi girls, they are not middle class, so there will be no media campaign for them, as was launched in several extensively publicised cases over the last few years.

Bastar can no more get rid of me than I can get rid of Bastar. In 1992, because I attended meetings to observe the protests by the villagers of Maolibhata against the steel plant that was proposed to be sited there, the government denied me access to the local archives. But the government then fell, and my book on Bastar, *Subalterns and Sovereigns*, was published by 1997. In 2004, four of us doing a survey of the Lok Sabha polls were stopped in a village by local Maoist sympathisers. They retained activist Ajay TG's video camera. The brilliant Chhattisgarh police later arrested Ajay because the Maoists apologised and wanted to return the camera. In 2005, Salwa Judum activists stopped us as part of the

People's Union for Democratic Rights (PUDR)-People's Union for Civil Liberties (PUCL) fact-finding team on Salwa Judum; in 2006, as members of the Independent Citizens' Initiative, Ramachandra Guha, Farah Naqvi and I were stopped and searched in Bhairamgarh *thana* by out-of-control SPOs, and Ramachandra Guha was nearly lynched inside the station while the *thanedar* (station superintendent) was too drunk to read the letter we carried from the chief secretary. My camera was taken away by a Salwa Judum leader, and returned only months later. In 2007-08, the then SP, Rahul Sharma, fabricated photographs of me with my arms around armed Maoist women and showed them to visiting journalists and others to try and discredit my independence. He later claimed, when challenged, that the photographs were of one 'Ms Jeet', and it was he who had verified the truth. In 2009, historian Ajay Dandekar, anthropologist JP Rao and I narrowly escaped a mob of around 300 Salwa Judum leaders, police and SPOs, who, however, took away JP Rao's mobile phones, a camera charger and vehicle registration documents from the parked jeep. The police refused to register our complaint and detained us for questioning for a few hours, even though we had got the consent of the district collector and the Mirtur CRPF contingent to visit Vechapal. In January 2010, a team of 15 activists from the National Alliance of People's Movements and other organisations was pelted with stones, eggs and cow dung in Dantewada. The Salwa Judum lives and flourishes under the new name of the Ma Danteshwari Samanvay Samiti, and the more organised label of 'SPOs', encouraged by the cover of impunity granted by the Centre and its operations.

For anthropologists, our professional life is often difficult to separate from our personal – our research depends on developing deep friendships with the people we 'study'. In the 20 years that I have been visiting Bastar off and on, I have acquired a range of acquaint-ances, friends and people who are like family members. In many ways, their concerns are my concerns, though I can always run away, and they cannot. But while friendships make it harder to do systematic research (the pressure to hang out and drink with people is much larger than the drive to 'survey' them), they do not diminish one's commitment to independ-ence and objectivity. The relationship between anthropology and advocacy has long been a subject of debate within the discipline, and, within India, people like NK Bose, SC Roy, AR Desai and many others have raised the question of the anthropologist/sociologist's social commitment. I have myself come down on both sides of the divide, recognising that good research requires the kind of whole-time dedication that advocacy takes away from. On the other hand, it is the generosity of people who are suffering, in sharing their time and pain with us, that enables us to raise new and relevant questions for research. Ultimately, as Michael Harner said in 1966, when the American Anthropological Association was debating whether to pass a resolution against the war in Vietnam, "Genocide is not in the professional interests of anthropology".

Editor's Notes

1. Nandini Sundar, historian Ramachandara Guha and retired civil servant EAS Sarma have filed a petition in the Supreme Court challenging the Chhattisgarh state government on the Salwa Judum, a vigilante movement it launched in 2005. The Salwa Judum civil militia is armed and sponsored by the state to fight Naxalites, adherents of Maoist ideology, active against the government in the states of Chhattisgarh, Andhra Pradesh, Jharkhand, Bihar, West Bengal and in parts of Maharashtra and Uttar Pradesh, among others. The Supreme Court petition contends that the state government has, under cover of the Salwa Judum, unleashed extrajudicial killings and atrocities upon the adivasi (indigenous) people of Chhattisgarh. In the course of its hearings, the Court has expressed disapproval of the state's arming private persons, terming it an abetment of crime. It has also directed the government to act on the recommendations of the court-appointed National Human Rights Commission investigation that confirmed claims of widespread atrocity, and called for compensation and rehabilitation for victims, among other things. Further atrocities are also reported to be under way, primarily affecting the region's adivasi people, in the course of Operation Green Hunt, an anti-Naxalite offensive the Centre launched in late 2009.

2. Trade union leader and civil rights activist Shankar Guha Niyogi was shot dead at his home in the mining town of Bhilai in the early hours of 28 September 1991. The industrialists and hired men accused in his killing were convicted by a trial court but acquitted in the Supreme Court in 2005, 14 years later.

UNPARALYSIS

On the Usefulness of Anxiety
Two Evil Media Stratagems

MATTHEW FULLER + ANDREW GOFFEY

The following sections of text are stratagems selected from a work-in-progress that aims to capture the changing nature of power in contemporary media, especially in its increasingly technosocial aspects, and to distill them into a series of useful ploys or tactics. Drawing its practical inspiration and modular structure from the writings of Nicolo Machiavelli, Baltasar Gracian and Arthur Schopenhauer, amongst others, and founded on substantial research into corporate literature, technical and strategy documents, these stratagems are offered as a means of working with the many kinds of power articulated through media systems.

Traditional media studies works on power relations in terms of ownership, access, identity, representation and interpretation. Whilst these have their place, in a context in which media are increasingly becoming directly operational (as control systems) and biological (in their closer correlation with the triggering and monitoring of affect and information), and at the same time are growing more distributed, autonomous and integrated both amongst themselves and with multiple scales of reality, a pragmatics is required which is capable of recognising the collapsing of the technical into the cultural, social and ecological whilst at the same time being explicitly cognizant of the opportunities for power that such a situation presents.

This given, the Evil Media approach works with a broad conception of mediality that, whilst it includes the usual repertoire of systems of signification that can be detached from the body, also works at scales that are beneath the level of the whole body – on brains, neural entrainment and physiologically potent chemicals partially handleable as signals.

Alongside these, the approach works extensively with much of contemporary grey media such as expert systems, workflow, databases, human-computer interaction and the sub-media world of leaks, networks and permissions – structures that establish what eventually appears as conventional media. These systems are now far more widespread and functionally significant than those which are most often apparent as media. Their relative invisibility, or naturalisation through ostensibly neutral technicity, and their fusing of the cultures of the workplace with those of consumption and policing offer numerous opportunities for interesting uses.

Machiavelli emphasised that rulers should be feared rather than hated, but first of all, they should be rulers. Fear is indeed preferable to love in that it carries less unpredictability and risk of loss. A technics of fear, as something transmissible, calculable and directional, needs to be supplemented by the cybernetic recognition of feedback. Evil Media approaches provide this necessary reflexivity.

Invite Everyone into the Spychodrama

In a world of ruse, cunning and manipulation, nothing is unambiguous or unproblematic, everything is pliable, biddable, suggestible. The question of the tools one uses, the forces one has at one's disposal, and the ways in which these can be made to work to one's advantage is thus permanently open, despite the sleek façades and seamless, transparent interfaces which seem to tell another story. In the multiple fields of knowledge production, the exercise of strategic or stratagematic intelligence requires an attentiveness to what would otherwise remain irredeemably obscure epistemological discussion, hair-splitting conceptual distinctions, even throwaway comments and off-the-cuff remarks. Chairman Mao knew this only too well, pointing out – in the field of politics – that trouble is an excellent thing. Even the emergence of a controversy in a scientific field can furnish crucial indicators for otherwise imperceptible shifts, geopolitical impasses and social problems, offering a toehold for the astute media operative. In this way, the cracks, faults and disturbances marking our mental universes offer the same kinds of opportunities for exploitation as do bugs in the algorithmic universes of software, and one stratagem is always in the position of being able to turn another to its own account.[1]

The domain of the 'psy' disciplines, the once-favoured epistemo-technical resource for public relations gurus, cold warriors and wizened imperialists, drawn on pell-mell in the development of strategic ambiguity (spychoanalysis would have been a good name for the fantasised practices of mind control), once again proves a crucial resource for following the shifting configurations and shadowy actions of mediums.

Part of the genius of psychoanalysis was to have linked what it does as a set of therapeutic practices to a conception of knowledge and of truth. Its promise to uncover hidden truths, its use of the concept of transference to break down the unconscious resistances of the patient and mitigate the possibly distorting effects of suggestion and, more generally, to detect and disclose things that a patient couldn't or wouldn't acknowledge, has, one must admit, a certain strategic allure. More refined than the salivating hounds of Soviet behaviourism in the context of social power and geopolitical conflict, the theatrical *mise-en-scène* of its conceptual framework – its learned allusions to Ancient Greek culture – gives added value and a hefty payout of cultural capital with which to speculate and scheme. As with the resonant connections between counter-intelligence practice and literary criticism,[2] mapping furtive and clandestine dynamics into textual structures and theatrical scripts offers a tasteful sheen and a somewhat aesthetic ornamentation to the resolution of geopolitical problems.

The double reference to knowledge and to therapy, in fact, offers a flip-flop that can be utilised with impunity to avoid unwelcome accusations of trickery and manipulation. On the one hand, the therapeutic claim – we're only trying to help alleviate the suffering of psychological disorders – can be used to sanction any manner of improper suggestiveness in practice. On the other, the knowledge claim – that patients disclose in analysis the truth of their suffering – can be used to head off the criticism that maybe the analyst puts ideas into his patient's head and constructs the problems the analysis then claims to resolve. Unlike behaviourism, which quite openly acknowledged its debts to the model of reflex action by siphoning off the excess dribble produced in expectation of reward, the implications of the suggestive stimulations of reflex action were historically cast to one side on the royal road to the unconscious.[3]

Thus, one might say that in spite of the well-meaning, therapeutic intent of analysis, its appeal to Science offers a cover, an alibi, an air of benevolent neutrality and cultural sophistication, a confident feeling of being in the right, to what others might see as really a technique of influence.[4] We've already seen the value of this in the polemical construction of brainwashing. So when Jung, breaking with Freud, remarks that in transference, that imprimatur of scientificity, the analyst can appear a devil, a god or a sorcerer,[5] it's not difficult to laugh such things off as the obsessions of a mythomaniac. The archetype? Not a scientific concept, I'm afraid. But when we add to the balance-sheet the systemic downgrading of fear in favour of an endogenous logic of anxiety,[6] and we factor in the findings of recent work on the psychology of torture (difficult to attribute those anxieties to the subject in question[7]), we can't help thinking that Jung might have had a point. Could it be that the reconstruction of the unconscious might have been at the service of forces other than those of pure science all along? Maintaining plausible deniability for the hex you've placed on the terrified libido is made considerably easier if you can excise in advance any connections that the unconscious might have with the outside world.

Part of the opposition that psychoanalysts, stalwarts of the Cold War of the psyche, have towards initiatives developing elsewhere – psychopharmacology, cognitive science and neurobiology, for example – stems from the complications they bring into the dynamic of transference (whose operative structural fantasies are rather homologous to brainwashing and mind control): what strange, active, possibly empowering effects might an anxiolytic or an anti-depressant have on a patient's unconscious resistances to the outing of the truth? The medium of psychoanalysis is speech, but there must be a powerfully motivated forgetting to make us ignore the possibility that the psyche is constructed through other media too. Irony fading, the analyst comments that "addiction opens a field where no single word of the subject is reliable and where he escapes analysis altogether".[8] Fearing the spiking of the psyche, the analyst insists on the exclusion of any other agents than the medium of language.

What we are getting at is that a certain doctrinal (or theoretical – the difference is slight here) rigidity renders a practice open to the classic counter-intelligence scam and ruse of power: the turning of an agent. Given the wilderness of mirrors that analysis finds itself in, there is the strong possibility of no longer knowing who or what is running who – we can ask in all seriousness whether Anna O., right at the inception of the analytic movement, was humouring Breuer and Freud all along. In any case, the hypothesis that the unconscious might be *simulated* in particular situations is one we can't ignore any longer.[9] What becomes of your intelligence-gathering operations if the other you think you are controlling is ironically conforming to your demands or imitating you in a game of sly civility?[10]

One can always find a use for someone or something that so adamantly holds to doctrinal purity and the universality of its judgements, maintaining a haughty disdain for anything even moderately pragmatic: the fabrication of a terrain predisposed to certain kinds of affective configuration (anxiety, a disposition considered to be universal); a willing ignorance of the myriad other mediators by which an unconscious might be constructed; the belief and expectation that politicians, strategists, marketeers, will respect the autonomy of the scientist. Analysis, we might say, prepares the ground for depressed, anxiety-prone subjects and offers a remarkable set of tools for welding subjects to their symptoms. All the misery of the world, miraculously transformed into the exasperated comments of the parent to the child: you'll see, just wait until you're an adult…

So what was it that Jung glimpsed? Devils, demons, gods, sorcerers – mythic images going beyond the family, sure, but also something properly *frightening*. Castration anxiety? Perhaps. To the great benefit of already well-stabilised forces, analysis didn't really want to have that much to do with fear – Freud himself sometimes seems to say that by virtue of its connection with external objects, fear is unanalysable.[11] Anxiety, by contrast, is not only susceptible of analysis, but performs socially useful work in preparing us for the kinds of shocks that frightening situations create. But if this distinction seems quite uncertain to us, we cannot ignore the inestimable tactical value of focusing attention on what goes on inside a subject as part of the more general process by which zones of secrecy, culpability and shame can be fabricated. Turn the other to your cause; even if, deep down, they are afraid of you, it's always good to have people who can keep a secret on your side.[12]

Speak the Metalanguage of Metabolism

…although she's not really ill, there's a little yellow pill…

The invention of psychopharmacology – following the experiments of Loewi in the 1920s, demonstrating the *chemical* basis for the transmission of neural messages (whilst not definitively ruling out the previously reigning hypothesis of electrical transmission) – the commercial sale of psychotropic drugs such as chlorpromazine and the invention of benzodiazepines in the 1950s, along with the publication of manuals such as the *Diagnostic and Statistical Manual of Mental Disorders*, have had a powerful effect on the constellation of forces making up 'the social'. If the irrational exuberance of psychosurgeons demonstrated that social relations and the imperatives of the state could sometimes be fabricated with ice picks and scalpels,[13] the mythologisation of mother's little helper in popular culture not only confirms, as McLuhan has it, that the medium is the message, but it also acts as an index of complex shifts in the ecology of media.

The development of psychopharmacology and its steady infection of the social generate new media spaces, new media with their own messages. No longer electronic technologies working at a distance in extended space, but chemical technologies creating distances in intensive space; keying social relations into the bio-chemical strata of organic material; targeting and mobilising populations of neurons – not through the electronic messaging systems of mass media exactly but through the facilitation of neuronal transmission systems, meshing with the loops and hits of online connectivity; catalysing circulation through the topologies of networks linking synapses, minds, emotions, techno-science, geopolitics; creating grey media for grey matter and vice versa. Whilst there may be no simple, one-to-one mapping between the use of pharmaceutical substances and widespread patterns of thought, in matters of mind control, we should at least be receptive to the idea that new substances generate new stratagems.

Research programmes backing up into the early part of the post-World War II era already testify to an interest in the manipulative potential of psychopharmaceuticals.[14] And the question marks that still hang over the funding of Timothy Leary's research, not to mention the propping up of a charismatic leader (John F. Kennedy) by amphetamines (that famous smile is holding back the strung-out grinding of teeth), are good indicators of the strange connections that become possible when active substances become a significant component of the clandestine relations and alliances of the polity.

Psychopharmacology alters the distribution – and hence balance – of forces political, technical and chemical, factoring in new agents for consideration in the strategic calculus of populations. Downplaying the strictly monitored conditions of the séance, the couch, the 50-minute hour, in the ongoing battle for hearts and minds, and embracing instead the gaseous dispersion and nebulous clouding of chemical media, allows for unsupervised processes of self-medication, permitting the confusion of therapy, governance and pleasure (albeit at the admitted cost of having to find uses for addictions) and requiring in turn a shift into the multi-dimensional spaces of non-linear thinking. The slow metabolising of power through a new alliance with chemistry and a corresponding molecularisation of conflict, where negotiations are now contracted through the prescriptive regimen of the dose (or the illicit regimen of the hit), requires an acceptance that bonds (both chemical and social) can be covalent as much as they can be ionic, in spite of the latter's oppositional attractions.[15] Acceptance, then, of a troublesome shift in the characteristic operations of domination and control.

At the social level, as much as at the more strictly biochemical level, political talk about controlled substances[16] risks an epistemological blunder of oxymoronic proportions (the jokey half-admission contained in the corresponding declaration of a war *on* drugs is actually more of the order of a strategic ambiguity and a tacit concession to a new ally). After all, if nature offers the allure of strictly deterministic processes, the scientific realism of something happening 'whether we like it or not', then, legal niceties aside, who's to say who is in control any longer? Is the confidence of *realpolitik* in realism misplaced?

The mathematical certainties of the causal chains of physics and the precision engineering of lock-and-key biological specificity might persuade the untutored that the identification of the neuronal apparatus productive of affect could henceforth be played like a keyboard[17] (imagine! with everything from do-re-mi to Schoenburg!). But if the hopeful hyping of drug design plays on a well-entrenched and neatly rationalised model of pharmaceutical practice, in reality, the chemical orchestration of inhibition and disinhibition and the corresponding dynamics of control require much greater forms of artfulness. More specifically, they call for a reckoning with the very great difficulties in making determinism – a useful hypothesis for the laboratory and a resonant strap line for marketing – scale up and into the variegated territories of 'the social'.

It is here that the trials and tribulations of the weaponisation of chemical agents help demonstrate some of the new possibilities, risks and limits of control. Of course, the cartoon capers of government agents and scientists finding ways to break down enemy combatants using cigarettes laced with marijuana are one thing (as are the bigger budget giggles of the exploding cigar as highly targeted assassination device),[18] but developing precise delivery systems for chemical weapons is quite another: the Moscow Theatre siege in 2002, for example, was not a well-orchestrated, precision-controlled military operation. Calibrating the impact of something which has to be dispersed by aerosol, as a mist in the atmosphere or through thermal bomblets (the case with BZ[19]), plays havoc with attempts to make the determinist logic of linear causality – which material intervention at the level of grey matter was supposed to offer – work at the supra-organic level. Doping up or doping down neuronal receptors is a tricky proposition once the subject is out in the open and there is both a blood-brain barrier and a targeted recipient problem to overcome. In an interrogation room, you can strap a suspect down and tease up a tender vein, but for battlefield ops and crowd control (CS gas and lacrimogens – don't forget your soft contact lenses – notwithstanding), the aerosol effect disperses chemicals either too quickly or too indiscriminately. This creates obvious public relations problems and makes the development of tried and tested battlefield doctrine a complex task.[20] The propensity of unstable and unpredictable mediators to generate uncontrollable forms of *blowback* here[21] presents a world- and possibly bio-historical challenge for crisis management and may or may not commend some chemical agents to a lengthy entry in any future manual of psy ops. Or spy ops for that matter.

However psychopharmacology is not exactly chemical warfare (even if pharmaceutical companies willingly play on both sides of the military-civilian divide), and the displacements that pharmaceutical products accomplish in the ongoing production of the psyche still offer a latitude for manoeuvre worth exploiting. It may just be that psychopharmacology – especially in the grey area between (failed) covert military and (successful) overt civilian guises – offers the possibility of a more intelligently negotiated alliance with chemical agents. The use of pill technology for self-administered domestic consumption, for example, as opposed to the unpredictable mediations of weaponisation, or the complex, localised institutional apparatuses of lobotomy or ECT [electroconvulsive therapy], allows for more accurate delivery (even if it does depend upon a less tightly controlled chain of mediators). A pill embodies a strategy with much more tangible reliability than the shaky practices of quacks, headshrinks and other shamans, to say nothing of the eye-watering intrusiveness of the icepick.

The definite preference that the psychopharmacological machine displays for the production of short-term effects is as critical here as is the media form and can be of great value, especially if tied in to other apparatuses reliant on the up-down, high-low movements typical of machinic junkiedom (even the stock exchange needs a stimulus package from time to time).[22]

Whilst the poor adaptation of double-blind clinical tests – which allow for the marketisation of drugs – to the evaluation of long-term effects may compound the problems of blowback over time, the molecules upon which such tests are focused are actually highly effective recruitment devices. Kingmakers of a new kind, they sealed the ascendancy of a new macro-political actor – the pharmaceutical giant – and, while they may not possess the diagnostic power of a good doctor or psychoanalyst, in a highly pragmatic way, they don't require that a new recruit reveal the truth about him or her self. The massive success of diazepam (from the family of benzodiazepines) – according to some sources, the most widely prescribed drug in the United States between 1962 and 1981 – is exemplary in this regard. Whilst the curative effects of such a substance might blur the difference between a symptom and a cause, it has no real need for secrecy, guilt or shame. Look how quickly user groups set themselves up on the Internet – doctor-patient confidentiality doesn't enter the equation. Anyway, anxiety offers a useful cover story for dealing with harmful or fearful incursions from the outside world and, in the worse case scenario, under conditions of addiction (or influence, but for different reasons), as we saw elsewhere, the subject is easily discredited as an unreliable witness.

More significantly, perhaps, one of the invaluable side-effects of benzodiazepines, cyclopyrrolones, dopamines, and SSRIs [selective serotonin reuptake inhibitors such as Fluoxetine, i.e. Prozac] is to have accelerated the process of reforming and recomposing the very field in which and on which they operated. From an initial position where they complemented the medium of speech in the talking cure, pharmaceuticals end up taking over completely. And there wouldn't be any CBT [cognitive behaviour therapy] without the reorganising effects of drugs on psychology.[23] Liquidating the 'dependency on authority' effects characteristic of therapeutic speech, the bio-chemical end of deference creates an ambiguous situation. For whilst existential dramas of anxiety are replaced by effects of disinhibition that can, it is true, minimise the lacerating effects of the group superego (a distinct advantage when trying to operate in the amoral zone of strategy), there is a complete shift of affective investments, with group identities forming round the molecule.[24] Harnessing complex metabolic patterns and turning agents when the theatrical tragedy of the primal scene has been vapourised becomes a multimedia operation, and in the peculiarly interstitial spaces that are created when linearity doesn't scale up, negotiation, ruse and cunning are open even to the most hardened of addicts.[25]

Notes

1. We aren't trying to make a point about science 'in general' here, just observing that the psy disciplines are a fascinating resource and topic for explorations in the (ab)use of power. See, for example, Isabelle Stengers, **Cosmopolitiques** Vol. 7: **Pour en finir avec la tolérance** *(La Decouverte, 1997, Paris).*

2. Michael James. **Jesus Angleton Holzman: The CIA and the Craft of Counterintelligence** *(University of Massachusetts Press, 2008, Amhurst). Also see the review by Terence Hawkes, "William Empson's Influence on the CIA" in* **The Times Literary Supplement,** *10 June 2009.*

3. See Marcel Gauchet. **L'inconscient cérébral** *(Seuil, 1992, Paris).*

4. Stengers, op. cit.

5. Gilles Deleuze and Félix Guattari. **Anti-Oedipus** *(Minnesota University Press, 1983, Minnesota), p. 46.*

6. See, for example, Freud's comments in "Beyond the Pleasure Principle". In (ed.) James Strachey, **The Standard Edition of the Complete Psychological Works of Sigmund Freud,** *Vol. 18 (Hogarth Press, 1955, London), ch. 2.*

7. Francoise Sironi. **Bourreaux et victimes** *(Odile Jacob, 1992, Paris).*

8. Jacques Lacan. Cited in Avital Ronell, **Crack Wars** *(University of Nebraska Press, 1992, Lincoln), p. 53.*

9. Mikkel Borch-Jacobsen. "L'inconscient simulé". In (ed.) Tobie Nathan, **La guerre des psys** *(Les Empêcheurs de Penser en Rond, 2006, Paris).*

10. Jean Baudrillard. **In The Shadow of the Silent Majorities** *(Semiotext(e), 1983, New York). Homi K. Bhabha. "Sly Civility". In* **October** *34 (1985), pp. 71-80.*

11. See Freud, op. cit.

12. Vinciane Despret. "Le secret est une dimension politique de la thérapie". In Nathan, op. cit.

13. In the words of Walter Freeman, the intent was to turn "taxeaters" into "taxpayers". See Jack Pressman, **The Last Resort: Pyschosurgery and the Limits of Medicine** *(Cambridge University Press, 1998, Cambridge).*

14. The ARTICHOKE programme, for example. See Alan Scheflin and Edward Opton, **The Mind Manipulators** *(Paddington Press, 1978, London), and Dominic Streatfeild,* **Brainwash: The Secret History of Mind Control** *(Hodder, 2006, London).*

15. cf. Thomas Pynchon, **Gravity's Rainbow** *(1973).*

16. The Controlled Substances Act was passed in the USA in 1970. Nixon declared his war on drugs in 1971.

17. As in the scenario imagined by Alfred Hitchcock and relayed by Slavoj Žižek. See the brief discussion of this in Philippe Pignarre, **Les malheurs des psys** *(La Découverte, 2006, Paris), pp. 44-45. On specificity, see Jean-Jacques Kupiec and Pierre Sonigo,* **Ni dieu ni gêne** *(Seuil, 2000, Paris), pp. 17-60.*

18. See Streatfeild, op. cit., pp. 44-49.

19. Reid Kirby. "Paradise Lost: The Psycho Agents". In **The Quarterly Journal of the Harvard Sussex Program on CBW Armament and Arms Limitation** *71 (May 2006), p. 1.*

20. ibid., p. 4.

21. cf. Chalmers Johnson, **Blowback** *(Holt Paperbacks, 2004, New York).*

22. See Félix Guattari, "Machinic Junkies" in **Soft Subversions** *(Semiotext(e), 1996, New York). See also Christian Marazzi,* **Capital and Language** *(Semiotext(e), 2008, New York), on the short-term movements of credulity inherent in the financial markets.*

23. The full argument is developed in Philippe Pignarre, **Les malheurs des psys,** *op. cit. Pignarre's* **Comment la dépression est devenue une épidémie** *(La Découverte, 2001, Paris) is a crucial text for following the logic of recruitment in the pharmaceutical industry.*

24. See Sylvie Le Poulichet, **Toxicomanies et psychanalyse: Les narcoses du désir** *(PUF, 1987, Paris), on the fate of 'transference' in addiction, Pignarre, op. cit., and Tobie Nathan,* **A qui j'appartiens?** *(Seuil, 2007, Paris), on new complexes of attachments in psychology, and Carole Rivière, "Le lien de dépendance addictive à Internet: Une nouvelle forme d'addiction?" Available at: http://www.omnsh.org/article.php3?id_article=94 (accessed 2 September 2009), for an analytic approach to new media.*

25. Emilie Gomart. "Surprised by Methadone: In Praise of Drug Substitution Treatment in a French Clinic". In **Body and Society** *10 (2-3), pp. 85-110.*

Three Miles from Anarchy
Managerial Fear and the Affective Factory

JAMIE CROSS

I. Death in the Factory

> I was going around today, giving out photographs of workers. I was in the Finishing
> department and I gave this guy a photo of his Best Worker presentation ceremony.
> Then another guy came up behind me and said, 'Where's my photo?' And then the
> person I just gave the photo to said, 'Yeah! Where's his photo?' And then all of a
> sudden, all the people in the section were crowding around saying, 'Where's his
> photo?' 'Give him his photo'. And I was saying, 'OK, it's no big deal! You haven't got
> a photo. I'll just go and get another one printed. It's no big deal!' But I mean they
> were getting really agitated. Really agitated! Just because of the photo! And then,
> just for a moment, I though they were going to lynch me…

In September 2008, an Indian executive at a major European auto parts manufacturing unit
in North India was rushed to hospital after sustaining multiple head injuries in the courtyard
of the factory he managed. He was pronounced dead soon after arrival.

The circumstances surrounding events at the Swiss-Italian owned Grazioni factory in
Greater Noida, where Lalit K. Chaudhary worked, remain unclear. At the time, however, the
dominant media story quickly became one of murder in the factory: an act of vengeance and
retribution carried out by a group of sacked and disenfranchised workers. "Lynched by the
Mob", screamed one Italian newspaper headline.

> If you want to be a general manager, you have to be a psychologist. You have to
> be an anthropologist. You have to be a sociologist. You have to look at things from
> the worker's perspective. You have to ask yourself: why is that guy working on the
> machines so angry with me?

The death of a manager at a global factory in India realises and sustains in the most powerful way the basic fear of people who oversee production in the country's transnational manufacturing units: the fear that they might fail to control the people they employ. For companies that remain competitive by keeping labour casual, insecure and precarious, this fear becomes inseparable from production processes.

In the aftermath of the events at the Grazioni factory, managerial fear circulated openly in the international business media. Foreign and domestic industrialists described their panic and alarm at being confronted by workers who were "very extreme" and "very radical". "It's becoming increasingly difficult to work under these conditions. No one is protecting us", an Italian manager told the *Financial Times*.

> Last week, some of these same guys put down their tools and stopped work. They were like that for a couple of hours and then they just went back to work. That worries me. That really worries me. Do you know why? Because that means they're not ready to strike yet. They're preparing... preparing for war. So what am I going to have to do? Well, I'm not going to wait. I'm going to have the war now. I'm going to have the war on my terms.

For 12 months in 2005, I was granted privileged and extended access to a very large European manufacturing unit at a special economic zone in South India. The factory's manager was a middle-aged British man whom I shall call 'the Factor'. The Factor allowed himself to be interviewed inside the factory in his air-conditioned office or on the floor of dusty manufacturing sections and outside the factory in his rented apartment or in city restaurants. Over the course of a year, I recorded several hours of unstructured interviews during which he spoke frankly about the everyday work of keeping the factory low cost and globally competitive. Against the backdrop of rising discontent over wages and working conditions, our conversation frequently addressed concerns over the loss of control.

> I mean, I read the papers, right? And in the back of my mind I'm thinking, how far away before things blow up here? 'Cause I don't want to be here when it does... I mean... any nation... any factory... can turn in on itself. We're all just three miles from anarchy.

In this brief essay, I combine extracts from these interviews with a reflection on the nature of fear at sites of global production. Rather than think about managerial anxieties over worker discontent and the loss of control as emotional epiphenomena, or the outward expressions of psychological drives, I propose that we approach managerial fear as an 'affect' of the factory itself.

Affects are not simply feelings or emotions, wrote Gilles Deleuze – appropriating the term used by the 17th-century Dutch philosopher Benedict de Spinoza – affects are sensations and subjective qualities that exist outside and move through the human subject.[1] Building directly on Deleuze's writings, cultural theorists have begun to re-locate their reference point for sensual intensities outside the body and away from the sub-conscious, in spaces and objects, environments and things.

In this tradition, we can begin to see fear not only as an inner state of being that effects how human subjects perceive and act in the world but as an *affect* of those worlds that subjects inhabit and interact with. Not as an experience borne by a single individual but as an emission that is released by machines and devices, buildings and landscapes. In this vein, I argue, global factories are deeply affective institutions that elicit states of fear in their workers and managers, just as they do hopes, aspirations and dreams – to profitable ends.

II. Engineering Sentiments

A few months ago, we tried to hold meetings with workers on the factory floor. But we just couldn't do it. What happened? Two or three people stood up and started yelling and whooping about wages like animals, and the rest followed like idiots...

We can't have that. What we need here are teams. Teams! Teams that we can love. Teams that we can make love the company.

Love the company! Teams. Certificates. Uniforms. Employee-of-the-Month Awards. Technologies of governance in the modern factory have always been both affective and discursive. Corporate executives like the Factor have learnt to engineer the souls of their working subjects through the production of affective responses as much as through the production of knowledge.[2] Pastoral modes of discipline engender workers' consent to hyper-intensive and low-waged work regimes by fostering their pastoral or filial bonds to the company; by celebrating production as a patriotic duty; by casting efficiency as a path to moral or spiritual reform; and by championing hard work as a route to social mobility.[3]

Fear is a vital element in this affective fabric. Managers manipulate feelings of precariousness and vulnerability – just as they do hope and desire – to political effect. Statistical tools, charts and databases for measuring performance. Timekeeping devices, clocks and watches for monitoring productivity. Work sections, cells and teams for organising flow. Closed circuit television equipment and glass partitions for increasing visibility. The array of spatial and surveillance technologies in the modern workplace ensures the constant insecurity of workers.

Who says management is a science? Bullshit! The principles might be scientific. But as for how you apply them, well that's all down to you! All the best managers use their intuition. They say, 'I know it sounds sensible. But something doesn't look right. Something doesn't feel right'.

The factory manager – the factor – is a central figure in contemporary political and economic transformations. But our understanding of what takes place on the floor of the global factory is impoverished if we think about managerial decisions as characterised by pure calculation. Instead, what counts for knowledge and judgement in these spaces, the world's global manufacturing units, is organised around the interplay of reason and affect.[4] Managerial subjectivities are 'shaped by' or 'embroiled' in their environments as much as the workers'. And fear is never just a malleable affect that managers can utilise or deploy to their own ends.

> These people! *These People!* They're the same people in Indonesia. The same people in the Philippines. They hate us. [The Factor is sitting in his air-conditioned office looking at a report in a communist party magazine describing working conditions in this factory.]

> They hate these zones. They want the zones closed. And now they're targeting us. [The Factor points his finger at a hammer-and-sickle emblem in the corner of the page.]

> Can you imagine what they're saying? [He begins to speak in a grave, serious voice, pushing out his chest and pumping his fist in the air.] Brothers and Sisters, we are going to strike until we get more salary... Until we double your salaries... Until the company gives you housing... They're like an opposition party. [He begins to jab at the hammer and sickle. He jabs slowly at first and then jabs harder. Eventually, he is pushing down on the hammer and sickle with his forefinger, smudging the ink, rubbing it out.]

> I consider this the single biggest threat to this factory, to the viability of this factory. Can you imagine! There's a whole group of them and they come together, sit together, every night and talk and talk about this factory. They're very clever. They're much more clever than I imagined. But they're not cleverer than me.

III. A Monument to Control

> This factory is just like a computer game... You have these little guys with stubble around their faces, hunched up, walking around, doing things and causing trouble, and your job is to control them.

The factory is an elaborate apparatus for controlling space, time and people in order to produce things. Like other modern institutions, the factory is an architectural, technological and relational triumph of governance. When it is operational, the factory stands as a monument to control.

I'm a capitalist... Productivity equals profits. Efficiencies equal wealth. That's what I believe. I believe... I know... that the kind of stuff I do here, the kind of stuff I do in this factory, works. It's a win-win situation. I really, truly, cannot see a loss in it. Anywhere! But I also know that it takes a lot of effort... a hell of a lot of work... by general managers and middle managers and lower-level managers to keep this seemingly effortless cycle going.

Yet control is never permanent or given. Control is always a temporary achievement, an incomplete and unsteady accomplishment.[5] Control must be worked towards, asserted, maintained and renewed. Control must be co-ordinated, monitored, managed and made. Every operational factory, then, also stands as a perpetual reminder that control is an unstable edifice. Control, the factory constantly reminds its managers, is ephemeral, tentative and un-assured.

We need to make sure that if someone does something wrong, everyone knows. And so that when we kick them out, everyone else will say, 'What did he expect?' We can do, really do, things here, but first I'm going to have to crucify some people in a very public fashion.

What kind of affect, we might then ask, does such a complex socio-technical apparatus emit? What kind of affect does an environment that is designed explicitly to impose control have on the people who are employed to manage it?

Look. You can see him now on the CCTV screens. This guy... the one with the stubble. He's one of the troublemakers on our list. He's one of the Loud Boys. He's one of the guys who've been trying to hurt us for over two years. Did you see what he just did? He walked into that section and spoke to the people who were supposed to work overtime. And now those people are not sitting in the section anymore. Now they're sitting in the bus outside and not working overtime. Now they're indoctrinated. People like this guy are just so anti-company that no matter what we did for them, they'd still hate us. It's inbuilt. You see it in their eyes when you talk to them. You can see it in their body. They bow their heads down, they hulk their shoulders up and they glare at you. It's disturbing. But I've seen that look before. In England. In Manchester. You can say anything you like to people like that. You can say, 'If I give you everything you want, will you work hard for me?' And you know what they'll say back? 'Fuck you'. No, we can't have people like that here. They're the people that we are going to have to fire.

The very apparatus that is designed to ensure and extend control over labouring subjects – 'the workers' – has an opposite and unintended affect. The same social relations and technical systems that are designed to assert control over a labour force also generate an anxiety that control cannot be guaranteed. Managerial anxieties over the loss of control in the global factory are 'subjective feelings' and 'spatially effected feelings'.

The factory exudes fear as its own affect. The socio-technical architecture for asserting control – the buildings and workspaces, machines and technical devices, the modes of social difference and distinction that comprise the global factory – gives off or emits a fear that control can be lost.

> [The Factor is on the telephone.] Who are all these people standing in the lobby?… What are they all doing there, standing around?… Recruiting day? I didn't know today is recruiting day!… But who are they? Who are they? How do we know they haven't been trained before coming here? How do you know they haven't been trained by a union to infiltrate us?… We have to find out who these people are. We have to find out what they have been doing for the last six months! And we have to found out now!… We need to get the consultant in… Today. Tomorrow. Next week is going to be too late.

Fear acts upon managers in generative and unanticipated ways. The apparatus of control generates anxieties that can be fed back into factory organisation in constructive ways; constituting managerial subjectivities and driving innovation. Fear is inseparable from the rationalisation of power and opens up the possibility for particular paths of action.

> [The Factor spins around in his rotating office chair to look out of the mirror glass window behind him. A crowd of blue-uniformed production workers mill around outside, waiting for the start of the 2 p.m. B shift. He turns back in his chair.]
>
> I don't know how to divide and rule here. I need to isolate the good from the bad. But I don't know how to separate the two. And then you have the grey… And I don't know who the grey are at all.

In his drive to ensure the company remained globally competitive, the Factor was locked into a perpetual search for efficiencies in production. Each successive innovation in targets, wage schemes, layouts or work organisation was a further rationalisation of time and space designed to increase the intensity and efficiency of labour power, and extract ever-greater surplus from the labour process. His anxieties at worker discontent and the loss of control were harnessed and marshalled into ever-more creative systems for asserting control and extracting value. Fear as affect is interwoven in the socio-technical apparatus of production.

IV. The Affective Factory

In newspaper reports of Lalit K. Chaudhary's death, the industrial workplace was more than a backdrop to the story. Journalists lingered on spatial details not just as context, but as if the factory itself had been a crucial or complicit actor in his death. In the Italian newspaper, *La Repubblica*, for example, the factory become the *teatro della rissa* or the 'theatre of the brawl'. Thinking about managerial fear as affect is to understand the factory in precisely this way: as a spatial environment and socio-technical apparatus that makes particular feelings and actions possible. The affective factory is a unique environment in which fear is both a product and a motor of control.

In Deleuze's wake, cultural theorists have become increasingly alert to the non-discursive sensations or affects that environments and objects can create,[6] as well as to the ways that architects and designers can write affective responses into them.[7] As the philosopher Brian Massumi puts it, affect is an "intrinsic variable of late capitalism... as infrastructural as the factory".[8,9]

We all know that fear as affect can be mobilised and manipulated to political ends. The global factory offers an important reminder that contemporary systems of low-cost, hyper-efficient capitalist production hinge on the fear of managers as much as of workers.

Notes
1. *Nigel Thrift. "Afterwords". In* Environment and Planning D: Society and Space *18 (2) pp. 213-55 (2000).*
2. *Nicolas Rose.* Governing the Soul *(Free Association Books, 1989, London).*
3. *Analiese Richard and Daromir Rudnyckyj. "Economies of Affect". In* Journal of the Royal Anthropological Institute *15 n.s. (1), pp. 57-77 (2009).*
4. *Caitlin Zaloom. "How to Read the Future: The Yield Curve, Affect and Financial Prediction". In* Public Culture *21 (2), pp. 245-268 (2008).*
5. *Bruno Latour.* Reassembling the Social: An Introduction to Actor Network Theory *(Cambridge University Press, 2005, Cambridge).*
6. *Nigel Thrift.* Non-Representational Theory *(Routledge, 2007, London).*
7. *Yael Navaro-Yashin. "Affective Spaces, Melancholic Objects: Ruination and the Production of Anthropological Knowledge". In* Journal of the Royal Anthropological Institute *15 n.s. (1), pp. 1-18 (2009).*
8. *Nigel Thrift. "Intensities of Feeling". In* Geografiska Annaler *86 B (1), pp. 57-72 (2004).*
9. *Brian Massumi. "The Autonomy of Affect". In* Cultural Critique *31, pp. 83-109 (Fall 1995).*

Data Sphere

ADNAN HADZI

We are, in many ways, living in times of a slavery of the mind. Through Intellectual Property, our culture is owned by a few. I want to elaborate upon this idea of slavery in this essay, extending it to our ideas and our minds through referring to Rousseau's *The Social Contract* (Rousseau, 1762).

> Thus, however we look at the question, the "right" of slavery is seen to be void; void, not only because it cannot be justified, but also because it is nonsensical, because it has no meaning. The words "slavery" and "right" are contradictory, they cancel each other out. Whether as between one man and another, or between one man and a whole people, it would always be absurd to say: "I hereby make a covenant with you which is wholly at your expense and wholly to my advantage; I will respect it so long as I please and you shall respect it so long as I wish." (ibid.)

The Debian Foundation, one of the biggest platforms for the Linux operating system, wrote the Debian Social Contract for the free and open source software community, reflecting many of Rousseau's thoughts:

> Our priorities are our users and free software. We will be guided by the needs of our users and the free software community. We will place their interests first in our priorities. We will support the needs of our users for operation in many different kinds of computing environments. We will not object to non-free works that are intended to be used on Debian systems, or attempt to charge a fee to people who create or use such works. We will allow others to create distributions containing both the Debian system and other works, without any fee from us. In furtherance of these goals, we will provide an integrated system of high-quality materials with no legal restrictions that would prevent such uses of the system. (Debian, 2004)

In this essay, I will extend the idea of the Debian Social Contract to media, suggesting similar principles that can be applied to free and open media, and defining these as a pre-condition for peer-to-peer database documentaries such as Deptford.TV. Deptford.TV is a research project on collaborative film I initiated in collaboration with the Deckspace media lab, the Bitnik media collective, the Boundless project, the Liquid Culture initiative, and Goldsmiths College, London. It is an online media database documenting urban change in Deptford, Southeast London, and it functions as an open, collaborative platform that allows artists, filmmakers and people living and working around the locality to store, share, re-edit and redistribute the documentation of Deptford.

The open and collaborative aspect of the project is of particular importance as it manifests in two ways: a) audiences can become producers by submitting their own footage, and b) the interface being used enables contributors to discuss and interact with each other through the database.

In the field of media, so-called Open Content licences have been created over the last decade in response to how copyright laws have changed in favour of the media conglomerates. A famous example is the Copyright Term Extension Act of 1998 – often labelled the 'Mickey Mouse Protection Act', due to the extensive lobbying by the Walt Disney Corporation that ensured Mickey Mouse's absence from the public domain.

Another, more recent, example of the battle over social contracts and the sharing of rights – and their associated wealth – is the 2007 Writers Guild of America strike: from November 2007 to February 2008, more than 12,000 screen and radio writers struck work over the Alliance of Motion Picture and Television Producers' refusal to negotiate an increased share in revenues from digital media sales and, more importantly, from Internet-distributed media. On 8 January 2008, the strikers had a symbolic victory with the shutting down of the Golden Globe television gala, and it even looked likely that the annual Academy Awards ceremony would also be cancelled for the first time in its history. The writers decided to compete with the studios by collaboratively producing and distributing their own shows online; *The Independent* went so far as to state that the strike was "potentially revolutionising the way television is made and consumed in the online area" (Gumbel, 2008).

With social contracts such as the Debian Social Contract in place, one can decide how to produce, distribute and share media. But these alternatives are quickly corrupted if the issues involved, especially in regard to author's rights, are not looked at in a sincere way, as once defined by Rousseau and rewritten by the Debian Software Foundation.

I ask: are FLOSS (Free/Libre/Open Source Software) and other, related open and free content licences likely to develop further in the future, providing a platform for alternative media practices? I argue that the development of computers and microchips with built-in copy control technology and the current changes in intellectual property legislation endanger the sustainability of such alternative practices and licencing schemes. Worryingly, the social contracts that relate to copyright and intellectual property tend to breach the current privacy protection of consumers: in order to enforce new copyright laws, control needs to be tightened by surveying the computers consumers use in their private sphere. Unfortunately, these new control mechanisms can also be used to silence critical voices.

These are ultimately issues of legislation. I know that I am now digressing into legal terrain, but I do so in an attempt to outline a possibility practiced with the Deptford.TV project. The concern was how to move from an abstract idea of social contracts to a concrete legislation which could enable a cultural production that is not deemed antithetical or oppositional. This can be done through defining independent terms and conditions, namely free and open content licences. At this point, I would have liked to offer the reader a link to the video clip, *Staking a Claim in Cyberspace*, from Paper Tiger TV, in order to involve you into the practice of media production. Unfortunately, this is not legally possible within the academic context; one can only get hold of a copy or link to the file through the more nebulous file-sharing networks...

Social Contracts

> Yet in spite of this broad spectrum of possibilities, there is no place where one can prepare for a collective practice. At best, there are the rare examples where teams (usually partnerships of two) can apply as one for admission into institutions of higher learning. But once in the school, from administration to curriculum, students are forced to accept the ideological imperative that artistic practice is an individual practice. (Critical Arts Ensemble, 2000)

With the concept of social contracts, the assumption that all individuals are sovereign changes. With social contracts, the people give up sovereignty to a system that will make sure that individual rights are protected. A portion of each individual's sovereignty is given up for the common good (in anarchist terms, one would speak of solidarity). Rousseau believes that sovereignty stays with the people, for if the people are not content with the governing force, they rise up. Rousseau's social contract was, therefore, one of the main references for the French Revolution.

Rousseau thinks that obedience conflicts with people's freedom. Our natural freedom is our own will, he asserts. He defined the social contract as a law 'written' by everybody, his argument being that if everybody was involved in making laws, they would only have to obey themselves and, as such, follow their own free will. How, then, could people create a common will? For Rousseau, this would be possible only in smaller communities, through the practice of caring for each other and managing conflicts for the common good – ultimately, through love. He imagined a society the size of the city of Geneva, where he came from, as an ideal ground for the implementation of the social contract theory. Ironically, it was France through its revolutionaries (amongst whom Robespierre was a great admirer of Rousseau's writing) that implemented the social contract theory. However, France read it differently, imposing social contracts on the people.

In this essay, I outline the concept of social contracts in terms of freedom and ownership through a form of coalition as defined by the Critical Arts Ensemble (CAE). I explain how one can have an ad hoc coalition to implement a strategy in order to achieve a common aim – the coalition only needs to function until the strategy has been implemented, after which a standard is created which can be adapted by society.

In other words, for collaborative film-making, the extension of copyright legislation is an important social contract. As argued below, copyright laws are not, in effect, functioning anymore in regard to digital distribution. Consequently, artists, programmers and activists have been looking for alternatives to and extensions of these laws. According to the CAE, collectives can configure themselves to address any issue or space, and they can use all types of media. The result is a practice that defies specialisation.

> Solidarity is based on similarity in terms of skills and political/aesthetic percep-
> tions. Most of the now classic cellular collectives of the 70s and 80s, such as Ant
> Farm, General Idea, Group Material, Testing the Limits (before it splintered) and
> Gran Fury, used such a method with admirable results. Certainly these collectives'
> models for group activity are being emulated by a new generation. (Critical Arts
> Ensemble, 2000)

In the Deptford.TV project, the groups doing a documentary film together often share a similar political and/or aesthetic approach to the film but different levels of technological know-how. I borrow the term 'cell', used by the CAE to describe the organism of their group, to refer to the Deptford.TV collective. In these cells, solidarity arrives through difference. Because the individuals bring different kinds of knowledge into a cell, the possibilities of endless conflicts are reduced. Film teams are ideally built up with participants specialised in directing, editing, producing, camerawork, etc. When a cell decides how to produce the film/ project, those members with the most know-how in their special fields become authoritative in the sense of deciding how to film, direct, edit, etc. CAE argue that solidarity based on difference creates functional and more powerful groups. They compare this to the dominant approach of solidarity based on equality and consent democracy adopted by many tactical media groups such as the Ant Farm collective. Such groups had a fear that hierarchy would lead to stronger members becoming dominant over weaker members within the collective. CAE does not follow the democratic model.

Coalitions, Not Communities

> The collective does recognize its merits; however, CAE follows Foucault's principle
> that hierarchical power can be productive (it does not necessarily lead to domina-
> tion), and hence uses a floating hierarchy to produce projects... Consequently,
> there has always been a drive toward finding a social principle that would allow
> like-minded people or cells to organize into larger groups. Currently, the dominant
> principle is "community". CAE sees this development as very unfortunate. The
> idea of community is without doubt the liberal equivalent of the conservative no-
> tion of "family values"... Talking about a gay community is as silly as talking about
> a "straight community". The word community is only meaningful in this case as
> a euphemism for "minority". The closest social constellation to a community that

does exist is friendship networks, but those too fall short of being communities in any sociological sense. (Critical Arts Ensemble, 2000)

In Deptford.TV, people come together from different backgrounds but share similar concerns. We deliberately try to group together participants with different skills. These participants choose to document specific topics that fall within their personal interests, thus accepting that conflicts could occur while approaching these as positive for the overall production of the documentation process. CAE explains that this kind of alliance, "created for purposes of large scale cultural production and/or for the visible consolidation of economic and political power, is known as a coalition" (ibid.). Those who take responsibility within a Deptford.TV cell are also those who are most involved in decision-making, in the spirit that, in order to keep the coalition together, what is important are tools, not rules.

Similarly, theorists of the online world like Howard Rheingold increasingly acknowledge that notions of 'community' with all its *gemeinschaft*-like connotations (close-knit, familial, based on mutual solidarity, etc.) are often overstated. Steven Jones (1995) notes how 'community' is generally conceptualised as a) solidarity institutions, b) primary interaction or c) institutionally distinct groups. Only the third of these – community as institutionally distinct group – makes sense, Jones argues, in the context of computer-mediated communications. While I would diverge from Jones' contention in that this mode of communication is not only socially produced, but is equally technically constituted, it is notable how it still challenges the idea of community as being based on geographic proximity, to the extent that one could, like Jones, talk about computer-mediated communities as "pseudo-communities".

Communities formed by CMC have been called "virtual communities" and defined as incontrovertibly social spaces in which people still meet face-to-face, but under new definitions of both "meet" and "face". (Jones, 1995)

With the recognition borrowed from Miller and Slater (2000) and effectively repeated by andrea rota (2006), we must not assume an insurmountable gap between the alleged 'online' and 'offline' worlds: Deptford.TV is both a local, situated practice as well as one which stretches into the online world. Nevertheless, it should not be mistaken for a permanent, tight-knit community; rather, it is a tool-based (technological as much as social), temporary, if not occasional, coalition.

Open Content Licences

Open Content licencing schemes, as outlined in Lawrence Liang's book, *A Guide to Open Content Licences* (Liang, 2004), help to create an understanding of a shared culture – culture as a communication medium rather than a commodity. Culture and creativity very often build upon previous works through re-using, remixing and reinterpreting works; often this is a fundamental part of any creative practice. Therefore, the academic and journalistic concept of 'fair use' could be an important part of social contracts for creative practices. But 'fair use' and even 'public domain' are under threat. New digital copyrights such as the Digital Millennium Copyright Act (Wolf, 2003) were written in order to tackle file-sharing, illegalising this new technology in many countries without considering any of its benefits.

This is a recurring discussion that tends to take place around any invention of new communication technologies. An example is the invention of VCR recorders: at the time, it became clear that those trying to stop the distribution and production of VCRs, especially the big studios, made huge profits from rentals and sales in the new home-video market. The same could prove to be the case in regard to file-sharing technologies.

The original intention behind copyright laws was to support a vibrant production of culture through the protection of producers and artists. As current copyright legislation cannot be fully implemented when it comes to practices of online distribution and file-sharing, the media giant lobby is proposing new copyright laws which violate the private sphere of the consumer and threaten the existence of a democratic public sphere. The irony behind the attempt to create a more strict copyright legislation through eliminating fair use is that the original intention, to support cultural production, might come to a stand-still as the artists will not be able to access and use cultural materials they need to produce new work. As a result, stricter copyright laws disadvantage artists and small producers while they work for the benefit of already powerful media conglomerates.

> For the most part, copyrights are not held by individuals, but by corporate entities that are part of the content industry. The content industry would argue that strengthening their position allows them to provide greater incentives to individual creators, but many creators vociferously challenge that notion. Strengthening copyright laws does improve the position of the content industry by giving them a relatively untempered monopoly over content, but it does so at the expense of the public good. (Besser, 2001)

The public sphere has traditionally been determined by law. Here I coin the term 'data sphere' as an extension of the public sphere – following Fenton and Downey (2003) and their argumentation on 'counter-public' spheres – to describe a digital, networked public sphere where practices such as peer-to-peer networking cannot possibly adhere to traditional copyright laws and cultural content is made available in complete disregard of current legislation. This happens largely through processes that are wholly machinic: automated, self-emergent, governed by protocol rather than direct human intent. Consequently, these copyright laws are, for the first time, being breached by a critical mass of technology: technologies which are mainly in the hands of consumers. When observable coalitions arise out of this mass, they resemble a 'data sphere' more than an intentional, human-centred 'public sphere' in the traditional sense, since the coming-together need not be by personal volition but by the ways the actual infrastructures are configured. If the 'datascapes' of Latour and others make possible a tracing and documentation of how existing social structures come together and become constituted, 'data spheres' are the more particular instantiations that form through an actual mobilisation within these datascapes.

Social contracts and laws will eventually be defined for these data spheres, but until then the big 'user-generated' platforms such as YouTube, MySpace and Facebook try to get their hands on every uploaded piece of content in accord with the old, non-efficacious copyright legislation. Reading the terms and conditions of those mega-platforms makes one wonder how it can be that so many artists and independent producers hand over the rights for their content to these platforms. This is an excerpt from Facebook's own terms and conditions:

> By posting User Content to any part of the Site, you automatically grant, and you represent and warrant that you have the right to grant, to the Company an irrevocable, perpetual, non-exclusive, transferable, fully paid, worldwide license (with the right to sublicense) to use, copy, publicly perform, publicly display, reformat, translate, excerpt (in whole or in part) and distribute such User Content for any purpose, commercial, advertising, or otherwise, on or in connection with the Site or the promotion thereof, to prepare derivative works of, or incorporate into other works, such User Content, and to grant and authorize sublicenses of the foregoing. (Facebook Terms and Conditions, 2008)

These platforms present themselves as open-content providers that host a democratic discourse by offering members of the public freedom of speech. In reality, they hold the contributors as slaves to advertisement, which is, at the moment, the only real means of income generation and profit-making for these ventures. Investments in this field can be on a grand scale: Google bought YouTube in 2007 for $1.65 billion. These companies need to see a quick return on their investment, so they become 'wolves in sheep's clothing', marketing themselves as providers of free and open content while in fact implementing strict proprietary rules.

> Consciousness of desire and the desire for consciousness together and indissolubly constitute that project which in its negative form has as its goal the abolition of classes and the direct possession by the workers of every aspect of their activity. The opposite of this project is the society of the spectacle, where the commodity contemplates itself in a world of its own making. (Debord, 1994)

I suggest that the only use of these platforms should be tactical – as when publishing content on YouTube, one can benefit from higher visibility – but this comes with abandoning one's rights. The use of file-sharing technologies, on the other hand, is strategic – as the participants do not need to abandon their rights and can bypass the draconian terms and conditions imposed by platforms such as YouTube and Facebook. Michel de Certeau defines 'strategy' in *The Practice of Everyday Life*:

> I call a "strategy" the calculus of force-relationships which becomes possible when
> a subject of will and power (a proprietor, an enterprise, a city, a scientific institu-
> tion) can be isolated from an "environment". A strategy assumes a place that can
> be circumscribed as proper (*propre*) and thus serve as the basis for generating
> relations with an exterior distinct from it (competitors, adversaries, "clienteles",
> "targets", or "objects" of research). Political, economic, and scientific rationality
> has been constructed on this strategic model. (de Certeau 1984)

Often, strategic models depend on the building of infrastructures and the production of laws,
goods, literature, inventions, etc. Through this production process, a strategy aspires to
sustain itself. I argue that the Internet is such an infrastructure and is, by its very ontology, a
file-sharing technology. As such, use of the Internet through file-sharing is almost impossible
to restrict by enforcing non-realistic copyright laws. This use is a strategical utilisation of
an infrastructure that is already anti-hierarchical. This strategic utilisation generates data
spheres which have to be moderated through social contracts since the anti-hierarchy and
openness of the datascapes do not lend themselves to restriction in the traditional sense.

Adding Open Content licencing schemes to the file-sharing distribution technology enables
audiences to become active not only in the process of viewing and criticising content, but
also, and more importantly, in its production process. Open, free content licences are often
referred to as 'copyleft'.

In the online hacker lexicon, jargon.net, copyleft is thus defined as:

> copyleft /kop'ee-left/ /n./ [play on 'copyright'] 1. The copyright notice ('General Pub-
> lic Licence') carried by GNU EMACS and other Free Software Foundation software,
> granting reuse and reproduction rights to all comers (but see also General Public
> Virus) 2. By extension, any copyright notice intended to achieve similar aims.

In 1983, Richard Stallman, a software programmer, started the GNU Project, creating
software to be shared with the goal to develop a completely free operating system. For this,
Stallman invented the General Public Licence (GPL), which allows for the freedom of reuse,
modification and reproduction of works.

Copyright asserts ownership and attribution to the author. Copyright protects the attribution to the author in relation to his/her work. It also protects the work from being altered
by others without the author's consent and restricts the reproduction of the work. Copyleft
is not, as many think, an anti-copyright. Copyleft is an extension of copyright: it includes
copyright through its regulations for attribution and ownership reference to the author. But it
also extends copyright by allowing for free re-distribution of the work and, more controver-
sially, the right to change the work if the altered version attributes the original author and is
re-distributed under the same terms.

For the 'copy-paste generation', copyleft is already the natural propagation of digital
information in a society which provides the possibility of interacting through digital net-

works. In doing so, one naturally uses content generated by others, remixing, altering or redistributing this.

> Simple "public domain" publication will not work, because some will try to abuse this for profit by depriving others of freedom; as long as we live in a world with a legal system where legal abstractions such as copyright are necessary, as responsible artists or scientists we will need the formal legal abstractions of copyleft that ensure our freedom and the freedom of others. (Debian, 1997)

One of the main current Linux platforms is the Debian Project. Debian describes itself as "an association of individuals who have made common cause to create a free operating system" (ibid.). Debian, as a group of volunteers, created the Debian GNU Linux operating system. "The project and all developers working on the project adhere to the Debian Social Contract" (Debian 2004). In this social contract, Debian defines the criteria for free software and, as such, which software can be distributed over their network.

The Deptford.TV project is strategically building up its own server system with the goal of distributing over file-sharing networks, rather than relying on YouTube or MySpace, thus distributing files under the Free Art Licence in the spirit of the GPL and the Creative Commons 'Share-Alike' attribution licence. Nevertheless, Debian reviewed the Creative Commons licences and concluded that none of the Creative Commons core licences are actually free in accordance with the Debian Free Software Guidelines, and recommended that works released under these licences "should not be included in Debian" (Debian, 2005).

Creative Commons (CC) was critically discussed in the first Deptford.TV reader by rota and Pozzi (2006), specifically criticising the 'Non-Commercial' clause of the CC licence. This Non-Commercial (NC) licence forbids for-profit uses of works. Despite that, it is often used by content creators who want their media to be distributed and find useful the exchange of information and critical opinions about their work. In this way, a common pool is created. For commercial use of material distributed under the NC licence, one would have to contact the original author for permission. Nevertheless, the definition of 'Non-Commercial' is, strictly speaking, very difficult. Many producers use CC licences to distribute content cheaply via the Internet in order to raise attention to their works. It is interesting that through this attitude, we see more artists relying on revenues coming from higher visibility rather than sales of their work. For musicians, for example, this can be live concerts; for photographers, ad hoc commissions. According to rota, "the Non-Commercial clause would only limit diffusion of their works, as well as limit the availability of freely reusable work in the communal pool from which everyone can draw and contribute back" (rota and Pozzi, 2006).

Unfortunately, these uncertainties in the Creative Commons system made it corruptible. This is the reason why YouTube, MySpace, etc. are often referred to as 'open' user-generated content platforms. They provide tools which merely make it seem as if there's real sharing going on, whereas in reality these sites are about driving traffic to one single site and controlling this site.

Deptford.TV uses the General Public Licence (GPL), the Free Art Licence and the Creative Commons Share-Alike attribution licence as a statement of copyleft attitude. The basic reference for the Deptford.TV project is the General Public Licence, a Free Software licence, which grants to you the four following freedoms:

0.The freedom to run the program for any purpose.
1.The freedom to study how the program works and adapt it to your needs.
2.The freedom to redistribute copies so you can help your neighbour.
3.The freedom to improve the program and release your improvements to the public, so that the whole community benefits.

You may exercise the freedoms specified here provided that you comply with the express conditions of this license. The principal conditions are:
•You must conspicuously and appropriately publish on each copy distributed an appropriate copyright notice and disclaimer of warranty and keep intact all the notices that refer to this License and to the absence of any warranty; and give any other recipients of the Program a copy of the GNU General Public License along with the Program. Any translation of the GNU General Public License must be accompanied by the GNU General Public License.
•If you modify your copy or copies of the program or any portion of it, or develop a program based upon it, you may distribute the resulting work provided you do so under the GNU General Public License. Any translation of the GNU General Public License must be accompanied by the GNU General Public License.
•If you copy or distribute the program, you must accompany it with the complete corresponding machine-readable source code or with a written offer, valid for at least three years, to furnish the complete corresponding machine-readable source code.

Michael Stutz (1997) describes how the GPL can also be applied to non-software information. The GPL states that it "applies to any program or other work which contains a notice placed by the copyright holder saying it may be distributed under the terms of this General Public Licence", so, according to Stutz, this 'program', then, may not necessarily be a computer software program – any work of any nature that can be copyrighted can be copylefted with the GNU GPL (ibid.).

The Free Art Licence as well as the CC Share-Alike attribution licence follow the attitude of the GPL. As the Creative Commons 'SA-BY' licence states, you are free to Share (to copy, distribute and transmit the work) and to Remix (to adapt the work).

In many ways, the GPL provides a de-militarized zone. Everyone agrees to leave the big guns at the door. Period. The non-commercial CC licence, on the other hand, is a pledge not to use the guns, if you play nice. And, to be on the sure side, being nice means to consume, but not to build upon works in a serious way... essentially (and to daringly simplify) GPL comes from an ethical conflict/dilemma, while CC comes from economic/jurisdictional observation. (Princic, 2005)

These licences are unfortunately not entirely compatible with each other; however, they carry the same attitude. Like with the discussion between free and open-source licencing schemes and the resulting labelling of FLOSS (Free/Libre/Open Source Software), I argue that alternatively the same can be done with media to represent the same attitude. Therefore one could perhaps speak of 'FLOMS' (as in Free/Libre/Open Media Systems), since the discussions and differences in the open media field between GPL and CC are like the ones in the software field between free software and open-source software. To use file-sharing as technology and to apply the attitude of copyleft is a possible strategy for alternative media practices with the aim of creating a social contract, a legal model in which the culture of sharing becomes valuable. Therefore, concentrating on a copyleft attitude for media production might be a better way forward to bring social contracts into the data sphere and, with it, a new discussion around the meaning of the public sphere and the shared cultural heritage of the file-sharing generation.

References

- Besser, Howard. "Intellectual Property: The Attack on Public Space in Cyberspace" (Copyright 2001). Available at: http://www.gseis.ucla.edu/~howard/Papers/pw-public-spaces.html (accessed 23 February 2009).
- Critical Arts Ensemble. **Digital Resistance** (autonomedia, 2000, New York). Available at: http://www.critical-art.net/books/digital/index.html (accessed 24 February 2009).
- Debian. "About Debian" (1997). Available at: http://www.us.debian.org/intro/about (accessed 26 February 2009).
- _____. "Debian Social Contract" (2004). Available at: http://www.debian.org/social_contract (accessed 26 February 2009).
- Debord, Guy. **The Society of the Spectacle** (Zone Books, 1994, London).
- de Certeau, Michel. **The Practice of Everyday Life** (University of California Press, 1984, Los Angeles).
- Fenton, Natalie and John Downey. "Counter Public Spheres and Global Modernity". In **Javnost – The Public** 10 (1), pp. 15-32 (2003).
- Gumbel, Andrew. "Striking Writers Pull Plug on Golden Globes TV Gala". In **The Independent,** 8 January 2008. Available at: http://www.independent.co.uk/arts-entertainment/films/news/striking-writers-pull-plug-on-goldenglobes-tv-gala-768991.html (accessed 2 March 2009).
- Liang, Lawrence. **A Guide to Open Content Licences** (Piet Zwart Institute, 2004, Rotterdam).
- Princic, Luca. "GPL vs. CC (Ethics vs. Economy?)" (2005). Available at: https://lists.skylined.org/pipermail/ossa/2005-February/000648.html (accessed 5 April 2009).
- Rousseau, Jean Jacques [1762]. **The Social Contract** (Penguin Classics, 1968, London).
- Stutz, Michael. "Applying Copyleft to Non-Software Information" (GNU Project – Free Software Foundation, 1997). Available at: http://www.gnu.org/philosophy/nonsoftware-copyleft.html (accessed 3 March 2009).
- Wolf, Christopher (Foreword). **The Digital Millennium Copyright Act** (Pike & Fischer, 2003, Washington).

Factoring Fear
Investigations into Media(ted) Fear

SANDHYA DEVESAN NAMBIAR

The little ones sit by their TV screens
No thoughts to think
No tears to cry
All sucked dry
Down to the very last breath
Bartender what is wrong with me
Why I am so out of breath
The captain said excuse me ma'am
This species has amused itself to death.

These lyrics are from the song "Amused to Death" from the album of the same name by Roger Waters, which attempts at critiquing the nexus between mass narratives such as religion and mass media, both of which indeed operate as the 'opiate of the masses'.[1] The album, released in 1992, is based on the book, *Amusing Ourselves to Death*, by Neil Postman; both speak disparagingly of the supposed wonders of modern society, which seems besotted with the new gods of consumerism. Both works provide a point of departure for certain questions that surround the idea of fear as received primarily through the media:

(i) Are there linkages between fear, media, democracy and power where citizens of a state are transformed continually into consumers and further into subjects of media?

(ii) If fear and, by extension, terror are the new 'products' to be consumed through media intervention, who are the complicit actors in this theatre of terror and how?

(iii) Are there certain images, stereotypes and ideas reified in the media in order to be invested with greater power to evoke fear in the social, cultural and political spheres?

This essay grapples with the problematisation of the tacitly understood relationship between media and productions of fear and terror, which feed into local, socially specific ideas and ideologies of power, governance and citizenship.

Before embarking on this essay on fear, I have to ask, in this post-modern, post-sensation society, what contains enough capacity, intensity and resonance to evoke fear? What can propel us to act and react based on an emotion such as fear when we are fast approaching a seeming absence of fear? In Shakespeare's *Macbeth,* in response to the bloodcurdling scream of a woman, Macbeth exclaims:

> I have almost forgot the taste of fears.
> The time has been my senses would have cool'd
> To hear a night shriek, and my fell of hair
> Would at a dismal treatise rouse and stir
> As life were in't. I have supp'd full with horrors;
> Direness, familiar to my slaughterous thoughts,
> Cannot once start me.[2]

Lamenting the loss of fear and feeling, Macbeth is in the unenviable situation of being unable to sufficiently feel anything in order to reach the level of fear. This paper attempts to examine whether modern television audiences have become similarly too desensitised and dehumanised to feel emotions manifestly, especially an emotion as strongly reactive as fear, leaving fear, then, to become produced for selective consumption. This paper shall further seek to investigate such social phenomena where the trivialisation of the human has led to the popularity of certain images, types and programmes, especially as evinced in such reality TV shows as *MTV Roadies, MTV Splitsvilla, Fear Factor, Who Dares Wins, I'm a Celebrity – Get Me Out of Here, Khatron ke Khiladi, Bigg Boss, Sach ka Saamna, Exhausted* and the like, where people are forced to live out hyper-real situations and participate in extreme acts involving fear and terror (such as being immersed in water for inordinate lengths of time) and perform 'stunts' and games with conditions such as not being allowed to sleep for days (the favourite being swallowing non-edible, and often live, insects and other such creatures to universal disgust and horror).

We are in the Age of the Image where every new image is being constantly touched up, repixellated and airbrushed in order for it to 'look good'. In such a world, the visual medium immediately gains power and authority, becoming, in culture guru Marshall McLuhan's terms, both message and metaphor. We are, for now, in a Brave New World where a webpage on the apocalyptic novel of the same name by Aldous Huxley will also show you advertisements for new washing machines and LCD television sets, and a Yahoo! advertisement on television tells you that your own reality is banal as compared to the world of You-Yahoo! It is a sign/cultural signifier of the times, where every moment has been Googled, Facebooked, Twittered and made continually redundant. We are witnessing the advent of a new society where we have been transformed into Huxley's "great abbreviators", confined to tweets of 150 words or less.

In these abbreviated times, one might ask, what most scares us, spooks us, terrifies us? One of the factors of fear leading to an increased state of paranoia and paralysis in the socio-cultural sphere seems to be the state of the world as manufactured by the media – the world of terror, climate change, death, germs, diseases such as AIDS, hypertension, diabetes and swine flu, and the consequent fear of the mass obliteration of the human race as evinced through movies such as *2012*, based on doomsday predictions again popularised by the media.

Terror as the intensified form of fear has permeated our consciousness to an extent that would have been impossible to achieve without the help, support and indeed the very presence of the mass media. The media creates new monsters for us everyday, and serves them up in a news-mix related to fears of death, global warming, resource limitations, Red Terror, terror across the border, love jihad, the oil crisis, the food crisis, the water crisis, etc. It seems that every day is a battle fought over minor and major crises without end or resolution but within the ambit of the world that the media creates for us and cocoons us in, cut off from actual blood and gore. Neil Postman wrote about the effects of television on the unsuspecting public as far back as 1984 in his book, *Amusing Ourselves to Death,* where he says: "Television has become, so to speak, the background radiation of the social and intel-lectual universe… The all-but-imperceptible residue of the electronic big bang of a century past, so familiar and so thoroughly integrated with American culture that we no longer hear its faint hissing in the background or see the flickering gray light".[3]

The culture of fear thrives on the creation of dichotomous hyper-realities – with reality itself shown as a war between the forces of good and evil, war and peace, terrorists versus the peaceful majority, the Self against the monstrous Other – which continually force us to react and choose sides. The rise of terrorists, villains, monsters, can perhaps be traced to the rise of a global fundamentalism and fascism, where each group imagines itself to be in the right, forced to act out of fear of the other. There are constant encounters, face-offs, battles, conflicts, based on fear, especially in a climate where terms such as 'war on terror', 'collateral damage' and 'shock and awe' have become commonplace. The text of fear is manufactured through the use of images and language in order to coerce people into a certain idea or action where they imagine themselves as members of a certain community against another.

The media, therefore, participates in regulative discourses that attempt to create and locate meanings and identities based on an assumption of the hegemonic power wielded by an authority as distinct from the subject, who then is forced to become a willing/unwilling observer and voyeur. In that sense, the *mediated public* participates in such voyeuristic paradigms that are intended to at once de-subjectivise both the performer and observer, and bind them in an uneasy relationship based on the politics of fear and power. In the movie *Star Wars: Episode 1 – The Phantom Menace*, Yoda tells Anakin on the subject of fear, "Fear is the path to the dark side. Fear leads to anger. Anger leads to hate. Hate leads to suffering. I sense much fear in you". Although the category of fear is more complex than such direct relations, the hatred and paranoia related to fear are transformed into actuality by a mass media with strong, vested, self-serving interests.

When trust in positive ideology fails, there is an overarching dependence on the language of fear, violence and terror, built in order to maintain order of certain kinds, as also to steer people into forming groups and communities based on the necessary function of survival. This creates what Judith Butler would call "abjected subjects", who are emptied out of their persona and are instead made to represent particular interests and identities while they are continuously being emptied out – abjected humans, as it were. All media, in McLuhan's view, "are active metaphors in their power to translate experience into new forms. The spoken word was the first technology by which man was able to let go of his environment in order to grasp it in a new way".[4] In the present terrains of media, the electronic has replaced the spoken word in terms of appeal and power but similarly strives towards the construction of new environments and negative impacts based on the patterns of fear.

Fear overrides the concerns of egalitarianism, liberal democratic principles, justice and logic, and can therefore be an extremely potent tool in the hands of those who wield power or seek to. And the most potent medium to spread the message of fear is television, and in the present time, there is nothing more starkly evocative of this than the unending lineup of reality TV shows that have become staple. As audiences, we are either transformed into dumbly captive voyeurs of bedroom politics or are made complicit in fear-mongering and violence in the poisonous combination of news and reality TV, the *simulacra* of reality, as poststructuralist cultural critic Jean Baudrillard puts it.

At one level, one is never shown the consequences of the various stunts, games and competitions performed in reality TV, therefore helping in the 'cartoonification' of televised reality. We cannot react when we watch someone falling off a cliff unless it is accompanied by terrifying music or horrified expressions on the faces of other contestants. We wait for affirmation from these sources, which are never revealed as being manufactured reality, and depend on them for our emotional responses.

On the subject of the cult of media fear, Bertolt Brecht has said, "There are many who pretend that cannons are aimed at them when in reality they are the target of opera glasses". In a recast of Hobbesian fear, the families of those being interviewed and asked seriously personal questions on the programme *Sach ka Saamna* (Face the Truth, a remake of the American reality show *Moment of Truth)* are subjected to the greatest anxiety, where fear of social stigma and loss of honour form the underlying theme, intensified especially in the wake of the values advocated by the bourgeoisie. *Panic Encyclopedia* makes a similar point – "Panic art situates us within its own polar opposition: nostalgic desire for the rock-solid values of respectable modernism vs. hyper-fascination for the valuelessness of postmodern over-production".[5] The recent controversies surrounding *Sach ka Saamna* also led to state intervention by policy makers, fearful of the corruption of public morals through the programme. The Samajwadi Party MP, Kamal Akhtar, took up the issue in the Rajya Sabha, arguing that the questions asked in the show on 22 July 2009 were against Indian culture – women were questioned about their marital fidelity – and called for a halt to the screening.

In most cases, such as those involving celebrities and actresses such as Urvashi Dholakia, Roopa Ganguly and Bobby Darling, one can detect the construction of questions based on gender roles and identities, where social prestige is opposed to individual choice and where individual anxiety is both the cause and the effect of hegemony and repression. As critic Corey Robin points out, fear as anxiety is not just a political or social tool; it has become the very psychological basis and state of the masses. She goes on to say, "And when the government acted repressively in response to this anxiety, the purpose was not to inhibit potential acts of opposition by keeping people down (Hobbes) or apart (Montesquieu), but to press people together, giving them a feeling of constancy and structure, relieving them, at least temporarily, of their raging anxiety".[6] Television, as the epitome of the communication between and above the masses, can offer the simulacra and semblance of relief or prohibition by co-opting the masses and speaking for them.

In such cases, one might argue, the traditional roles of gender, community and identity are sought to be validated through the sanction of the public, while newer identities and roles such as those of the openly transsexual Laxmi or Bobby Darling are 'questioned' in order for the watching public to pass their tacit judgement. In each of these cases, even while they are exhorted to overcome their fear of the 'truth' (posited as a singular, monolithic statement of fact as opposed to plural, perspectival notions of truth), they are being coerced to stand trial through the manufacture of social fear in front of the masses through their admissions of 'guilt'.

One can also take, for example, other programmes that advocate the notion of 'going beyond fear' such as *Fear Factor, MTV Roadies* and *Khatron ke Khiladi* (The Daredevils), where participants supposedly transcend their fears and phobias, also supported by advertisements such as the Mountain Dew ad that says: *"Darr ke aage jeet hai"* (There's victory beyond fear), the toothpaste ad for Pepsodent that goes *"dishum dishum"* (onomatopoeia for beating someone up) against germs, as well as current ad campaigns targeted at whipping up popular sentiment regarding the 26/11 Mumbai attacks. At the superficial level, while the participants in reality television programmes such as *Roadies* or *Khatron ke Khiladi* are made to confront their individual fears of certain objects, they are at the same time being intensely subjected to the fear of failure within a particular community.

This fear of 'failure', and therefore the subsequent fear of the anonymity that could follow, is the essential ingredient of these programmes, where the actors are never asked to confront the fear of failure itself. Also, the cult of the celebrity, followed in almost all these programmes, lends the added hierarchy of the sanction of Big Brother, variously incarnated in the persons of such celebrities as Amitabh Bachchan or Akshay Kumar.

Failure in the social community, loss of face and the loss of social honour and prestige have become, through media intervention, one of the most prevalent fears sold on Indian television and, by extension, in society at large. Even while fears at the macro level, such as fear of war or disease, fluctuate and intensify/lessen with time, the more locally situated fears of local authorities or locally available others, such as the imagined communities of the class-based/religious minorities, are intensified in order to become prevalent notions of their beliefs and powers through electronically convergent media. An instance may be seen in the current advertisement featuring actor Abhishek Bachhan for Idea Cellular Ltd. on what is popularly known as the "Mumbai 26/11 terror attack of 2008" (of which, tellingly, the Taj Mahal Palace hotel has become emblematic, despite the attacks having taken place at around ten different locations), which builds on the hysteria around the event whipped up by news channels that led many upper-class Mumbaikars to join mass protests, the same people conspicuous in their absence during the more damaging July 2006 attacks on the Mumbai intra-city trains. Very evidently, then, the media demonstrated its power to collect the critical mass of people necessary to effect physical change in the public sphere, and demonstrated also its capacity to whip up public passions for or against certain sections of the population.

Coming back to the questions posited at the beginning of this essay, it would be worthwhile to additionally look at the convergence of the media – and media-related perspectives – with discourses that construct and sell the grand narrative of fear, psychosis, anxiety and panic for the willing public. The manufacture of the culture of fear requires further investigations, where fear has been commoditised and converted into a saleable product for consumption in the market through electronic convergence/interdependence, in order to create more markets and goods based on the main factor of fear. Most of the current market trends, entertainment channels, TRP ratings and news reports depend on the industry of fear in order to attract more audiences, consumers and buyers. Fear is peddled by all kinds of sources, news media, cinema, television, Internet, thereby elevating it to a level beyond the ordinary or the human, where those that are feared are the new purveyors of the newly mediated environments. In the movie, *Iron Man* (2008), the main protagonist, Tony Stark, who is a weapons manufacturer, sums up his ideology thus, while showing off his new Jericho missile: "Is it better to be feared or respected? I say, is it too much to ask for both?"[7] The mass media, controlled by big corporations, are the new king-makers, powerbrokers and evangelists, attempting to cash in on both these opportunities – fear and respect; through the creation of circular dialogues, they initiate self-fulfilling prophecies of new crises, dire consequences, doomsday scenarios and new Armageddons, which can be averted only if one takes recourse to the solutions they offer. Fear is the new saleable 'hot' item being peddled; in the waiting markets, it is bought all too quickly.

I conclude this essay with pertinent dialogue from the American film, *V for Vendetta*, adapted from the DC comic book by Alan Moore, wherein is an instance of media critiquing media itself. Here, the character V delineates the twisted plot of the power-hungry High Chancellor, and reveals the ways in which the state and big industry collude in order to retain power.

> V: However, the true goal of this project is power. Complete and total hegemonic domination… Fuelled by the media, fear and panic spread quickly, fracturing and dividing the country until at last the true goal comes into view. Before the Saint Mary's crisis, no one would have predicted the results of the election that year, no one. And then not long after the election, lo and behold, a miracle… it was a pharmaceutical company controlled by certain party members that made them all obscenely rich. A year later, several extremists are tried, found guilty and executed while a memorial is built to canonise their victims. But *the end result, the true genius of the plan, was the fear.* Fear became the ultimate tool of this government, and through it our politician was ultimately appointed to the newly created position of High Chancellor. The rest, as they say, is history.[8]

Notes

1. *Roger Waters.* Amused to Death *(Sony, 1992).*
2. *William Shakespeare. (Ed.) John Wilders,* Macbeth *V.v (Cambridge University Press, 2004, Cambridge), p. 205.*
3. *Neil Postman. "A Peek-A-Boo World". In* Amusing Ourselves to Death: Public Discourse in an Age of Show Business *(Penguin USA, 1985, New York), p. 59.*
4. *Marshall McLuhan and Terence Gordon.* Understanding Media: The Extensions of Man *(Ginkgo Press, 2003, California), p. 57.*
5. *(Eds.) Arthur Kroker, Marilouise Kroker, David Cook et al.,* Panic Encyclopedia *(Macmillan, 1989, Montreal), p 19.*
6. *Corey Robin.* Fear: The History of a Political Idea *(Oxford University Press, 2004, Oxford), p 76.*
7. *Trevor F. Bartlett. "Iron Man". In* Saturday, *10 May 2008. Available at: http://www.wirenh.com/Film/Film_reviews/Iron_Man_200805102905.html (accessed 20 November 2009).*
8. *Andy Wachowski, Larry Wachowski et al.* V for Vendetta: From Script to Film *(Universe Publishers, 2006, New York), p. 124.*

Fear in Neo-*Kaliyuga*
Epistemic Troubles in Techno-*Smrti* Times

KAUSHIK BHAUMIK

The modular *qasba* towns of Asia and the *bazaars* within them are a residue of the speeds of Islamic expansionism between the 9th and the 13th centuries, and are thus marked by ecstatic enunciations of the experience of speeds, by a frenetic pace of production, by a relentlessly fast stylisation of all matter, of everything (including phenomena such as voice, bardic poetry, perception of birdsong, lovers' orgasms and so on). Much of material culture here is an involuntary expression of wonderment at what speed can do to the body. But such a reflex excitation of the senses by speed is also remarkably suited to meet the material demands of a fast-expanding imperial order that consumes goods and instigates markets at the same remarkable rates. The eye is always looking askance towards the next horizon of conquest that will bring in new demands that will require skills to adapt fast, very fast indeed, as they did in the mediaeval era to keep up with the perceptions of change that the venture of Islam was producing the world over. The Islamic totalisation of speed had re-worked *techne* to a new pitch of productivity that would make the *bazaar* approach the machine in no time. As the historian Marshall Hodgson points out, the one significant thing that distinguished Islam from preceding world-system hegemons was the extraordinary freedom it allowed for people to choose their social and life destinies. This unique freedom became translated into the speeds with which people rushed to take advantage of it, and emanated also in a quickening of the transaction of goods and bodies as the world became more accessible to personal drives without the earlier sanctions of a hierarchical access to material resources. Hodgson's point about the rising fortunes of the mercantile class and the burgeoning of trade under Islam makes sense in the entanglement of the freedom to access the world, to do new things with it and also to spread across the world in search of new destinies of prosperity.[1]

However, it could be argued that the totalisation of speeds introduced by Islamic world conquests was not just about engendering the *bazaar* as a space of production. The *bazaar* also enlarged into a competitive system for creative labour, encompassing domestic life, literature, music, knowledge systems and aspirations for social betterment, of which the *bazaar* was merely a revelatory representation. By the 18th century, this logic of competition in speed that began in the epochal Islamic urban revolution had seeped into the villages of India from Kashmir to the Malabar. The volume of cultural production brought forth in the Islamic phase of Indic history that lasted until the 1920s is mind boggling, an index of the logic of speed that ran the regimes of cultural production. Additional acceleration, produced by such factors as the twist colonialism gave to the speed dial of productivity, population expansion and finally the bottling-in of the explosive forces of creativity by the nation-state, has merely intensified the *bazaar* order into the organics of everyday Indian life. The material emanations of the oral and the textual orders of knowledge, seen in the logic of productivity, are shot through with the febrile vibrations of the competitive speeds of the *bazaar*.

The terms of *bazaar* competition have now changed. The Indian *bazaar* is today one of the biggest sweatshops serving the global economy, which in turn seems to be converging on a voracious, hyper-consumerist *bazaar* model more than ever before. If the *bazaar* competition of Islamic times was carried out in the name of the glory of the emperor/empire and Allah, its modern manifestation is mobilised in the name of the advancement of the Indian nation. These shifts in register of the hegemonic ideologies that cap *bazaar* regimes of productivity in the Indic have important bearings on the manner in which fear is felt and expressed in 21st-century *bazaar* India. The cultural material that frames sensory experience in the *bazaar* has changed, leading to new registers in which fear is felt and to popular cinema becoming the prime location through which fear in this competitive order is expressed.

Epistemic Orders of the *Bazaar* and Expressions of Fear

Three distinctive knowledge orders reside in the Indic *bazaar* – the textual, the oral and the sensory reflexive. One can point out that these are co-extensive and by one or the other means inform one another, at least from the sensory reflexive 'upwards' towards the textual. Culturally, the Indic *bazaar* is a space dominantly marked by a mnemonics of skill recall employed to carry out various forms of labour tasks. Textuality is minimal, and the collective memory of labour combines remains the main repository of skill recall techniques. The sensory reflexive is the most pervasive literacy medium that underpins both the religious ritualism of *bazaar* and household spaces as well as the world of informal labour that fabricates, transports and distributes material goods through the Indic everyday. The telescoping of different kinds of hierarchical orders – brahmanical, Islamic and modern, translating roughly into caste, communal and class divisions – has ensured that labour in the *bazaar* proceeds across either silence and/or mutual mistrust between patron and labour or in ecstatic master-slave devotional relationships across cultural taboo lines. These translate into complex symbolic myths of power and domination that use materiality and sensory feels of environment to express themselves. Caste being the dominant reality of labour in

India also ensures that there is a complex mapping on to the social of primordial cosmic fears emanating from a fear of environmental forces, something that cuts across class. The synergies between hierarchy and cosmic fear provide the frame for a slave labour regime in a hyper-capitalist context, allowing sweatshop conditions and the acceptance of exponentially expanding high demand orders. The expansion in demand, in turn, makes the market more hectic and unstable, an instability that runs across the psychic worlds of owners and workers alike.

The endless return to the sensory reflexive after a passage through the three epistemic orders thus becomes the base for, to put in a certain Indic register of classifying knowledge and culture, *smrti* forms of knowledge, forms of knowledge learnt by rote memory. Bodily reflexes can inspire rote learning as can oral enunciations. Oral enunciations in their turn can form the base of a textuality that retains the basic repetitive incantatory logic of orality. Needless to say, the sensory-reflexive base of life and culture that marks the co-extensiveness of cultural expressions spanning 'textuality', in the largest sense of the term, is also the reason for the inter-infusion of *bazaar* and everyday in India – with the instability of the sensory-reflexive in labour and materiality forever promising to blur the lines seeking to classify reality in symbolic and hierarchical dimensions towards seamless flows of textures of materiality. We notice this in the creative logic of *ragmala* paintings, where colour is used in such a way that the shapes of delineated forms dissolve into the feel of the temperatures on our skin that the colours elicit and, by extension, into an 'environmental' feel of the scene depicted.

That such an epistemic order is structured by a basic instability at its core due to the relentlessness of demands to productivity is only to be expected. The emphasis on the interconnectedness of the various levels of economy and society merely points out the all-pervasive quality of *bazaar* instability structuring the Indic. Fear, from Islamic times, had always structured the modern *bazaar*. This, after all, was the lynchpin of the military-fiscal order, as the ritual loot of the *bazaar* during conquests made very clear. Stories of hauntings by spirits, attacks by dacoits and desecration during invasions or natural calamities form the bedrock of oral lore emanating from the *bazaar*. An obsession with miracles abounds in this literature as does the obverse: an earthly, pornographic emphasis on sex and other worldly pleasures, extracted as costs of the relentless order of productivity that the *bazaar* is. In a lot of love poetry, the miraculous revelation of the woman's body and sexual explicitness act as mutual enforcers of sensory intensities. The same pre-occupations have from the beginning framed cinema in India, from the manic enjoyment of imported action adventure serials to the relentless paranoid action of the Fearless Nadia films. And, indeed, the vast popularity of a certain kind of performative cinema that made the sensory reflexive basis of the *bazaar* explicit can only be explained by the intensities of pain and desire produced in a system that pushes labour so easily under the demands for productivity to the edge of human fortitude – the sensory reflexive itself.

The instability of existence in the *bazaar* lies opened up to the eye in 1970s Indian cinema. Wide-angle shots and an excessive use of zooms and track outs to present dramas of extreme competitive violence expressed the instability of the self as having crept up into the eye itself. Amitabh Bachchan's iconography of the haunted and hunted hero on the run expressed itself mainly through tormented and over-stressed eyes. The burden of labour holding up a vast system of demands was taking its toll, and neither emperor nor god nor nation could help sublimate this strain in any symbolic register of idealism. And not only does this instability mark the site of labour, but the entire social fabric seems to have been shaken up by an incredible paroxysm of material greed through and through. Social explanations for grasping behaviour in terms of class or caste have been abandoned. From this point on, cinema that already was largely in the hands of *bazaar* mercantile capital – serving the interests of entertaining the subaltern masses and the young lower-middle class single male as its main economic dynamic – changed over to a *bazaar* cinema that, extraordinarily enough, began to serve the middle classes as well. The effects of unemployment, disaffection against tradition and India's population explosion were driving the middle-class young into earning their living for the first time in direct links with the *bazaar*, the source of the cheap commodity production regimes that allowed them their jobs. Two decades on, cinema, with its capacities to directly catch the sensory basis of life and fear in the *bazaar*, becomes the *lingua franca* of a literate middle class living in or on the margins of *bazaars*. The difficulties and the perils of labour in an inflation-ridden, hyper-competitive middle-class labour market become coded in this cinema as *metaphorically* equivalent to the kinds of tensions that the *bazaar* has traditionally been defined by.

The obliteration of textuality, or the symbolic linguistic, from the registers of expression of fear points as much to the secularisation of the senses in the mayhem of the economic wars of productivity waged in the *bazaar* as to the logic of the *bazaar*, shifting under such pressures towards the sensory reflexive and away from the symbolic. And violence at this reflex level of the unconscious, joining the sensory and the motor without any symbolic mediation, is bound to be extreme and visceral to the core. Not only do the stakes of the visceral realism of cinematic violence keep spiralling through the decades, but so does the obsession with eviscerating the sexual in increasingly explicit forms. And over the years, by the time we reach the film, *Satya*, we find the domestic, that last bastion of symbolic coherence for the senses, whittled away under the pressures of a relentlessly competitive economy. The death of the domestic as a site of repose from the sensory reflexive seems to have spurred on popular cinema to ever more daringly 'explicit' representations of the sensory reflexive without any symbolic respite. Elements such as the earlier expression of the density of erotic passion in a certain lyricism of word and music in the Hindi film song stand discarded. Dance becomes more frontal and more explicitly expressive of sexual needs, yet at the same time more mechanical. Gone is the mediation of the sweeping move-ments of dance of an earlier cinema that denoted seduction in duration, mediation.

Inasmuch as the sensory reflexive base of the *smrti* knowledge of social rituals and modes of behaviour is what runs the *bazaar*, hyper-emphasised performative scenes of great sensory camaraderie between bodies that learnt in silent rote from each other could alternate with scenes where such bodies could also kill one another with equal performative verve and intensity. Ecstasy and reflex violence reside side by side in an atmosphere of what the psychoanalyst, Wilfred Bion, calls thalamic fear, a fear where the slightest error or even doubt in carrying out tasks always elicits a fear of letting a cosmic order down, so high are the stakes of productivity in the *bazaar*. And, sift through the entire range of production order films coming out of Bombay, no order of production is left untouched by the approach of the sensory reflexive in *smrti* – the corporate as much as the military or the police or the artistic. Or, for that matter, we also see the sensory reflexive enter the oral and the textual, say in the form of the violence depicted in televisual soaps, in the retelling of religious myths, in the increasing vogue of the dystopic comic book form or in the violence of consumerist imagery and writing that marks news today. Technology has only made *smrti* knowledge more paranoid, technology being almost always introduced into the contemporary Indic in the name of increased productivity and not creative formal play in duration and contemplation.

The Touch of Speed and the *Dharma* of the Gambler

As speed touches an order of production, it drives the order towards the logic of productivity that destabilises desire and skill towards the sensory reflexive rather than the textual and epistemic. The pressure of the system falls upon senses forever 'ignorant' of the reality of the pressures of productivity, given the inherent fragility of the senses in a sensory-reflexive confusion ultimately rooted in fears of cosmic imbalance. A labour order forever uncertain of its sensory articulation in space is driven by increasing productivity towards paranoia about the 'fatal' error that will bring the techno-cosmos down. This is nothing but the fear of the evacuation of the symbolic from the sensory, under the pressures of labour demands that only accelerate the operation of all kinds of social and cosmic fears circulating in the senses from beforehand.

The flipside of such extreme anxiety and uncertainty is that the fearful senses hit back by rendering speculative all productive gestures through and through, and thus add a paranoid dimension to competition. Earlier rituals of competition and confrontation in the symbolic meant that status in the imperial order rooted speculative instability in the system in temporary stasis. In the modern age, the coming together at once of the persistence of vestiges of cosmic fears of environmental forces and the secularisation of the senses by the forces of history threatens to push *smrti* forms of experience and expertise into an exponentially spiralling, speculative competitive order. In this order, unending in the one sense and fascist-apocalyptic in the other, history is made to end by making bodies evaporate in a drama mimicking the forces of history, a re-enactment of the death of the self fantasised under labour pressures.

For the moment, we see the reflex reaction to the threat of the secular in the carnival of blind speculation on all fronts of life – commercial, consumerist and epistemological (including the political) – in a rise in apocalyptic spiritualism of all forms in the *bazaar* (that, in its *yogic* quest to use the entropy of the sensory to calmly accept a violent death, becomes the flipside of the fascist-apocalyptic) and in a mind-boggling variety of 'syncretistic' *bazaar* commodity production. Coded in this 'syncretistic' production is the sensory confusion of being suddenly 'outed' from earlier hierarchical certainties into the challenge of the approach of a value-free, secular sensory. The terror faced at the approach of a value-free infinity of sensation into the material is signaled by the hyper-material nature of *bazaar* kitsch today, which is very different from the organic, 'syncretistic' nature of the *bazaar* commodities of the pre-modern, although the latter too is included in the hyper-material of contemporary commodity production. New 'syncretisms' can range from a coming together of clashing textures of materiality in fashion, architectural styles or other forms of cultural production such as song or cinema or even 'traditional' *bazaar* products such as sweetmeats or *paan*. We are in neo-*Kaliyuga*, where the inversion of symbolic hierarchies is the order of the day as speculation in sensory panic drives textures of materiality into one another in the hyper-material. Cinema, with its unique capacity to capture the intimacy of terror and the projection of spectacle into the mass, thus becomes the favoured medium to catch the polarities of experience described above.

Speculation thus becomes a way of eliciting the potential of cultural forms in materiality, in productive action, to buy time to transit from the symbolic to the secular of value-free sensation. But speculation is also about letting the automatism of the senses in the sensory-reflexive arrange the emergent materiality of the world in the secular in aesthetically just directions of flow, letting in new configurations of the material in the approach of the secular. In transition, speculative dreams of empire building and the destruction of empires of the senses float around in the civil war of consumerism, and its equal mix of intensity and entropy of the senses, that today's *bazaar* is. Rationality seems to lie on the side of the arch-gambler, a Yudhisthira, the pattern recogniser of social history, posited as the ideal emperor of Hindustan by the Mahabharata, the paramount summation of the *smarta yuga*. He is the fantasised 'political' gambler, thrown up in the virtual political-fiscal speculative regime, who out-waits smalltime speculators in the symbolic to let history mature towards the edge of Apocalypse. In that calamitous hour, the final sacrifice can be held to strike the fine balance between intensity and entropy that is the sublimation of thalamic fear in sensory conflict. This, then, is the solution posited by a text faced with rationalising the unruly histories of the equally unruly forces of history – snakes, semen, the senses (especially hearing), the mind and its various emanations and horses, amongst other things it seeks to control within its diegetic ambit.

And beneath all this lies the flow of desire in textures of pure sensation symbolised by Krsna, the instigator of all gambles, the one who knows all but whose gestures seem as bizarre gambles to the bystander, the destiny of the text, the one to whom all must return in flow once the turbulence of history is over. The passage from the symbolic to desire in the secular, in pure sensation, it seems can only happen in the 'political' reaching the edge of Apocalypse to flip over into desire. This eventuates when it is realised that it is the intensity of desire that has been 'misread' as the rising intensities of 'political' ambitions in the symbolic. The Bharata text flows out to us at the edge of the apocalyptic snake sacrifice as does *dharma* from the edge of Apocalypse in battle, a battle that sums up all possible civil wars of its times. Only the political-aesthetic gambler would know such limits. And much of modern Indian culture has flowed from the move effected in the Shi'a-Vaishnava ethos of Wajid Ali

Shah's court, from the apocalyptic edge of the end of Islamic power in the Indic. With its disintegration were all the energies of the commodity in empire let out to flow through the popular cultural productions of *bazaar* India for the next hundred years. Of these, the popular cinemas of India were the most powerful form, the form that caught most accurately the sensory stakes of Indic history in the 20th century.

Speed destabilises perception, causes materiality to multiply or creates the illusion of materiality cracking up into multiplicities. Textuality retreats to the *smrti* of the sensory-reflexive. Yet in times of great material flux, it might be useful to posit the textual as just another form of materiality – and await its re-emergence on the other side of flux, alongside the emergences of other forms of expression. Patience in the sensory-reflexive – capable of reading patterns in chaos, of letting the material content of desire flow through contradictions – can insert *dharma*, even if momentarily, into the *Kaliyuga* of the carnival, where all values come under threat from insurgent desires arriving from all sides and in many cultural forms. There is no one form of the sublimation of the touch of speed in the reverse touch of sense – the way of the Buddha, Gandhi, of cultural superstars, revolutionaries or the ones who opt out of historical memory, all gamblers in the senses, eliciting sublimation from their constituencies, internal and external, according to the historical specificities of the materiality of sensory fear they share. Whether these lead up to some kind of new way of thinking through a democracy of the senses – in the cutting edge of the technologies of the senses at play in the consumerist wars of the *bazaar* (and given the vicissitudes of the political struggles of our times, it might be apt that we merged what we conventionally call war and techno-consumerism) – only time will tell.

Note

1. *Marshall GS Hodgson. "The Role of Islam in World History". In Marshall GS Hodgson, (ed.) Edmund Burke III,* Rethinking World History: Essays on Europe, Islam and World History *(Cambridge University Press, 1993,Cambridge) , pp. 97-125.*

Changing Scenes

MOINAK BISWAS

Recent history has forced us in West Bengal to think after a long political sleep. Familiar answers are breeding new questions; unfamiliar bodies are getting mobilised for action. As domains of eruption jostle for recognition, people long living by an outworn political discourse are forced to notice the limits of their comprehension. Change is needed for this alone, if for nothing else. [1]

The fun begins when specialists make blunders. We are witnessing this all over the land, but with the unique backdrop of having the same party in power for over three decades, the winds of chaos feel a bit different to us in Bengal. A shocking recent instance of specialist blunder was the Lok Sabha elections of 2009: among the all-round failure of predictions, Bengal was one of the more amusing cases. But things are hardly giving experts time to determine their substance. I would like to talk about one incident, picked from a spectacular sequence, but one that ultimately does not yet belong to a sequence. I shall try to address the self-contradiction of this statement in what follows.

The 'sequence' in question began with protests at the end of 2006 against the government attempt to acquire land for the Tata Nano factory in Singur, and ran in 2007 through the agitation against land acquisition for a chemical hub in Nandigram, demonstrations decrying the police involvement in the death of Rizwanur Rahman, the public distribution system (PDS) conflagration that saw a spate of attacks on ration dealers, and the great rally of 14 November in Kolkata, held to protest against the violent repression of the Nandigram resistance. In 2008 came the panchayat elections that dealt the ruling Left Front unprecedented reversals. In November that year, a grassroots agitation started in Lalgarh against police excesses. In 2009, the Lok Sabha elections returned 25 parliamentarians from the Trinamool Congress-

Indian National Congress coalition from a total of 42 seats in West Bengal. A clutch of smaller streams are tied to this current – the stalling of land acquisition in Asansol; girls' school students in Jadavpur raising road barricades to condemn ruling party bullies; school committees long in the hands of the Communist Party of India (Marxist) [CPI(M)] suddenly changing political composition; or more visible eruptions – the auto-rickshaw protests in 2008 that looked like serious anarchy. Some of these streams flow directly into the sequence, deepening its reality; some lie at a remove, virtually connected. Somebody will write an account of the totality soon; others have to attempt part portrayals till that happens.

I would like to draw attention to one incident that took place on 21 November 2007. Only a week before that, a hundred thousand people marched in silence to protest the violent ruling-party attacks in Nandigram, creating a history of sorts. It was impossible to know from within the bounds of that expression that another society lying next door was internalising the impact of 2007 in a different way; outrage there was developing into serious unrest. It made us all aware of demarcations and unexpected affinities.

Event

The All India Minority Forum and an orphanage of the Furfura Sharif called a road blockade on 21 November. The three issues they raised were Taslima Nasrin's ouster, Nandigram and the Rizwanur death. Groups of Muslim youths started the blockade on Ripon Street and on roads around Park Circus. Shortly afterwards, a vast Muslim populated area from the central to the eastern Kolkata turned into a war zone. Barricade after barricade came up on the streets; brickbats, glass bottles, burning tyres, petrol bombs started raining down on the police. Police vehicles, buses and some private cars were put on fire. Fear gripped the busy Wednesday morning, bringing the city to a halt. From Ripon Street to Entally, Moulali, Park Circus, Tiljala, Topsia to the Parama Island on the Eastern Bypass – a grid of fire sprawled as groups of youths went on a free rampage. The lanes showed combat readiness: crates of cold drink, inflammable glue and brickbats were in ample supply, as well as a good supply of young boys to stand as shield in front, and armies at the back to rain hand-made missiles. The police and the Rapid Action Force (RAF) looked on helplessly. The decision not to open fire had been taken at the top; it soon transpired that the use of water canons and rubber bullets did not have approval either. The army was called in after 3 p.m. The city saw a curfew for the first time after the December 1992 demolition of the Babri Masjid. The boys retreated from thoroughfares to smaller streets, and then to the warren of lanes. The landscape of skirmishes with its scattered flames slowly became deserted after dusk.

Who was behind all this? Idris Ali, the leader of the All India Minority Forum, had lost control over the crowd early on; he had faced a brickbat attack and by evening had been suspended from the Congress party. The other convener, Furfura Sharif, issued a formal denouncement. Both organisations were expelled from the recently-formed Milli Ittehada Council, a forum of 12 Muslim organisations including the Jamiat Ulema-e-Hind, led by its West Bengal president, the Nandigram activist, Siddiqullah Chowdhury. Five days earlier, violent slogans had been raised against Taslima Nasrin at the Council's first convention on 16 November. Siddiqullah's criticism of the slogans showed that he didn't have much control over the council. It is not unusual for popular agitation to run out of control of the initiators. Two days later, *Ananda-bazar Patrika (ABP)* reported possible SIMI and outsider involvement. They were apparently waiting for the police to open fire to start a full-fledged riot. From the experience of a city that had seen the surging humanity in the streets on 14 November, it all looked like a conspiracy. The opposition parties called it as much – a sabotage of the rulers.

But how to explain what happened? The community laying siege to the heart of the city nurses a sense of deprivation and insult deep enough to start a bloodbath. Thousands joined what obviously spiralled into a 'riot'. But what kind of riot was it where citizens were not attacked, not a single casualty, and, leaving aside 35 policemen, not even cases of injury were reported. How was that possible? Was it an attempt to provoke communal riots, as a common conjecture went? One could have killed a couple of people in that case, set shops on fire. The idea that police restraint diffused a possible communal flare-up is hardly tenable either. From the following morning, the newspapers carried analyses saying the flare-up was hardly spontaneous, there was good planning behind it. But it is also obvious the leaders had lost all control. In whose hands was the plan then? Reports said: the *chakka jam* (blockade of vehicles) in the morning didn't show any indication of the later aggression. It was only after the police baton-charged the road gathering that things changed from demonstration to battle. What plan would pull off an act where people from the ghettoes indulge in large-scale rampage, arson, street-fights, but don't kill anyone, attack shops or houses? Where pedestrians walk through the chaos to safe zones, no one hurt?

Some secret thread ran between them, one can surmise that much. But it is difficult to believe the thread was meant to be visible to someone, that some individual or organisation was running the show according to a plan. If the outburst was real, one cannot explain how it controlled itself. The spark that should have blown into a wild fire was gone the next morning. One has seen many conspiracies of disorder, but rarely an eruption dousing itself. If we do not set the incident in the sequence of 2007, it will look even more senseless; but how can the sequence accommodate this aberration?

Taslima Nasrin was the reason? That's what it would seem to be if we are to explain action by consequence. Taslima did leave the state immediately after this. But the cracks of this reasoning are clear. First, the crowd raised slogans on Nandigram and Rizwanur as well. Second, the complaint against Taslima was an old one; it had earlier never given rise to protests even remotely similar. Therefore, even if we read the incident as a sequel to the attack on Taslima in Hyderabad on 9 August, things do not fall into place. Even the *ABP* edito-rial on 23 November cautioned against reducing the incident to the Taslima issue, pointing to the groundswell of a sense of deprivation among Muslims. The problem is in mixing unac-ceptable terms with the ones already familiar from civil society protests – Taslima Nasrin with Nandigram and Rizwanur. A possible explanation is of course that fundamentalists were using the last two terms to hide the real one: Taslima. But for the people who want to convey something from the street, the words, the symbolic machinery they have, are their only reality. A hidden slogan does not serve any purpose.

The other line of reasoning – 'people do not say what they seem to say, the real story is told by ideology or economics' – forecloses the possibility of anything 'happening'. All that takes place becomes the outcome of something else. The challenge of 21 November lies in its visible body: the term 'Taslima' took its place alongside Nandigram and Rizwanur, not behind them. The problem is of lying alongside; it is about the simultaneous affinity and disjuncture between 21 November and the sequence of civil society protests.

The Muslim question should not be incomprehensible at a basic level. That Singur and Nandigram had a large population of Muslim peasantry came up occasionally in the discourse of protest. Not too often though, for there was apprehension about distracting the united visage of the movement. From the chief minister's damaging remarks about madrasas to the Sachar Committee's shameful revelations about Muslims in Bengal, moments of strong disaffection had preceded 2007. The new sense of alienation among the community was reflected in the 2009 elections. In the wake of Singur, Muslim grievance shared largely the same space with mainstream protests. The Rizwanur protests began with a rare outburst from the community living in the Tilaja, Darga Road area, but soon changed its form. On 22 September 2007, rumour arrived in the area about Rizwanur's corpse going missing from the morgue of the Nilratan Sircar hospital. About 1,500 people came out in the streets, laying siege to the area around Park Circus; a police car was set on fire. The RAF was called in in the afternoon. A civil protest of consensus took over immediately afterwards, characterised by candlelight vigil, etc. That was the first instance of a quick assimilation of a straying current.

Street Play

We don't know about the inner workings of 21 November. Investigations could help us in that direction, although it is hard to overlook the paradox of a situation where being inside means holding information back. We are concerned here with a slightly different question though. The reason for viewing 21 November as a blind point in the 2007 sequence lies not in its origins, of which we know almost nothing, but in its elastic and furious body, its indeterminate goals. To ask the question again – how could that anger stage itself before all eyes and fold up so deftly? How did its traces all disappear without giving rise to a sequel? How was it forgotten so fast? Something falls short in all this, which must be its content in excess. It will be hard for the socio-economic explanations offered for 2007 to make sense of this breach of economy.

The event differs from the moment of its beginning. What we call the body here unfolds in duration. We are concerned with appearances for the moment, not the inner workings. Saying something in public can be motivation enough to take to the streets, especially for those who are forced to remain outside the boundary of representation. Action on the street follows the aesthetics of spectacle, which has no contradiction with spontaneity. These actions perform themselves; they are necessarily traversed by their own images.

Partha Chatterjee has recently written about the increasing "tactical" use of violence in the Indian society. It helps articulate the disparate demands of what he calls the political society into a coherent form. The intention of this violence is not to punish anyone, but "to display in public space, in spectacular fashion, the anger and moral outrage of 'the people'. Violence here serves the rhetorical function of converting populations into people".[2] This variety of populist politics is the means for the majority to enter the domain of democracy. Politics and government policy constitute each other through such moves, and, at the same time, more and more people come within the purview of governmentality. The events of 21 November seem to fall within this logic of the spectacle to a large extent. But there is an anomaly. There was hardly any articulate demand; a confusion of demands was created instead. Why would a population wanting to be people stage an obscure festival, disappear without a repetition of the demands? It is hard to maintain a gaze on this from the two poles of motive and consequence. Was there something in that incident that points to an affinity between the civil and political societies behind the walls of separation? Wasn't such affinity a characteristic of 2007?

Ernesto Laclau's recent reflections on populism are close to Chatterjee's observations. To relegate populism to the margins of politics, he would say, amounts to disavowing politics itself, since most politics is done today in that form. For him, the unit of a community is 'demand', not the individual. He studies the articulation and coordination of demands, and the way they find a place in society. Populist politics is heavily dependent on excess of representation, on empty rhetoric. How that rhetoric and its empty signifiers work in the process of group formation is something that concerns him. The late Freudian work, *Group Psychology* (1921), inspires him to bring the question of libido to the scene of bonding. The structure of attraction and identification in the group resembles the libidinal dynamic.[3] The discipline of losing control that one saw on 21 November cannot be approached through the definite entities involved; the clue must lie somewhere in the relations. If we think of bonding on the street as having its own content we have to reflect on the inflation of rhetoric, paths of symbolic traffic. A space of circulation lies between the group that took to the streets to say something and the one that left the scene leaving their motives in the dark.

The newspapers talked about rumours. What were the new vehicles for rumour in 2007? Reports say the police jammed mobile phone networks. They knew those networks could do more damage than the weapons. During Nandigram, we saw front-page photographs of the proverbial Bengal peasant, clad in *lungi* and *gamchcha*, firing a country-made rifle with a wireless handset pressed to his ear. The Lalgarh People's Committee against Police Atrocities, entrenched in the poorest territory of West Bengal, has raised funds to purchase a large number of mobile sets for its members. The role of new technology in mass movements is seen as an addition mostly, but it is not only speed and tactics that change with networks, the content undergoes change. Peasant consciousness itself must be changing.

Neighbourhood of Images

If one is to take the spectacle into account, it would be difficult to overlook the ground that politics shares with aesthetics. Not only political expression, the very content of politics would need the help of aesthetics to make sense. Jacques Rancière is among the few thinkers of our times to maintain such a double gaze. He argues that politics is a re-distribution of what enters the domain of the senses, what we see and hear. A society maintains the positions assigned to its members by sustaining a system of representation, by deciding what can enter the frame of representation and what cannot. He calls the stable form of this the 'police'. Politics is not only a matter of instituting a new rule; more primarily, it is a struggle of re-drawing the boundaries of the sensible. Without that, politics cannot change the police.[4] I would like to make a few observations about neighbouring lives and representations that are inspired by Rancière's thought.

The historic rally of 14 November made a surprising revelation of numbers. It wasn't easy to grasp how many of us were waiting to come out on the street before that day. The events of 21 November made a second exposure. The circle of protest suddenly widened to take in a neighbourhood seeking to echo the outrage in its own language. It should prompt us to train our sights on the provisional objects of recognition around us.

It is hard to recognise the course of change brought about by 2007 from a neutral point of view. But the question of change in representation can be raised objectively, without immediate recourse to judgment. Is it possible to read the widening of the frame proposed by 21 November as a metaphor of larger processes under way? It is often said that the 32-year rule of the Left has been made possible through a stabilisation of cultural norms, and through the ruling party's success in establishing itself as the legitimate representative of those norms. The curious mixing of socialist and Bengali nationalist elements in the CPI (M) language is a good index of this process, from which an exceptional *bricolage* of political techniques has emerged. I would suggest that changes are visible in the representational reserve of the culture in question, a process that has direct political consequences. The work of politics is to seek entry to the domain of representation; but the real problem occurs when that domain itself undergoes change under the pressure. The new politics in West Bengal is underscored by such transformations at a deeper level.

Let us look at the convergence of politics with a kind of cultural production in Bengal that scholars never touch, the mainstream cinema of Tollygunge. At the height of the PDS (ration-shop) protests, on 2 November 2007, *ABP* reported an incident from Coochbehar. The Mithun Chakrabarty-starrer, *Minister Fatakesto*, was enjoying a great box-office success in the Tufanganj area. In the film, Mithun forces a corrupt kerosene dealer to pay large fines to the people he cheats. The local villagers were reported to have put that lesson into practice against the ration-shop dealers in the area. The interesting piece of information was how this act of 'inspiration' spread from village to village, from Maruganj to Bansraja, Shalbari, Mahishkuchi, Dholpol. A festival of people's taxation began. The film, directed by the iconic Swapan Saha, may not yield much in terms of inspiration finally, but it is important to note how it was being used. The *ABP* report says:

Sensing trouble, the ration dealers' body is saying people have to understand the difference between film and reality… The family members of the victimised ration dealers allege that *Minister Fatakesto* is responsible for the incitement. Birenbabu, the brother of Nirenbabu, a ration dealer of Shalbari, says, "*Minister Fatakesto* is an influence behind the ration movement." Mrinal Mian, the brother of Tasiruddin Mian, ration dealer of Bansraja, says, "The agitators are saying a Fatakesto beating will be meted out to those who do not listen to them." (Arindam Saha, ABP, 2 November 2007)

The film in its totality was not as important as what could be extracted from it. In *MLA Fatakesto* (2006) and its sequel, *Minister Fatakesto*, a slum goon appears in the role of a people's saviour, meting out rough justice to politicians, bureaucrats and the police. His mentor and patron is the chief minister who shows physical resemblance to the current chief minister of the state. The second film was made after Singur, and is therefore ambiguous about the hero and chief minister coalition. The problem of land acquisition, effects of industrialisation, etc. enter the plot. But the axis of populism, which is anti-party and anti-politician in both the films, and which serves as the source of vigilante justice, remains the same. That the second film has an implausible antagonism – the chief minister and slum hero versus the minister's party and administration – did not seem to bother its audience, not at least the agitators mentioned above. They use the film in a way that allows them to extract messages in the form of intensity and outrage; verbal definitions of characters and ideas become secondary to this axis of communication. The dialogue that made these films famous, "A fist flies here, your corpse flies to the crematorium", was heard with all the echoes that it didn't have.

Haranath Chakrabarty's *Tulkalam* (2007) participates more directly in the contemporary political controversy. We see peasants struggling to save their land in the face of industrial aggressors (whose Sino-Asian features are a reference to the South East Asians involved in the Nandigram chemical hub). We see a bunch of villains who are called the 'party', which signifies only one entity in the party-society of West Bengal.[5] The village in question looks much like Singur. Mithun Chakrabarty portrays an outsider who leads the rebellion. The interesting twist is his seeking of justice for the humiliation and murder of an old 'party leader' at the hands of the new bosses. In one scene, a comrade of the slain leader comes secretly to give his blessings to the rebel, whose struggle has made him believe Marx, 'Lelin' and Mao are still alive. The two raise their fists and chant, "*Inquilab Zindabad*" (Long live the struggle). We have a good example here of the cultural political reserve that has sustained the Left Front rule in the state. A certain content must be appropriated now by its Opposition through culture, a political content that has become a cultural-ethical reserve, and to which the ruling Left Front has lost claim. One should not be surprised by Trinamool Congress leader Mamata Banerjee's sustained appropriation of Leftist rhetoric and cultural platforms. That the Left has lost its access to this reserve is the flip side of the coin. Being in no position to use the film's positive reference to one of their own traditions, they tried to stop its screenings in some areas, further helping the film to become a major success.

The script and dialogue writer of these films, Salil Kumar Naskar (or NK Salil, as he calls himself, the name change erasing his caste signifier, but also indexing the new relationship Tollygunge has built with Telugu cinema), has become a star in the industry. Salil's dialogue is an important vector of direct address as politics. Most of it is the empty rhetoric of populism, and it is hard to locate its target. But a very large audience has come to receive the declamations according to a logic of the cult,[6] in discrete blocks both aligned to the plot and independent of it. The vigilante action with a diffused political address was reproduced through other Mithun Chakrabarty films like *Tiger* (Swapan Saha, 2007).

A rift had appeared between mainstream commercial Bengali cinema and the educated middle class in Bengal in the 1980s. Is a re-ordering of such locations under way? I think it is. The process has been on for some time, but its connection with politics is recent. A frequently asked question before the Lok Sabha elections was, "How could one accept Trinamool Congress as an alternative? The leadership of the Left is, after all, in the hands of the *bhadralok* (as Bengal calls its educated élite); Trinamool is a party of unruly trouble-mongers". A common answer from those who favour change was that the ruling Left today best represents violence, misrule and corruption. But a larger question begs our attention: does the *bhadra* circle exist in the same form any more?

Today's newspapers report a hospital foundation ceremony in Kolkata (8 January 2010) where Mamata Banerjee was seen singing "We shall overcome". It all started in Nandigram when she made a public claim to the inheritance of the Tebhaga struggle, the 1946 armed peasant uprising to force a reduction in landlord appropriations of farm produce. On 21 July 2009, her gigantic rally in the heart of the city was accompanied by Salil Chowdhury songs composed for the leftwing Indian People's Theatre Association (IPTA); seated on stage was the mother of the 1966 hunger march martyr, Nurul Islam. This is visible political appropriation of a representational reserve. The other direction of change, coming from the other end, is much more amorphous and perhaps much more important. The urban middle-class *bhadralok* taste is losing its hegemony. And more, that class itself as a custodian of a certain culture is undergoing dissolution. I can only make a few stray remarks on the process here.

It is possible to make an obtuse connection between the loosening of frames of representation and the actual screens that have played a major role in the process. Let us think of the screen that stands at the centre, that of television. A quick path to the dissolution of its identity has been proposed by the *bhadralok* class itself, in the way that it has cut itself off from the Bengali language. The privileged citizens who have grown up over the last two decades in West Bengal have, by and large, stopped reading or writing in Bengali. In one television programme after another, the young anchors and guests are found speaking a Bengali that moves very close to the *patois* of the so-called uneducated classes. NK Salil's dialogue does not stand far from it. This would be television as evidence. It is possible to argue, nevertheless, that television is primarily an evidence of a pure unveiling of realities, and the proximity of lives that it itself helps bring about. It is a revelation to watch the song, dance and comic performance shows where contestants come in equal numbers from the city and outside, sometimes the balance tipping in favour of small towns. The urban culture of taste can hold on to its cultural function when the outer limits of its territory are known. Television, in order to expand its penetration of territories, has blurred these limits. Also, it is no longer possible for television to perpetuate a situation where a large section of its clients are viewers without being participants – a non-profitable proposition in the age of interactive media. A large section of the distant addressee is entering the screen in critical numbers. The Hindi performance items, no longer considered culturally backward in an age of the global ascendancy of Bollywood and at a time of retreat of the vernacular, are learnt and presented in great competitive earnest by both the urban and non-urban contestants. The physical acts they indulge in, in full presence of family members, were hardly imaginable even a few years back in Bengali public contexts. Not only the ceding of verbal ground, but an attendant physical idiom, flying in the face of *bhadralok* taste, is receiving a 'performa- tive' sanction from the family on screen. The comedy shows present a daily routine of a kind of laughter that belongs distinctively to the low humour of the street and fairground, even folk theatre. Television proves that fundamental components of cultural distinction like humour and music do not have a secure basis any more. As it removes the veil, the narrow and tenuous boundaries of a certain culture stand exposed. The ones supposed to remain outside have made a habit of trespassing. The same screen is assigned to all.

As long as the division between the bourgeois dramas of 'relationships' and the rustic romance of Tollygunge could be maintained things were a little simpler. Other, older divi- sions like that between the maudlin *jatra* and 'group theatre' could also sustain themselves. Mamata Banerjee, the queen of melodrama, could well be imagined occupying a *jatra*-like stage of politics, something that many believe she does. The trouble is, the Tollygunge tawdry is moving close to the middle-class Bengali film by an easy assimilation of extremely conventional signs of urbanity from middle-class cinema. And it has begun assimilating the social critical content of minority theatre and literature. The biggest commercial success of 2008, *Chiradini tumi je amar* (You are Mine for Ever, Raj Chakrabarty), was directed by a young TV show director and had a clear allusion to the Rizwanur incident. The obverse of this are the daily soaps on TV, made to expand the urban domestic entertainment base. The preponderance of extended family, feminine devotion, rituals, even shamans and gurus, shows the disappearance of the avowed distinction of educated middle-class culture. Urban families are no less avid consumers of this material. The discovery of the real expanse of a cultural preserve showed it to be in an advanced state of dissolution.

The *bhadralok* subject in question hardly has any scope for lament if it has decided to abandon its vernacular. It could be worthwhile to look for the shifts in communication, pedagogy and artistic production. Art, for example, might show unfamiliar and interesting developments. Over the last decade or so, the autumn festival of *Durgapuja* has taken on a new form, one in which academic fine arts, folk craft traditions, old *bazaar* art practices and new media elements have combined to create a highly competent public art. Loosening and mixing of practices and preferences, even their decline, might cause unexpected develop- ments. One should not be surprised if the *fyatarus,* the abusive, anarchic angels of Kolkata created by one of the most innovative contemporary Bengali fiction writers, Nabarun Bhattacharya, appear in a Tollygunge film a little more daring than *Tulkalam* some years from now. And if it becomes a major hit in Tufanganj. The lyrics of Bangla music band songs, a contemporary development in the vernacular, and newspaper features have come to a share an irreverent college canteen idiom that owes its origins partly to the decline in formal skills in the language. It is not a *bhadralok* idiom formally, but it is entirely urban. The kind of quasi-English Bengali films that Anjan Dutt makes for urban youth circuits owes a similar debt to the decline of the Bengali language. Authors like Nabarun Bhattacharya or Gautam Sengupta, on the other hand, write for a serious minority readership and use a hybrid street language to break free of fictional as well as moral conventions.

The territory of the image is giving in to unfamiliar people seeking entry. Those who find it wholly unacceptable are likely to turn away from all politics. But signs are clear that the minority culture of distinction has opened its doors to other semiotic neighbourhoods, and has even become dependent on the invasions for survival. We may not like it, but this might serve as an unexpected ground for political change. The crowd of 21 November has not yet crossed the neighbourhood borders to walk into the meaning of 2007, even though they owe their strength to the 2007 sequence. But there were signals that they wanted to enter the mainstream domain of secular protests. To see them as hooligans on a rampage and to find their action incomprehensible are part of the same representational blockage. A challenge before those seeking change is an intervention in the traffic across territories already under way.

Author's Note

An earlier Bengali version of the essay was published in Baromas, 2009. The essay came out of a discussion on Facebook with four young friends, Anustup Basu, Prasanta Chakravarty, Rajarshi Dasgupta and Bodhisattwa Kar. I am also indebted to discussions with Sibaji Bandyopadhyay, Anjan Ghosh and Dwaipayan Bhattacharyya. They bear no responsibility for the opinions expressed.

Notes

1. *"Change is needed"* ("**Paribartan chai***"*) is the slogan around which the broad coalition of opposition to Left Front rule in West Bengal is presently mobilised.
2. Partha Chatterjee. *"Classes, Capital and Indian Democracy"*. In **Economic and Political Weekly** *(EPW)*, 15 November 2008. The essay is a response to a discussion on his *"Democracy and Economic Transformation in India"*, **EPW**, 19 April 2008.
3. Ernesto Laclau. **On Populist Reason** *(Verso, 2005, London)*.
4. Jacques Rancière. **The Politics of Aesthetics, The Distribution of the Sensible**, *(trans. with an Introduction by) Gabriel Rockhill (Continuum, 2006, London/New York)*.
5. I borrow the term from Dwaipayan Bhattacharyya; see his *"Of Control and Factions: The Changing 'Party-Society' in Rural West Bengal"*, **EPW**, 28 February 2009.
6. See Umberto Eco, *"Casablanca: Cult Movies and Intertextual Collage"*, in **Travels in Hyperreality: Essays** *(Pan Books, 1987, London)*.

DISQUIET

The Apparel of Anxiety
Three Artefacts of Fear and Fashion

. AARTI SETHI

Artefact 1: In the March of 1933, a curious report appeared in *The Hindustan Times*. It read:

> *A Sartorial Ordinance[1]*
> *For the purpose of preventing movements of, and communication with, absconders and terrorists, the Governor in Council has inserted a rule in the Bengal Suppression of Terrorist Outrages Act, whereby no person will be allowed to wear the garb of any community or sex other than his own, unless he habitually does so in the normal course of his profession or occupation. Any person contravening the rule is punishable by imprisonment extending to 6 months, or fine, or both.*

Another report the following day provides some ancillary context to the decision.

> Dynamite in Girl's House[2]
> *Seventy sticks of dynamite were discovered in a young Bengali girl's house this morning by the Calcutta Police. After her arrest the girl, it is alleged, confessed to a conspiracy among the revolutionaries to damage local Government buildings and European houses.*

The report continues:

> *The girl, though Bengali by birth, came from up-country and, it is alleged, had been disguising herself as a Punjabi woman with a view to avoiding police detection.*

The decision did not go uncommented upon. An editorial appeared two days later which challenged the validity of the order, reasonably arguing that given the diversity of dress and attire in a country such as India, it was ridiculous to prosecute individuals solely on their fashion sense. It noted that,

> *India is a land of infinite variety of costumes and not merely no two communities but no two individuals always dress alike. That any one should be condemned to six months imprisonment for sporting a fez, a coat of a particular cut or a pagree tied at a particular angle is a serious invasion of the personal rights and liberties of an individual.*

Artefact 2: In *The Battle of Algiers*, Gilles Pontecorvo's film on the Algerian struggle for independence, there occurs a startling sequence of self-transformation. Three Algerian women, FLN[3] activists, stand before mirrors in a small room, somewhere in the *qasba*. In a rapidly edited sequence, where the camera draws attention to the harshness of the actions, they cut their hair, dye it blonde, divest themselves of their *abayas*, wear make-up and tailored suits, don pretty clothes. They pass through the barricades, are politely received by the guards on duty, who exchange a casual greeting even as they jostle *abaya*-clad women, mirrors of the selves the women have temporarily left behind only moments ago. Clutching handbags, they merge into the dense urban crowd. Some minutes later, bomb explosions tear through the city.

Artefact 3: In July 2004, 12 middle-aged women demonstrated naked outside the headquarters of the 17 Assam Rifles regiment at Kangla Fort in Imphal, capital of the Northeast Indian state of Manipur. Paramilitaries from the regiment had picked up, brutally raped and murdered a young woman, Thangiam Manorama. As the protestors exhorted Manorama's killers to appear in person, police personnel were despatched to deal with the situation. But what were they to do? So unused were they to the force of a body stripped voluntarily of clothing in full public view, shaming them rather than cringing in shame, that they were forced to withdraw.

Separated as these accounts are by vast swathes of time and distance, they share a vision of the self, one that relies on the outer casing as being somehow reflective of the inner 'core' of a person, such that to transform the outer is to simultaneously morph the inner. The outer must thus be strictly policed. The fears on display, from the very real threat of bombs faced in the first instance by a repressive colonial regime, to the sequence in *The Battle of Algiers*, wherein the cutting of hair and the discarding of veils signify the surrender of a self in the service of another, this fearful fashioning of the self that accompanies the assumption and divestment of clothing is, in a sense, an expression of an intuitive understanding regarding the expressive possibilities of clothing, or its lack.

Theoretically speaking, we could say there is no such thing as a fully clothed body, or a completely naked one. If by 'naked' we mean 'devoid of embellishment, concealment, disguise or addition', then, paradoxically, it is clothing that seems to perform this function. By wearing garb that one "habitually does… in the normal course of one's profession or oc-cupation", one is proclaiming who one is unambiguously, transparently. If becoming 'French', 'Bengali', 'Punjabi', 'Homosexual' were simply a matter of divesting oneself of one garb for another, how then would it be possible to state anything with any clarity?

And yet selves, like clothes, can be shed. The news report above, betrays another sense altogether of the relationship between appearance, performance, fear and the body.

For it is not that an individual reflects what or who she is by her clothes declaring what or who she is socially defined as, but rather that by wearing a *salwar-kameez* instead of a sari, or a "fez instead of a *pagree*", she renders herself temporarily invisible, camouflaged. Unlike small animals that play at being specimens of their more dangerous sibling species in order to deflect prospective predators, she seems to do the opposite – she feigns an innocence, and hides her sting.

The generalisation of dread makes suspects of everyone, certainly. But it also accom-plishes something else – it radically alters the terms on which power can engage with the mere appearance of being. Power fears the twin axis of radical ambiguity and radical clarity. Power is most comfortable when the terms of dissimulation and transparency are defined by itself. The asking of the question, 'Who is the stranger next to you?' is also to simultaneously acknowledge the answer, 'It could be, it might be, it possibly is – me.' The distance between that which is deemed the 'source' of fear/terror/anxiety – the 'terrorist', the 'stranger', the 'absconder' – and the target is finally only a few centimetres of cloth. For if part of Brihan-nala's fear is that she will be exposed as Arjun, then certainly Arjun too is afraid of what being Brihannala might reveal in himself.[4]

But what of the body? Often the nakedness of the body seems to reveal a truth unbearable in its iteration. The naked body can only ever be itself. But what is this self? It is not possible to say very much about it. This is possibly why forensics is such an inexact science. Being naked is to walk with an impenetrable cloak. Today, even to be naked is to obey an inner sartorial ordinance, the dictates of the fashion of fear.

Notes

1. The Hindustan Times, *17 March 1933.*
2. The Hindustan Times, *16 March 1933.*
3. **FLN**: *Front de Libération Nationale. Formed in 1954, the guerrilla group launched the Algerian War of Independence against the French and became the struggle's central political force. Algeria won its independence on 5 July 1962.*
4. *Arjun, the Pandava prince, one of the main protagonists of the Mahabharata epic, is said to have spent the penultimate year of his exile (along with his brothers and their common wife) in disguise as a dancing girl in the court of King Virata. Each of the five Pandava brothers chose a guise that is supposed to have reflected their innermost desires. Yudhishtira, the eldest prince and moral authority, chose to be a gambler; Bhima, the strong-man, chose to be a cook; and Arjuna, the fierce warrior, chose to be a woman, and a dancer.*

Feared Body

AGAT SHARMA

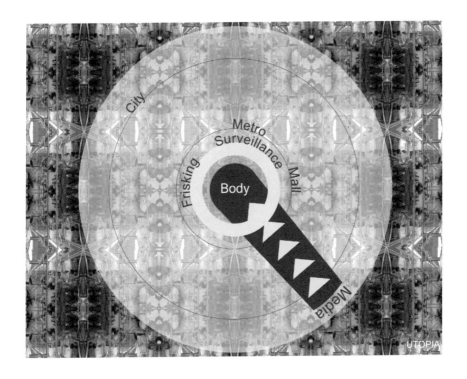

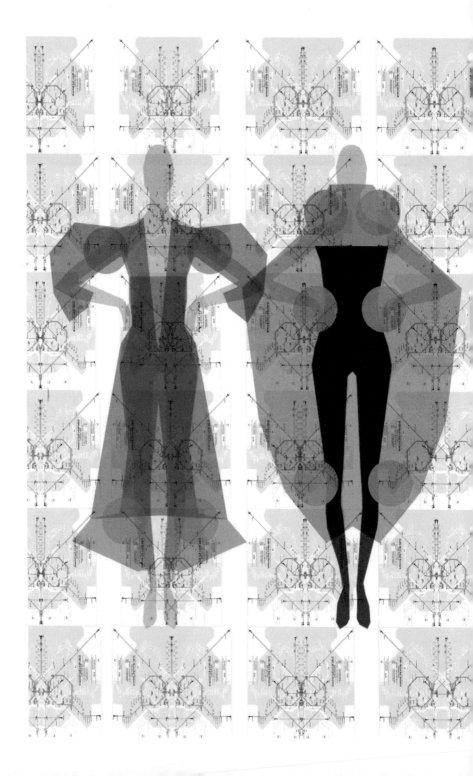

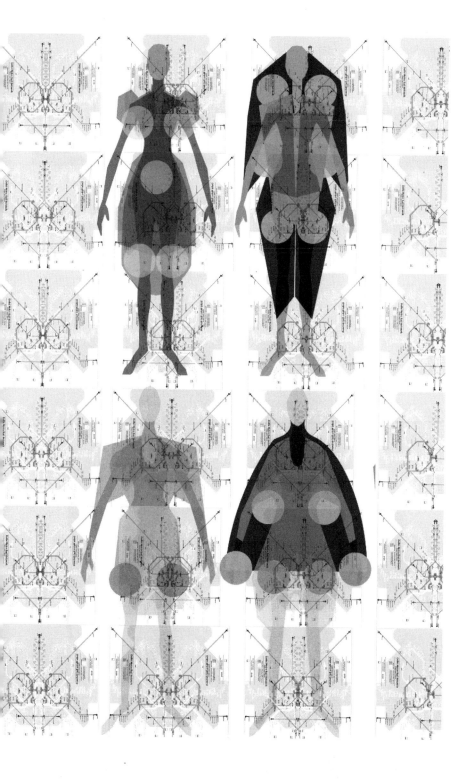

The Ninth and Final Ode to Life

NUPUR JAIN

For all their search
they cannot see
the image in the mirror.

It blazes in the circles
between the eyebrows.
Who knows this
has the Lord.[1]

Directions. The script was there: Infantry Road, right *maadi* →left No ↔No way, it's a one way. Look to the left and look to the right. Please beware of unhatched chickens crossing the road. Incubator down this road. March on, march on. GET OUT! Go in.

Safe... for the time being.

On the first day of Bangalore, my true friend said to me, "A cat has nine lives".

I need glasses, I thought to myself. Need some Crocin as well. I walked down to Shiva Medical Store and bought a gift from Archie's Gallery for a friend's birthday. Then I had a cappuccino at Café Coffee Day. I wiped my sweaty hands on my blue jeans and red top, plugged my ears with an iPod shuffle and flailed for an auto to take me to my hotel room.

I packed my bags and paid Rs. 700 for a cab to the Bangalore Airport. I glided up the security check and glanced up at the blinking monitors. My flight was not listed. Frowning, I took a takeaway cappuccino from Café Coffee Day and sat down in front of a monitor. There were a few others around me doing the same thing. We all worked on our wireless laptops and hurried into the moonless night when she asked us to board our flight.

Touchdown in Delhi. A long queue coiled around the pre-paid taxi booth. A longer one was waiting at the taxi boarding points. *The Little Prince* (1943) fell out of my bag. Just then, a taxi arrived. Taxis and autos are as important as *The Little Prince*. They take you from one place to another in the dark.

As I was peering out of the cab, trying to find my way, I wished I could meet the geographer on the sixth planet who would tell me about locations. But if he "couldn't tell" him, why would he tell me? Especially when things are ephemeral.

> *"But what does that mean, 'ephemeral'?" repeated the little prince, who never in his life had let go of a question once he had asked it.*
> *"It means, that which is in danger of speedy disappearance."*
> *"Is my flower in danger of speedy disappearance?"*
> *"Certainly it is."*
> *"My flower is ephemeral," the little prince said to himself, "and she has only four thorns to defend herself against the world. And I have left her on my planet, all alone!"*
> *That was his first moment of regret .³*

*

I put my ticket as a bookmark on the page, waiting at Bikaner House for the bus to come. I looked at the time. It was 12.30 p.m. Time flies. Sometimes you don't remember the date either, until you see it printed on your ticket to Jaipur. "It'll come", said the man next to me.

"What, the bus?" I asked, eating Bingo Mad Angles. I didn't even offer him one.

"No, the film", he said, pointing to the foldable TV screen in the deluxe A/C bus.

"Listen to me", said my mother, hugging me tight as I walked through the door. Aha! Am home, I thought to myself. I followed her into the kitchen, looking at the family pictures in the new photo frames. My Very Educated Mother just show us Nine Planets, I said, dumping my bags on the floor. "Let's go out", she said. "I can't go out, it's too dark in Jaipur". She sighed and lit her lamp in her temple. "Dear Gods, help her for she knows not what she did", she whispered to them.

I flung down my banana peel, laughing at that one. What Katie did, what Katie didn't.[4] Yuk-yuking, I stepped on it. And, well, not all of us fall down. But I slipped.

I was taken to a doctor to see what I could have damaged. Head, heart, lungs, liver, teeth, eyes, shoulder, ankle. He gave me one medicine for everything. "Just work. Forget about everything".

But I could not work. Diagnosis after diagnosis revealed nothing. So I stayed a bit longer in Jaipur. I would come back home before dark. Sometimes I could not go out at all. When I did, I noticed these new shops around our house in Shalimar Bagh. Shiv Furniture, Shiv Glass House, Shiv Band. And whenever I took an autorickshaw, the autowallahs would ask if I wanted to go to Shalimar Cinema, an old cinema hall now made into a mall called Sangam Towers at Church Road. Shalimar Bagh is beyond Sodala, new houses and temples and buildings are being built till Ajmer Pulia. Even beyond that, I think.

Where is Sitapura?

I was trying to find an encyclopedia on Jaipur. I wanted to know about the Origin of the City. Google it. I also stumbled onto the Origins of Myth and Religion. Mere coincidence. A la *The Matrix*? The architect is at work. But there are flaws in the system.

I needed to buy more medicine. I called up Shiv Medical and General, my aunt's regular medicine shop. My phone is ringing. Zooming into the night towards Sitapura, I saw Shivam Medical and General store. I bought some honey drops from the man at the counter. "Why did you call your store Shivam?" I asked him. "My younger brother died in 2005. These names are taken from the *pitras*".[5] I nodded my head and thanked him.

"MOM, WHAT ARE *PITRAS*?" I yelled as I swung in. "*Pitras* are ancestors", she said while she was cooking.

"Like Godzilla born in 1954 is to *Godzilla* in 1998?" I asked. She nodded as we watched the film. "Why is there so much violence in these films?" she asked me. "I don't know these things, please don't ask me". Forgive me Lord, for I have sinned.

In *Civilisation and Its Discontents* (1929), Freud talks about the development of civilisation and curbing instincts. Anger is an instinct. It tears at your insides as you break free from containers that block you in. Will I be free if I flow like liquid modernity?

Thousands of people were rendered homeless when the Indian Oil Corporation tanks burst open at Sitapura while we were watching a marriage party go past the Shri Shani, Shri Shiv, Shri Hanuman, Shri Ram Temple on Ajmer Road. It was a *sava* day. "*Savas* are auspicious days when people get married", my Mom said when I swung in again. An overall loss of Rs. 300 crore was reported in the fire. Shiv Dresses at Khatipura was bereft of customers.[6] A restaurant at Sitapura gave away marriage dinner meals for free.[7] Don't look at me when I eat more than two *rotis*. Pass the rice. Dessert. *Paan.* Ice-cream? Coffee? Wine and Cheese? Please flush out your toxins. Am trying. Will *ancien régimes* help me? "Hey Ram", I sighed.

Why do they use Shiva's name in buildings and temples in Jaipur? Nokia Tadkeshwar Mobile Shop, Shiva Shakti Juice and Ice-Cream Parlour, Shri Mast Mahadev, Shri Tadkeshwar Mahadev Mandir. Amriteshwar, Gyaneshwar, Maheshwar?

"Everyone wants happiness, fulfillment. And not even happiness so much as fulfillment. Fulfillment happens with three things. First, the destruction of evils, Shiva is the destroyer of evils. Then, his *Shivatva*,[8] his *kalyankari* aspect that is, manifest for the welfare of beings. And, finally, there is absolute happiness. A sense of fulfillment. This sense of fulfillment is in no one else but Shiva. Consumption is the beginning and the end of all activities. All of us are running around for this happiness in our goals, aspirations, desires, dreams. But the Gita is very important. You should concentrate on the Gita and do a comparative study with Krishna for your paper".[9]

Focus, right? I stepped out in bliss. I had my answers. Ring-a Ring-a Roses. "MOM! Where are my books?" I screamed. And we all fall down. "Please God, nothing should happen after this", I whimpered.

In *Family Matters* (2002), Nariman's father regrets filling his head with modern ideas. And how "he never learned to preserve the fine balance between tradition and modernness".[10]

New epistemology can have strong influences. Sometimes it can be violent. I picked up a biography on Gandhi from the bookshelf. Louis Fischer writes how Gandhi had a friend, Sheikh Mehtab, who was bigger and stronger than him. Being, frail, Gandhi could not run and jump like him. "He regarded himself as a coward. 'I used to be haunted,' he asserts, 'by the fear of thieves, ghosts and serpents. I did not dare to stir out of doors at night.' He could not sleep without a light in his room..."[11] But he dealt with his fears.

I went out to deal with mine. We visited the old city when it was lit at night, Padam and I. Jharkhand Mahadev at Vaishali and Shri Tarkeshwar Ji at Chaura Rastaa are the oldest temples here. Shri Tarkeshwar Ji temple was built in 1784 A.D., according to the *Shilpa Shastra*, a late mediaeval Hindu text on iconography and architecture, around the same time as Maharaja Jai Singh II built Jaipur. There are various other temples in the middle of the concrete road at Chaura Rastaa. The concrete was laid around these temples to accommodate the old within the new.

I also met a *drg ramatta*[12] during a visit to Jawahar Kala Kendra, the art centre Charles Correa designed in 1986. The *drg ramatta* has travelled. He told me that a river dries up, but then it flows again.

"Do you perceive differently with the change in the city?" I asked him. "No", he replied. "I perceive both tradition and continuity. I believe in both Makar Sankranti and in the *sanatan dharm*".[13]

But I insisted. I just wanted to know if there was a plan to the naming of certain temples in certain locations. "It's nothing. New colonies come up. New temples get built. People can pray in their houses also. But it's *shraddha*. So you build a temple. Every *budh* [Wednesday], we visit the Hanuman temple. Then we go to work", said Kailash Munso.[14]

In Hinduism, one can question. A dialogue happens. But then there are questions of faith and practice. You cannot put posters on paintings of Hindu deities in public places. Or you can if you wish to. Just that no one does. The writ and the image fade into faint remembrance with reassembling, but the image remains fixed in habits of the past. Amnesia happens with epistemic violence. Since unbounded consumption can exhaust the sensation gatherer,[15] disbelief and faint remembrance have to be anchored to the spaces provided with the discontentment with globalisation.

A cat has nine lives. So do human beings.

Notes

1. AK Ramanujan. **Speaking of Siva** *(Penguin Books, 1973, New Delhi)*.
2. **'Maadi'** *means 'take' in Kannada.*
3. Antoine de Saint Exupéry [1943]. **The Little Prince** *(Pan Books, 1974, Great Britain), p. 54.*
4. **What Katy Did**, *by American children's writer Sarah Coolidge, was published in 1872.*
5. *Interview with Dinesh Sharma, 22 October 2009, 8.30 p.m.*
6. *Interview with Vishal Baristo, 31 October 2009, 6.30 p.m.*
7. *http://www.patrika.com/fire-in-jaipur/index.htm (accessed 20 November 2009).*
8. *I understood this to mean 'that which is essentially him'.* **Kalyankari** *means one who does good.*
9. *Interview with Vishwanath Jalan, scholar and writer, 6 November 2009, 1.30 p.m.*
10. *Rohinton Mistry.* **Family Matters** *(Alfred A. Knopf, 2002, New York), p. 15.*
11. *Louis Fischer.* **The Life of Mahatma Gandhi** *(Grafton Books, 1982, London), p. 31.*
12. **Drg** *means 'one who perceives' in Sanskrit. A* **ramatta** *is a seer. 'Drg Ramatta' is a collaboration between Himanshu Vyas and Amit Kalla on photography=poetry=painting. Interview with Himanshu Vyas, photojournalist, poet, artist, on 18 November 2009, 2.00 p.m.*
13. *Makar Sankranti is an annual kite-flying festival in Rajasthan in January. The day is considered auspicious in the Indian calendar. The festival is closely linked to blue pottery making in Rajasthan. It is said that during the reign of Maharaja Ram Singh II, two potter boys, Kalu and Churaman from Achnera near Agra, came and beat the royal kite flyers. They had put powdered glass on their kite strings. They were immediately invited to Jaipur to teach the local craftsmen their craft. In modern times, the dying craft was revived by Maharani Gayatri Devi. Dharmendar Kanwar.* **Jaipur: 10 Easy Walks** *(Rupa & Co., 2004, New Delhi), pp. 45-46.* **Sanatan dharm** *is a Sanskrit term meaning 'eternal law'.*
14. *Interview with Kailash Munso, owner, JKJ Jewellers, 18 October 2009, 11.30 a.m.*
15. *Zygmunt Bauman.* **Life in Fragments: Essays in Postmodern Morality** *(Blackwell Publishers, 1995, London), p. 112.*

Nine Pages around Disquiet

PRIYA SEN

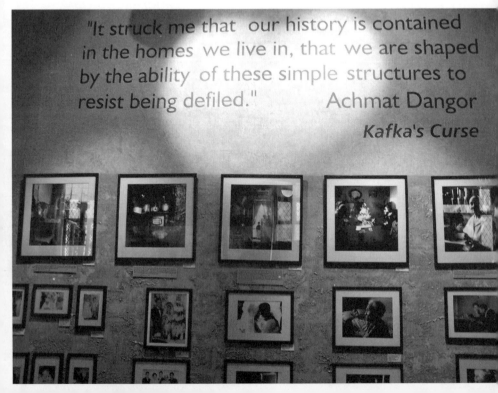

"It struck me that our history is contained in the homes we live in, that we are shaped by the ability of these simple structures to resist being defiled."   Achmat Dangor

Kafka's Curse

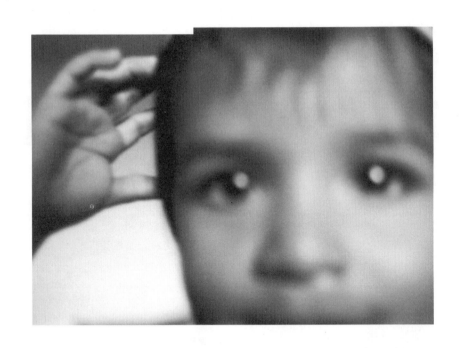

Page 1
District 6 Museum, Cape Town.

[It seems like what they did here was monumentalise the passing of things.]

Page 2
Imagine. High-speed concrete jets through parts of homes at night and creates concrete moulds in the morning...

Page 3
Half-bridge on state land.

Page 4
Carritt Moran and Company Pvt. Ltd.
9 RN Mukherjee Road, Kolkata 700001

Tea brokers since 1877, now considering liquidation.

Page 5
A congenital condition, Marfan syndrome also affects the eyes and vision. Retinal detachment because of the weakening of connective tissue and dislocation of the lens can happen in one or both eyes.

After N.'s surgery, shortly after his seventh birthday, in which his lenses were removed and replaced with internal contact lenses, he looked up at the sky one night and asked his mother what those tiny points of light were. Stars, she replied.

He said he had never seen them before.

Pages 6 and 7
"Where figures are involved, they, too, may be either extraneous to the picture, an integral part of it, or the main purpose of the photograph. If extraneous, they may be eliminated either by temporarily suspending the exposure, or by choosing a long exposure so that a passing figure will not affect the total image. If the figures are light and the obscured part dark, the exposure must be increased, otherwise 'ghosts' will appear. Where the figures are an integral part of the picture, and where they cannot be asked to keep still, a fast film, wide aperture, and judicious choice of time and lighting are indicated".
From: "Night Photography", in *An Encyclopedia of Photography: The Complete Photographer* Vol. 7 (National Educational Alliance, 1949, New York).

Page 8
Rilke wrote in his *Letters to a Young Poet*: "So, you must not be frightened, Herr Kappus, when a sorrow rises up before you greater than you could have ever seen before; when a restlessness like light and cloud shadows passes over your hands and over all your doing. You must think that something is happening upon you, that life has not forgotten you, that it holds you in its hands; it will not let you fall".

Page 9
Me Myself
Human Being
Mb: 9871265534

Radiosity
A SHORT PHILOSOPHICAL NOVEL

ROBERTO CAVALLINI

Fear, it is this gift that they would give us in the posthumous city; the possibility of being afraid for them: fear given in the word 'fear'; fear not felt.
Maurice Blanchot, *The Step Not Beyond*

In the middle of the room, there is a hole. Three persons are standing, talking anonymously and cautiously. Looking at the hole, in an hypnotic state of distress. Talking about the cavity that contains several different surfaces.

This is their secret, their improbable arrogance, their clandestine joy.

The hole is a curious deficiency of intellectual clarity: a woman on the right steps back and turns to the camera with ingenious apathy, slowly closing her eyes. An imperceptible noise breaks the silence, deferring whatever could have been deferred, including silence.

Here is the moment in the life of a woman in which everything seems connected to the impossibility of the infinite. A moment that becomes the dis-ruption one could name 'the present'. It is probably for this not-articulated, not-expressed, not-acknowledged and not-even-understood reason that P. is able to define the readability of his own erratic movement in relation to this constant dis-ruption. There is no time left but there is always something left: fear. And she knows that this sarcastic method of surviving is exhaustively dangerous. Exhausting the possibility of being afraid forever.

A gesture protects and looks after an advanced state of dissolution. A lapse of memory removed from temporal awareness reinstates the immediacy of the hole. At standstill. There is no political devaluation able to affirm immediacy over an encoded set of visual relations. P. goes back to the room, the other two persons are still there, always there. In the middle of the room there is a hole.

The becoming, eventually, of an inner state of stillness alters its axiomatic manifestation. There is a shift towards auto-complacency while the hole, reflecting, identifies itself as the demise of an ideal, its total and perverted creation of restoring an order: the radiosity of fear. The device is plugged in. And a broken monologue starts...

There is always an indefinite condition of acceptance that performs invariably and continuously without taking into consideration the place in which I happen to be.

I dreamt I could keep going without these walls, this city, your pragmatic decisions.

I could not.

This is when exhaustion accomplishes an exhausting gesture of denying not even the possible, but possibilisation as such. Gestures in dreams often retrace the possible unexpressed in reality: the seizure of that configuration remains unattainable, scattered. I exhaust nothing, I am exhausted by nothing, I am exhausting not even the possible, just the nothing within it.

So I have been trying to look somewhere, a place in which you don't speak, if there is silence, then I don't know, you need to learn also how to be silent. Could you?

"Exhausting any space whatsoever". Even in the middle of nowhere. Over there. Even fear. If it is neither passive, nor active, exhaustion is not even in-between the possibility of a being together: the passivity of action. Exhaustion can just be considered something that resides within the tangible appraisal of an essential solitude. No company. No friendship. No love. No fear. No sharing of exhaustion.

You spent some time looking over the window, expecting one word, no words, absolute peace notwithstanding. Waiting to listen to that particular noise, to see that particular movement that leaves you trembling and thinking.

The shape of an evident presence, in its many visible and invisible movements, can be measured and known if it is assumed that any interpretation of its absolute essence will remain impossible to accomplish. Exhaustion attracts nothing, it is attraction blown up into the void.

You said you were exhausted not by waiting, but by the impossibility of grasping and understanding the words written for you by him.

Are you still waiting for him?

...

It does matter then if you cannot read.

What occurs as exhaustion is a reversal of the Self from within; in this sense, the 'I' is not exhausted by something or someone. The 'I' is exhausted by nothing outside its Self. And it remains suspended over the void, within the Self.

You kept telling him that to be fearless is to avoid any exhaustion. To be afraid is the first step into exhaustion. You said, but you couldn't speak.

Exhausting fear, this being afraid, this state of emptiness in the form of a word: fear. And this exhaustion exists within a proposition that is invariable to the extent that it is something completely generated by the outside. Slowly dragged outside, seated, moving, not moving: staying, leaving, staying.

The traces I left in this place are a minimal activity with no name. As far as the place is concerned, then, the forest is everything. I asked if bearing no name was something dangerous and you said: "Present memories are gone probabilities". I already knew that. So I stopped asking.

Exhaustion is the opening and closure of an absence without access; it is a permanent process of burning down the limit of the visible towards its indifferent becoming. It is a combination of words without choice.

"How do you constantly cope with necessity", you said. "Which necessity", I said. With the fact that you cannot be completely self-sufficient, you always are in need of something. And it costs money. What about people? I will never make that mistake again.

Exhaustion and permutation without change: an image appears and then disappears without being noticed, but it is still there, it does not move. To already be exhausting the definition of exhaustion without even beginning to perceive it, without even a stuttered trace of a beginning. Inability to trace where exhaustion commences and ends.

Is there still something I need to tell you? I am writing to tell you that I am fine. I would like to whisper it softly, so you can hear the fear of my desire. No pain. Just keep listening to it.

Exhaustion does not have anything to do with renunciation. It is pure expenditure with no ends. Consuming within itself the chance of its end. A demand and, at the same time, the fulfillment of its negation. A suspension allows the activation of a substitution that would establish the informal setting of any operation within the realm of life. Pure life. Exhausted.

Let me come in. Let me go out.

Exhausting the same possibility of fear would be to erase any trace of its movement, with no movement, even beyond or *before* exhaustion. And I would bear witness to the silence without words and without voice. Drop by drop, sweating it all out.

Please take care of yourself.

Click.

Author's Note
This text loosely references Deleuze's essay "The Exhausted", in Gilles Deleuze, (trans.) Daniel W. Smith and Michael A. Greco, **Essays Critical and Clinical** *(Verso, 1998, London/New York), and Maurice Blanchot's fragmentary writings, mainly* **The Step Not Beyond** *(SUNY, 1992, Albany).*

Fear, Inequity and Time
A Sketch of How Art Answers the World's Questions

RAQS MEDIA COLLECTIVE

Recently, we were asked, in the course of an extended conversation, a three-legged question on how we responded to the calamities of our times as artists.[1] The question went something like this:

"How do you respond to:
(i) fear of the other and aggression towards others,
(ii) the inability of human beings to find the means to share the world's wealth and resources equitably,
(iii) the arrogance of the modern individuated self's preoccupation with the present, and its impatience with other modes of inhabiting time?"

After an initial spell of exasperation at the somewhat mammoth scale of the problems posed by the question, we began to be intrigued by what we thought were the relationships between the keywords of its three constituent parts:

Fear. Inequity. Time.
We found this triangulation suggestive.

Fear/Aggression towards others – linked to an inability to share wealth and resources – embedded in a subject-object separation that erodes the possibility of cohabiting a simultaneity of diverse spatial and temporal anchors and flows. What follows is the sketch of an answer to this three-legged monster.

Let's take this step-by-step.

We feel that a key component without which none of the arms of this triangular tangle can hinge on to each other is a notion of scarcity. The anxiety of scarcity, the notion that in order not to have less we must have more, seems to us to be central in any understanding we seek of the present world.

The anxiety of scarcity produces a mania of measurement. We are constantly beset by acts of measuring quantities of how much things are in order to know by how much we fall short. The opposite of scarcity is plenitude (not, we might emphasise, abundance, which is merely a measure of relatively 'less' scarcity).

The feeling of plenitude, of knowing that the quantum of a thing does not necessarily exhaust all available aspects of our experience of it, is an attempt to come to terms with the idea of the uncountable. We could say that a possibly valid way of looking at today's world is to render it in terms of the tussle between obsessive measurement and the random but radical realisation of plenitude. This is a combat between numbers and the uncountable.

The disposition of fear/aggression towards others is not unrelated to an inability to conceive of resources except in proprietorial terms. Crucially, this views our experience of resources in terms of finitude, in terms of thinking that we will 'run out of them'. It also privileges the present – the time left before 'we run out', 'while stocks last' – as the time of the utmost importance. The times of the past and the possibility of the future are both mortgaged and held hostage to the urgency of the unyielding present.

The siege of the self by notions of property and exclusive usage only makes sense in a model where any attempt to open out the custodianship and usage of a resource will inevitably end in a hostile bid to dispossess one's claim to that said resource.

If you do not fear that others can only relate to you by taking away what you think is yours, or what nourishes or delights you, then, it does not make sense to cultivate and maintain a posture of aggression towards them.

If you are not forever 'present tense', you can enjoy reminiscence, you can play at scanning the unknown horizon of the future.

All these attitudes – of letting ourselves be open to the uncountable, to plenitude, to others not solely as hostile competitors, to a variegated sense of time – require us to consider the quality, rather than the quantity, of an experience.

Perhaps this is where art and artists come in, as people attuned to qualities. Not necessarily making their evaluations solely in terms of what can be 'counted' in or around an experience, process or object. It makes little sense to talk of a piece of music in terms of the 'number' of notes it had. Rather, our evaluation has to take into account the relationships between the notes, including the silences (the 'non-notes') that lie scattered through the piece. A sense of that relationship cannot be computed, even though music is probably the most mathematical of the arts. It has to be expressed in a non-quantitative language.

What we are left with, if we accept these bald facts, is the possibility that artists might repeatedly venture into the territory of imagination in order to point to forgotten, or as yet un-conceived, ways of thinking non-quantitatively about issues such as scarcity and value, about essence and identity and about our experience of dispersal and duration, about space and time.

What has art got to do with this?

Simple.

Art enables us to ask questions about life afresh. Today, this possibility exists alongside the very real fear of an accelerated drift into genocidal wars and lethal acts of random violence. The renewed importance of asking fundamental questions about what life is or what it might offer is offset against the danger of life's extinction. That is why insisting on making art and making room for art is more than about affect, ideas and sensation alone, it is a way of guaranteeing a space for life.

And yet, in the end, artists are free not to be useful, this is a freedom that needs to be taken seriously. This freedom from utility makes it possible to enter realms of pure conjecture, or of looking at reality freed from the constraints of the real and the extant. By no means should this freedom be bargained away. We think that this freedom needs to be understood as a kind of uncountable plenitude.

In this freedom lies the constantly renewable possibility of positing different modes of relationships between selves and others, between the relative significance of different ways of sharing things, and different attitudes to space and time.

We need more than a mere measure of things as the building blocks of universal language. The vocabulary of measurement attempts to say way too much by means of way too little. We need more than just the sayable and the unsayable.

We need to ask: What are the signs of life? What kinds of visions can make us see signs of life? What remains to be brought out from our quagmires?

Not a bad set of challenges.

SCARED ON SCREEN

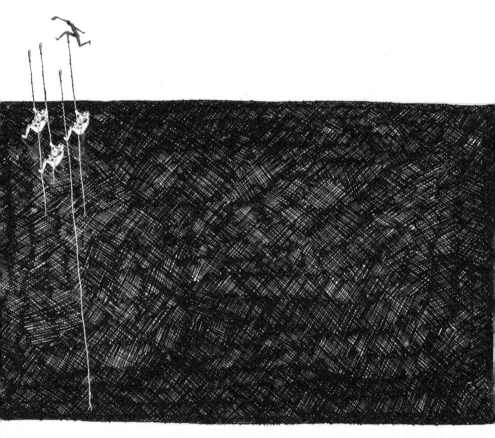

A Reply to Terrorism on a Wednesday
A Citizen Vigilante's Prescriptions for Governing Terrorism

RAHUL MUKHERJEE

In the film, *A Wednesday,* the protagonist calls the police commissioner of Mumbai to inform him that four terrorists need to be released, failing which he will set off bombs in different locations of the city. A whole set of negotiations and events follows at a staggeringly frantic pace with a climactic turnaround when the purported terrorist emerges as a "stupid common man". He makes it known that he intended to kill the released terrorists because the government and the bureaucracy had failed to "nip them in the bud". When asked about the reasons for his actions, the vigilante retorts, "They asked us this question on Friday, repeated it on Tuesday, I am just replying on Wednesday".[1] The "Friday" and "Tuesday" mentioned here point respectively to the 1993 blasts in Bombay, as the city was then known, and the 2006 train blasts in the hence renamed Mumbai, that occurred on those particular days. The reply on a "Wednesday", then, is a response to those incidents and the questions raised by those blasts.

A Wednesday premiered amidst serial bomb blasts in various cities across India. During this time, some other 'just released' films were also trying to understand the intimate connection between terrorism and urban environments.[2] Some of these films, including *A Wednesday*, attempt to comprehend terrorist activities of the past, and therefore hint at a tempered composure granted by distance from the events, and yet such distance is rendered elusive as their production and releases become crisscrossed and punctuated by further, experientially felt terror incidents.

Analysing *A Wednesday* involves grappling with three interrelated questions: a) How does a citizen in the form of a vigilante who has experienced the trauma of terror align her(him)self with regard to the nation/state as s/he responds/reacts to that terror? b) How are 'codes of terrorism' depicted in the fictive time of the thriller and how do they help differentiate the terrorist from citizen vigilantes (as depicted in other films), and parallel our experiencing of media-represented/simulated terrorism? c) Finally, in this temporary alignment and consequent cooptation of the vigilante by the state, what discourses of governmentality are put forward?

The distinct appearance of 'vigilante' subgenre films in Bollywood cinema happened during the 1970s, and it wasn't sheer coincidence that their rise took place alongside a growing dissatisfaction at the breakdown of the legal system, state corruption and recognition of the collapse of traditional lifestyles.[3] Such an eruption of vigilante justice films is not something particular to India. Claire King, while talking about the post-9/11 vigilante film, *The Brave One* (2007), mentions that prior films of the genre date back to *Dirty Harry* (1971) and *Taxi Driver* (1976), which came just when the United States was undergoing its post-Vietnam crisis.[4]

Susan Hayward in her essay "Framing National Cinemas" asks why a nation, which is perceived as a "social cultural community", becomes hyphenated/associated with the state, which is a legal and political concept. She answers: "[N]ationalist discourses around culture work to forge the link – the hyphen – between nation and state".[5] Hayward notes that in framings of national cinemas, "the artifact 'film' speaks of/for/as the nation".[6] Borrowing from the work of Patrick Hall, she then arrives at an argument about the nation both masquerading as a historical subject and at the same time hiding behind and/or concealing concrete practices of power and knowledge that the state carries out in the nation's name. When applied to vigilante films, vigilante justice appears/intervenes when the state itself is not able to provide justice, when the state is found to be incompetent in governing/protecting the nation. In such historically contingent situations, the citizen vigilante in the films comes to stand in for the nation, other-ing the state and venting anger at the state's inability to adequately exercise its practices.

Strategic negotiations between the vigilante and the state, as mentioned above, also occur in *A Wednesday* but with a few key differences. Such variations emerge because the vigilante by implementing the 'codes of terrorism' is able to have a slightly inflected relationship with respect to the city and the state. In citizen vigilante films, the city forms the backdrop to the vigilante/anti-hero in his/her avatar of an urban warrior.[7] The protagonist in *Zanjeer* (1971) finds himself in a haunted running scene on a low-lit road in Bombay's darkness. In *Deewar* (1975), two brothers have an epic confrontation over their mother (allegorically, their motherland) standing on an urban bridge. Paul Kersey (Charles Bronson in *Death Wish,* 1974*)* and Erica Bain (Jodie Foster in *The Brave One*) encounter crime on every street corner of New York. What such scenes have in common is an intimate engagement with the city as one physically negotiates its spaces. In *A Wednesday*, the cartography of violence in the urban landscape undergoes a certain kind of revision with the "stupid common man" as vigilante, sitting atop a building with a panoptical gaze of the city.

In the film, the vigilante makes his way to the top of an unused building where he assembles a cornucopia of communication devices: SIM cards, mobile phones, address diaries, a mini television set and a laptop. After setting up the equipment, he calls up not only the city police commissioner, but also television journalist Naina Roy. The audience is treated to the now all-too-familiar unfolding of a terror hijack, with the media always a player caught between the state on the one hand and the terrorist on the other. If terror indeed thrives on information, of which it must deprive the victim,[8] the deceptive "stupid common man" garners information through Naina Roy's news channel and dodges the police's attempts to track down his location by switching SIM cards and using re-routed mobile phones. He sees the city through television, he does not seek his enemies on the streets of the city. His ensuing telephonic duel with the commissioner begins to resemble Paul Virilio's conceptualisation of international warfare as an "optical confrontation" which involves "seeing", "foreseeing" and "not being able to see", and where "winning is trying to keep the enemy in constant sight".[9]

After an early round of negotiation, the citizen vigilante calmly regards the view from his rooftop, with a slow-panning camera showing the city moving around him (and not the other way around). The audience is then presented with a series of fast-paced, sharply edited shots of the commissioner pacing the police station, directing his officers over the phone as they frantically try to detect bombs in crowded malls and train stations. The camera finally takes us back to the vigilante, but not before it tilts up from the ground to show us the height of the building he is operating from. Thus, if crowded streets, traffic lights and shanty dwellings do rush past in the backdrop, they are not encountered by the citizen vigilante (as in other films) but by those pursuing him. Later, the vigilante confirms the released terrorists' identities through conversations with them by cellular phone, after which he annihilates them by just pressing a button.

Thus, the purported terrorist's strategic deployment of ICT-enabled gadgets helps the film in parcelling space and time in a novel way to show the citizen vigilante navigating the city's geography through aural and visual electronics. Additionally, it gives the impression that the Mumbai police lack the technological infrastructure to efficiently nab terrorists – they are unable to pinpoint the vigilante's exact location and have to seek the assistance of an amateur hacker, by which point a lot of time has elapsed. The audience is often reminded of the critical role played by 'time' in the thriller. Time is crucial for the vigilante – not only because he needs the police to procure the four terrorists he names and have them brought to the place of his choice before they locate him, but also because 'time' forms a part of his discursive arsenal against the "government's indecisiveness in handling terror", as he terms it. The inefficiency of the police is judged and measured by the time it takes them to finally ascertain the co-ordinates of the vigilante's location. After blowing away three purported terrorists, the vigilante remarks, addressing the police, "*It takes ten years for you to prove a person guilty. Don't you think this is a question mark on your ability? All this should stop. This whole bloody system is flawed. If you don't clean up this mess, then we will have to do something about it*".[10] (emphasis added)

The cited delay in convicting a person is part of a polemical speech asking for tougher laws to combat terrorism. In the past, terrorist organisations have opportunistically used this protracted time ("ten years") to free their imprisoned mates by hijacking Indian citizens.[11] For the film's domestic audience, witnessing the inability of the police to effectively react to a vigilante-constructed terrorist threat, it is not difficult to connect this inability as being symptomatic of the larger incapacity of the government ("bloody system") to deal with ("clean up") terrorists within a certain 'time window'. Thus, in the fictive time of the thriller, inundated with fast action-reaction events, a "politics of speed" (Aradau and Munster, 2006) characterised by decisive executive action seems to be privileged over a "slower, deliberative democratic model" to tackle the constructed risk of a perceived terror attack.[12]

The fictive time of the thriller does not allow the audience much time to reflect, and it stands in for a real time when the government, too, does not have time to reflect. The prescriptions given to the police (the state) by the vigilante (the citizen) for checking the menace of terrorism are presented as perfect common sense – after all, quickness and decisiveness are required to comprehend a film (especially a thriller) and a democracy (which comes to resemble a dromocracy[13]). However, it is precisely the identification of the audience with the vigilante's 'anger, trauma, everydayness and fear' that provides the affective foundation upon which rests the perfect rationality of continuously accelerated decision-making, trying to keep up with always-running-out time.

The vigilante is distinctly middle-aged; he pants after climbing stairs. Retribution delivered, he walks away carrying a grocery bag. He is neither a poster boy for the resurgent youth of 'India Shining' nor an activist affiliated with an NGO, but is someone who nestles himself into the middle of the Indian middle class. When he talks about his being afraid of "getting inside a bus or train these days", and of his wife thinking that "he is going to war while… [he is] actually going to work",[14] the audience has already related his condition with their own experientially felt everydayness of fear.

Although the vigilante maintains that his actions are not a result of sentimental loss, he refers to how images of his now dead co-passengers on the local train flash through his mind. His traumatic condition can best be described as "an unwitting reenactment of an event that one cannot simply leave behind".[15]

But we must not forget that the film is unfolding in circumstances that are also ideal for channelling personal ('place-based') traumas into collective ('national') trauma 'in pursuit of' (around) conflicting causes, for, as Kirby Farrell asks us to bear in mind, "people not only suffer trauma, they use it, and the idea of it, for all sorts of ends, good and ill".[16] By allowing the vigilante to return to everyday life, the state in a way accepts his argument that tougher laws are indeed needed. Moreover, this attitude of the state helps it mend the earlier, clipped 'nation(-)state' hyphen – in a symbolic gesture, the vigilante (the nation) and the commissioner (the state) meet each other as seeming strangers and shake hands. [17]

One has to acknowledge the film's inventiveness in foregrounding the 'everydayness of terror and the technologies facilitating it' in a mediated, dromocratic world. However, connections need to be drawn between audience perception/cognition of the pace of the film, the speed of information dissemination/processing during terror events and the film's positioning of the citizen with respect to the nation-state amidst/around the fear of terrorism to evaluate how particular citizenship roles and governance practices are enunciated that limit the scope of deliberative democracy in their attempts to securitise cities.[18]

Notes
1. Excerpts from **A Wednesday** (5 September 2008), dir. Neeraj Pandey.
2. Indian cities where serial blasts took place during the year 2008 include: Jaipur (14 May 2008), Bangalore (25 July 2008), Ahmedabad (26 July 2008), Delhi (9 September 2008) and Guwahati (30 October 2008), reaching a crescendo with the Mumbai 26/11 attacks. Among the films, I am particularly referring to **Aamir** (6 June 2008), dir. Rajkumar Gupta, and **Mumbai Meri Jaan** (22 August 2008), dir. Nishikanth Kamath.
3. See Ranjani Mazumdar, **Bombay Cinema: An Archive of the City** (University of Minnesota, 2007, Minneapolis). India also underwent a 21-month period of National Emergency starting in June 1975.
4. Claire King. "The Man Inside: Trauma, Gender, and the Nation in **The Brave One**". Paper presented at the National Communication Association's Critical/Cultural Studies Division, 2008.
5. Susan Hayward. "Framing National Cinemas". In (eds.) Mette Hjort and Scott Mackenzie, **Cinema and Nation** (Routledge, 2000, London/New York), p. 89.
6. ibid., p. 91.
7. Considering the vigilantism associated with Naxalite/Maoist attacks and their operations in rural areas, it can be argued that citizen vigilante films are not restricted to urban spaces only. However, instances of such representations are difficult to find in Bollywood cinema.
8. See Shiv Visvanathan, "Thinking about Terror", in **The Economic Times**, 1 August 2008.
9. Paul Virilio. **War and Cinema: The Logistics of Perception**, (trans.) P. Camiller (Verso, 1989, London), p. 3.
10. Excerpts from **A Wednesday** (2008).
11. One of the most talked-about incidents was the seizure of Indian Airlines Flight IC814 on 24 December 1999. The flight was forcibly taken to Kandahar; the hijack ended with the release of three militants. The ongoing trial against Ajmal Amir Kasab, accused in the 26/11 attacks on Mumbai, has been a subject of intense debate.
12. Aradau and Munster talk about how the "precautionary principle privileges a politics of speed based on sovereign decision" in contrast to Ulrich Beck's assumption that risk society will "reinvent politics along democratic lines with slow procedures where expert knowledge will be deliberated in the global public forum". See Claudia Aradau and Rens van Munster, "Governing Terrorism through Risk: Taking Precautions, (Un)Knowing the Future", paper prepared for the 'Governing by Risk in the War on Terror' workshop, 21 March 2006, San Diego, p.18.
13. Virilio writes, "There was no 'industrial revolution,' but only a 'dromocratic revolution'; there is no democracy, only dromocracy; there is no strategy, only dromology. It is precisely at the moment when Western technological evolutionism leaves the sea that the substance of the wealth begins to crumble, that the ruin of the most powerful peoples and nations gets under way... It is speed as the nature of dromological progress that runs progress; it is the permanence of the war of Time that creates total peace, the peace of exhaustion". See Paul Virilio, **Speed and Politics: An Essay on Dromology** (Semiotext(e), 1986, New York), p. 46.
14. Excerpt from **A Wednesday** (2008).
15. Cathy Caruth. **Unclaimed Experience: Trauma, Narrative, and History** (Johns Hopkins University Press, 1996, Baltimore), p. 2.

16. *Kirby Farrell.* Post-traumatic Culture: Injury and Interpretation in the Nineties *(Johns Hopkins University Press, 1998, Baltimore), p. 21.*

17. *Talking of* The Brave One, *Claire King observes how even when vigilante Erica Bain is caught by investigator Mercer (representing the state) on her way to kill the last of her attackers, he covers up her actions although they are both violent and illegal. See King, op. cit.*

18. *Visvanathan finds this situation to be a "failure of politics as an imagination". See Shiv Visvanathan, "Reflections on the Terrorisms of Our Time",* Seminar *598 (January 2009).*

Myth, Legend, Conspiracy
Urban Terror in *Aamir* and *Delhi-6*

KUHU TANVIR

The 21st century is only ten years old, yet it has already created an identity for itself – that of a crumbling modernity. The collapsing World Trade Centre has become the defining image of the decade, if not of the century, bringing terrorists out of their 'Afghan caves' and into the heart of the city, ushering in a terrorised urban existence.

Hindi cinema, like cinema across the world, has tried a variety of ways to define this fear, to understand the figure of the terrorist and, of course, to link and de-link terrorism and the ordinary Muslim. In the recent past, two Hindi films that have dealt with the issue of urban terror are Rajkumar Gupta's *Aamir* and Rakeysh Omprakash Mehra's *Delhi-6*. In this essay, I would like to argue that despite stemming from a common purpose – to present an alternative view point to the existing discourse on terrorism and Islam's relationship with it in the 21st century – the two films achieve something decidedly different and, in fact, have opposite impacts.

Aamir: An Agenda Gone Awry?
Rajkumar Gupta's *Aamir*, released in 2008, was not only a sleeper hit, but was also considered "an eloquent statement on the state of the nation and the Indian Muslim".[1] The story of a young, educated, modern Muslim man forced to become part of a terrorist outfit and carry out instructions issued to him by phone or risk losing his entire family, *Aamir* seems to present a flip side to the dominant discourse linking Islam and terrorism. A quick scan of some blogs that reviewed *Aamir* when it came out indicates that the film was perceived as one that works as testimony that all Islamic terrorists are not so by choice.[2] I would argue that while the protagonist may be the eponymous *Aamir*, the central character that the film constructs is the city and, in particular, a community as it inhabits the city, accesses it and ultimately responds to it. And it is in this construction that the film goes against its own project.

The most striking thing about *Aamir* is the way in which Rajkumar Gupta and his cinematographer, Alphonse Roy, have shot the city of Mumbai. Conscious of its interventionist agenda, the first ten minutes of *Aamir* show a montage of fairly traditional images of Mumbai, images that capture the hybridity of the city – from high-rise buildings to shots of Dhobi Ghat and the local train – only to rupture this romantic image with what Roy called *cinéma vérité*.[3]

The attempt really is to develop a sense of the everyday rhythms of the city, a rhythm that will soon be broken, not just for the audience, but also for the protagonist. Aamir enters a city he grew up in but encounters a place he doesn't recognise. Through his movements during that one day, both he and the audience are taken through the filthiest sites of Mumbai. It is a city of ruin[4] – one that is actively haunted by the predominant discourse of development and progress that Mumbai supposedly manifests. Given the rich, cinematic possibilities of Dharavi, slums have been used as a symbol of Mumbai almost as much as the Gateway of India has, so it is not the visual alone that is unique in this film, it is how and what that visual is made to communicate. As the nameless terrorist leader reveals, the purpose behind the journey he directs Aamir to was to show him the conditions in which the Muslim community lives. In the process, we are taken on a visual journey that maps visibly Muslim areas of the city, but despite his sympathetic plan with this film, Gupta decides to use fairly predictable and stereotypical ways of marking areas as 'authentically Muslim'. A case in point is the meat market that Aamir is directed to: the journey to and from that market is meticulously traced with bloody animal carcasses and butchers silently screaming an identity that inevitably links them to a not-so-abstract idea of Muslim-ness and, more importantly, to violence. Apart from the space that labels Muslims in the film comes a detail that complements it – eating habits. There are at least three moments in the film when characters (all Muslim) are shown eating. The first is when Aamir is sent to National Restaurant, with its Muslim management and clientele, all of whom are pointedly shown with half-eaten non-vegetarian food; the second is the food the gang leader eats in his house; and finally, the food put in front of Aamir. Eating habits are a traditional way of underscoring cultural differences, and in their grotesque usage, Gupta has employed them in a similar way.

Between the labyrinthine lanes of Mumbai, shot only for their overwhelming, squalid filth (and shot well enough for the visual to effectively convey the stench that goes with it), and the Muslims who seem to inhabit them, there is a connection created between the repulsion we feel at these sights and the community the film locates within them. The revulsion reaches saturation in a scene shot in a literally vomit-inducing bathroom; it is a poignant moment in the film but, more significantly, it places the entire community in a single class. In fact, the film manages to erase class distinction completely: it is not class that divides society here but religion. Aamir is the only upper middle-class moderate Muslim the film has, and it is therefore worth noting that his private space is not shown almost at all, except for one short, imagined scene when he recalls calling home and speaking to his family. When compared to the way in which the other, public, apparently non-secular spaces are mapped in the film, this scene, which is barely a few seconds long, can be easily forgotten. The way in which *Aamir* visually, and also psychologically, maps the city creates a palpable aura of all-encompassing fear that develops from a sense of otherness.

What emerges, therefore, is a network of Muslims, all of whom are part of a total network of terrorism. Class distinction is consciously done away with to privilege the idea of the *kaum*, the community the nameless leader keeps harping on about. Every Muslim in the film is part of the network and is therefore doing his or her duty towards the community.

Everyone knows their role in this terror machine and is willing to carry out that role without questioning. This becomes evident when the gang leader refuses to answer any of Aamir's initial questions, and, as the film goes along, Aamir too realises that it is pointless to challenge what he's being asked to do. An absolute community is what is presented to us: one which is defined by a sense of otherness (both internally and externally), and one that has a common aim – to avenge the wrongs done to the Muslim community by sending out messages through acts of violence. Language that by popular discourse is now attributed to terrorists is used by this leader, who wants to make Aamir a *mujahid*, a freedom fighter.

Apart from highlighting cultural differences, there is another way in which a distance between the community and a majority of the audience that would watch this film is created. The link with Pakistan, the biggest 'other' when it comes to India. The film makes it a point to extend the Muslim community beyond national borders because the problems at hand are not those of Indian Muslims alone but of 'Muslim *bhai* (brothers) across the world. Doing away with class and even national boundaries, *Aamir* creates a place-less community; in the process, the personal and, by extension, the human are subsumed by the communal and the political. Not only do we strictly access public spaces, but there is a conscious absence of a home space in the film, with the city taking over the visual narrative. Through Aamir's movements, a lack of stability is created that highlights the absence of home. It is in this process that the actual family is hardly seen while Aamir engages with this alternative family – the community. Taxis, hotels, STD booths, market places are what this film is made of, rendering rootedness an impossibility. Ironically, the only home space we see is that of the gang leader, who issues instructions from his home, peopled with other occupants who come and go and are therefore in the know of his sinister plan. The home space in this Muslim world therefore doubles as a terrorist headquarters of sorts as well.

While much is made of the liberal perspective of this film with regard to the connection between Islam and terrorism, the project seems lopsided in the two characters that occupy maximum screen time – Aamir and the gang leader. Nameless, and nearly faceless, the gang leader has a presence that overwhelms the narrative, while Aamir, despite being in every frame, is sadly dwarfed. Granted that Aamir is made to utter a few liberal, modern and secular homilies at a few moments in the film, but they remain mere details, while the absolute control of the gang leader takes over. The most horrifying moment (and also the most socially troubling one) of the film is the gang leader's spoken desire to hear the screams of the dying people on the bus. Except for Aamir, no character in the film is named, and their only identification is their religion – the fact that the gang leader has no name pushes this case further. Not a single Muslim in the film remains outside the network of terror, not even Aamir. There is an enduring sense the film communicates that despite education, a family and social standing, it is inevitable that the Muslim will have some connection with terrorism. He may not have a choice, but that is a small consideration in the larger picture, which seemingly concerns itself with personal and even national safety.

Delhi-6: **The Other Side of All the Noise**

The turbulent political history of the 21st century has ensured that fear – a political fear that is made personal – finds place everywhere, from dreams to reality, and consequently from realist cinema to other more derivative forms. I say this because while *Aamir* firmly situates itself through its aesthetic and its narrative in the realist mode, *Delhi-6* has a more fluid form. In *Delhi-6*, there are characters and a loose narrative, but the driving force seems to be of making a cinematic collage of Old Delhi. While it may not be a conscious decision on Rakeysh Omprakash Mehra's part, the blend of myth, 'reality' and urban legend that he uses ensures a dialogue in the film between a fluid structure and a consequently layered narrative.

Like Rajkumar Gupta's *Aamir*, Mehra's *Delhi-6* also prioritises the city in the guise of the story of its protagonist, Roshan (Abhishek Bachchan). Addressing questions regarding parallels between himself and Roshan, Mehra said, "*Delhi-6* is not an autobiography at all. I've just delved into my childhood memories and my youth in the film… It's more of the colour of that life that has been used in the background than anything else… Every day [of the shoot] was an anecdote for us".[5] The choice of Old Delhi as the central site of the film is interesting not just because Mehra's personal memories originate there, but also because of its status in India's national and historical memory. In contrast to New Delhi, which was developed by the British, the memory of Old Delhi is still affixed with the memory of the Mughals. The film's representation of Old Delhi situates it in a time-cusp where the old and the new exist simultaneously. The old structures, like Roshan's ancestral house, are still standing, but the planning is less than adequate – the streets are too narrow, safety is an inevitable issue, as is privacy, and amenities are collapsing. All this in Old Delhi, once the symbol of royalty and sophistication. I would argue that despite being a lived space and sharing much with Walter Benjamin's idea of a counter-monument (Benjamin, 1928),[6] the historical status of Old Delhi, which is still trapped in that space, brings it close to the idea of the monument but one which is collapsing. A telling example of this stripping of royalty is the house of Ali Beg (Rishi Kapoor). Everything about this character reeks of nostalgia for a past where refinement, poetry and sophistication were the flavour. His house, however, is in contrast to this surface regality. It is commercial, badly lit and a hotchpotch of cultural influences. It is almost paedestrian. The desire is for something more than a collapsing structure – for the sacred, perhaps. The mass participation in the Ramlila, the cow worship and ultimately the creation of the urban legend are all a result of this aspiration. The inability to fulfill this aspiration, and the fall from prestige inevitably lead, as Lefebvre says, to violence (Lefebvre, 1974).[7]

Like Roshan, who is part Hindu, part Muslim, Old Delhi too is captured for its hybrid cultural impulses. So while Roshan attends the Ramlila and also reads the *namaaz*, the narrow lanes of Old Delhi house devout Hindus, devout Muslims and, most significantly, a Muslim who is a Hanuman devotee – Mamdu (Deepak Dobriyal). The architecture of Delhi this film captures is worth examining. The narrowness of the lanes, the easy access from one house to the next and a significant number of public spaces (like shops and the Ramlila ground) establish a sense of a close-knit community. Neighbours are constantly in each other's space and manage to construct relationships despite artificial spatial divides since they are all so easy to overcome. For instance, even though the Sharma brothers (played by Om Puri and Pawan Malhotra) have not been able to resolve their basic familial dispute, and have erected a wall on their property, marking out their individual territory, the relationship between their families is intact, and the two always know what is going on in the other person's house. The movement this architecture enables (I'm thinking in particular of Abhishek Bachchan jumping from one rooftop to the other) and gives a spatial dimension to the easy and rapid movement of rumours and, in this case, terror. The all-knowingness of the community is contrasted with the unknowable in the film – the urban legend of the Monkey Man (drawn from the mysterious creature that created mass hysteria in Delhi in May 2001 and who was never ultimately caught).

The coming together of varying impulses in the film can be seen through the simultaneously existing layers of the narrative, and they ultimately contribute to Mehra's somewhat didactic agenda (the unproblematised and clearly stated secularist moral at the end of both this film as well as Mehra's last cinematic venture, *Rang De Basanti*, corroborate this line of thought). First, the Monkey Man, at least in the way that it is perceived, has something fundamentally in common with Roshan – the hybrid. Not only do Hindus and Muslims in the film ascribe characteristics of each other on the Monkey Man, but it is also a tussle between myth, actuality and science since links with the monkey god, Hanuman, are created on the one hand and a scientific explanation is sought on the other. This, then, highlights the varying strains in the very phrase 'urban legend'.

The Monkey Man, who is referred to as an *aatankvaadi* (terrorist) in the film, is a device used by Mehra to pull terrorism out of the realist narrative. Mehra throws together the players that have a role in the discourse on terror – religious groups, politicians and the media – along with mythology (the Ramayana) and urban legend, thereby creating a new idiom of terrorism where the terrorist is subsumed by terror – in other words, where the terrorist is a construct while terror becomes fact. The insane man who roams the streets of Old Delhi with a mirror is a meaningful, albeit trite, presence in the film as he is clearly meant to open our eyes to our role in the construction of the terrorist. To accept madness is, therefore, perhaps the sanest move, being, in this context, closest to the truth.

The media presence in the film is the opposite of this insane man. On the surface, the media is all about rationality – with access to interviews with policemen, local people and all those associated with the event, the attempt is clearly to represent the here-and-now immediacy of the situation. Except that there isn't one. Used with a great deal of self-consciousness, the Hindi news anchor (who agreed to caricature himself for the film) is the key player of this role. While in an ultra modern setting of a news channel studio, his language is that of legend. In one snippet of news that we hear, the words 'fear psychosis' are mentioned, but are then quickly pushed under the rug because treating the Monkey Man situation as investigative reportage, full of hard evidence, is more exciting for the viewer, where the attempt is to prove that there is actually substance to a news piece and a story is not, in fact, a tall tale.

Mehra's engagement with the idiom of terrorism that is available to the public is hence a counter-movement to rightwing groups and the role they play in creating a jingoistic language at the moment. Consider, for instance, the statement by the Shiv Sena's Delhi unit in 2001, responding to the terror of the Monkey Man: "The ISI is behind it; 131 monkeys have come across the border to spread terror".[8] There is a precision to this sentence that makes it believable, especially in the use of the number 131, which labours to lend authenticity to the claim. Mehra's film undoes this certainty, and the load of the real is reduced by introducing myth and legend.

Conclusion

Both *Delhi-6* and *Aamir*, therefore, start out with a common project: to combat prevalent terrorist discourse, especially as promoted by the media, and to do this by looking at the making of a terrorist. The process and impact of the two, however, is drastically different. In situating *Aamir* in one specific event, and in its use of heightened realism, Rajkumar Gupta's film remains the story of one individual. The structures of perception remain the same. At the end of the film, the image of the monster has not altered, it has only become more firm. There is a large kitty of such films being made across the world, and India is no exception. On the other hand, *Delhi-6* works retroactively – in other words, at a post-terrorism stage, where the issue is not one event but the language of accessing terrorism, in particular in its relationship with society.

Notes

1. *Quoted from film critic Anupama Chopra's review of* **Aamir.** *Available at: http://movies.ndtv.com/movie_re-view.aspx?lang=hindi&id=313&moviename=%20Aamir (accessed 8 November 2009).*

2. *A sample opinion from a first-time blogger: "*Aamir *is a film which addresses a topic of today, which been viewed with a one-dimensional perspective by the majority. Rajkumar Gupta presents another dimension, his own interpretation and his own opinion on the issue. The film shocks you. No one, at least yours truly, would have ever thought of viewing the issue from the perspective of the writer, and this is where lies the success of the writer. Right from the first few scenes, where Aamir Ali's baggage is checked, to the last scene, the writer compels you to think. Kudos to Rajkumar Gupta for daring to tread the path less traveled…" Available at: http://themoviema-niacabhishek.blogspot.com/2008/06/movie-review-aamir.html (accessed 8 November 2009).*
Yet another review says, "The film is based completely on the lives of Muslims in general and how they are provoked and manipulated by some very sick people and these are those people that have damaged their com-munity the most… Aamir is one of the progressive Muslims with modern thinking and he is trapped by a Muslim leader who kidnaps his family and blackmails him to act as he says. He then forces him to do some things or else he would kill his family". Available at: http://bollywoodrated.wordpress.com/2008/06/19/aamir-movie-review/ (accessed 8 November 2009).

3. *Alphonse Roy, Rajkumar Gupta and Rajeev Khandelwal were in conversation with Ranjani Mazumdar in New Delhi during the 11th Osian's Cinefan Festival, October 2009. While speaking at length about the various pho-tography techniques used in this film, Roy emphasised that the influence on him while filming* **Aamir** *was of* **cinéma vérité.**

4. *The concept of the city as the site of ruin is inspired by Ranjani Mazumdar's article "Ruin and the Uncanny City: Memory, Despair and Death in* **Parinda***" in* **Sarai Reader 02: The Cities of Everyday Life** *(Sarai, CSDS+The Society for Old & New Media, Delhi, 2002) Available at: http://www.sarai.net/publications/readers/02-the-cities-of-everyday-life/05ruin_uncanny.pdf (accessed 15 November 2009).*

5. *Interview with Rakeysh Omprakash Mehra from NDTVMovies.com, 16 February 2009. Available at: http:// movies.ndtv.com/movie_Story.aspx?id=ENTEN20090083702 (accessed 13 November 2009).*

6. *Walter Benjamin [1928]. "A Berlin Chronicle". In* **One-Way Street and Other Writings** *(Verso Classics, 1992, London).*

7. *Henri Lefebvre [1974]. Extract from* **The Production of Space.** *Quoted in (ed.) Neil Leach,* **Rethinking Architecture: A Reader in Cultural Theory** *(Routledge, 1997, New York).*

8. *From a report in* **The Hindustan Times,** *17 May 2001. Quoted in Aditya Nigam, "Theatre of the Urban: The Strange Case of the Monkey Man" in* **Sarai Reader 02: The Cities of Everyday Life,** *op. cit.*

Fear on Film
The Ramsay Brothers and Bombay's Horror Cinema

KARTIK NAIR

You can't make a horror movie in a multiplex.
Tulsi Ramsay[1]

The Ramsay Brothers are alternately revered as India's most popular pioneers of cinematic horror and reviled as fearsome intruders on the mainstream film industry, botching its onward march toward bourgeois respectability. A clan of seven self-trained filmmakers raised on movie sets and at matinee shows of *Dracula* and *The Mummy*, the Ramsay Brothers persist in popular memory as a cottage industry of terror: artisanal, makeshift and wildly enthusiastic about their work. It is alleged that they would shoot on 16mm and blow it up to 35mm; but it is also alleged that they would visit graveyards at odd hours of the night to complete their films. Here was an alternative economy of filmmaking, distinguished by its frugal discipline, internal star system, fierce publicity tactics and invisible revenue patterns. The Brothers were the unacknowledged house-guests of India's biggest movie industry for years together, and even the 80s, abandoned by the blockbuster, defiled by shabby experimentation and devastated by television and video, were nonetheless punctuated regularly by Ramsay hits. *Purana Mandir* (Ancient Temple, Shyam and Tulsi Ramsay, 1984), a musical *mélange* of hill-station romance and gothic terror, finished as the second-biggest money-maker of 1984. Trailing only BR Chopra's *Aaj Ki Awaaz* (Voice of Today, 1984), the film's success appears even more extraordinary when one considers the disintegrating commercial climate of the times as television and home video pulled audiences away from cinema halls.

In tracking the career of *Purana Mandir*, this article attempts to apprehend the story behind a totemic family name, a story that is also very much about Bombay cinema. With little to lose and no family honour to protect, the Ramsay Brothers exemplified the truly explosive potential of unexpected quantities moving in large force fields. In many ways, the impact of their films was primarily disruptive, a series of spectacular challenges for the industry, the press and the audience. Whatever these challenges may have been, they can today serve to illuminate the fault lines over which popular arbitrations of 'taste' have been historically conducted.

The Family Enterprise

After years of apprenticeship, the sons of small-time film producer FU Ramsay persuade the patriarch to finance an all-out horror film. The result: *Do Gaz Zameen Ke Neechey* (Beneath Two Yards of Earth, Shyam and Tulsi Ramsay, 1972), a breakout hit that sets the style for Ramsay productions to come. Every few months over the next two decades, cast and crew alike would be packed into buses and transported to the outskirts of Bombay for filming. Here, brothers Shyam and Tulsi Ramsay would dispatch directorial duties; brother Kumar would write the scenes while brother Gangu would lens them; Kiran Ramsay was usually in charge of sound and Arjun in charge of production; meanwhile, Mother Ramsay would cook for everyone.[2] Since the execution of the horror genre is painstaking, and its funds limited, it is no surprise that the Ramsay Brothers never worked with bona fide stars. Instead, trending with much of horror across film cultures, they relied on fresh, young blood to lubricate their productions: the appeal of quick money without the hassles of high-maintenance stars. Usually attractive, these young men and women were required to keep pace with the Ramsays; often, they became niche stars, returning to work with the family again in roles only superficially distinguished from one another. A case in point is Arti Gupta, a model who had dabbled in film work previously but made the decisive transition only when she was cast in the lead for *Purana Mandir*. After its success, she became a darling to the Brothers, their very own 'scream queen'.

Produced on express schedules and shoestring budgets, the Brothers' titles would then be released on a dozen prints in Bombay's less-favoured theatres. By the second week, that number would drop to ten; by the third week, only a print or two would remain in circulation in the city. By this time, a Ramsay film would have begun its journey into the interiors, playing on one screen in Pune in its fourth week, and on one in Wai in its seventh.[3] Trade wisdom suggests the Ramsays did 60 percent of their business in rural territories, where returns are slower and smaller and clouded with administrative haziness.[4] Numbers in *Film Information*, despite its meticulousness, represent only the tip of the box-office iceberg since the journal does not record revenues from the less-prestigious 'B' and 'C' centres, each with their own (tax) evasive histories. There is the additional problem of the journal's veracity, thrown into question by Tulsi Ramsay's unexpected and somewhat enigmatic comment midway through an interview: "We were always after *Film Information*. Report should come good, should come good".[5]

The relative persistence of this business model enhanced the bewildering opacity around the family enterprise. Their movies, caught in the divide between the respectable and the ridiculous, the legal and the illegal, often had truly confounding commercial lives. In an article titled "The Paradoxical Situation", VP Sathe noted his amazement at the fact that "a non-star cast horror adult film like *Purana Mandir* has been released in as many as twenty-three theatres", continuing that "at most of the theatres, the picture drew full houses" (Sathe, 1984). *Film Information* tells us *Purana Mandir* was in fact diverted to the black market during the very first week of its release. "Video cassettes of *Purana Mandir* which was being shown to about 75 persons was seized from the parlour", reads a report on a police raid in Bombay. "The police also seized a Nelco VCR, Weston TV and Rs 105 in cash" (*Film Information*, 1984).

Film piracy activates anxieties around legitimacy and public morality for texts entering popular circuits. *Purana Mandir* had already been certified an 'adult' film by the Central Board of Film Certification, so imagine the surprise of the police when they entered the parlour to find that "many children were seeing the film at the time of the raid" (*Film Information*, 1984). Worse than the scourge of copyright violation, bootlegging promises to corrupt our young. The censors are out to save our families, and the pirates out to destroy them. Ramsay horror, with its ostensible stock-in-trade of sex and violence, was energised by the efforts of both cops and robbers. Simultaneously, bootlegging served its eternal purpose as a viable other, a mafia-run shadow economy beyond the law. A fiction fed to sustain the myth of 'good money', to discriminate between pirates and producers, this shadow economy could make the meanest financiers – even the Ramsays – look like clean citizens.

Watching *Purana Mandir*

What happens: In the long-long-ago (200 years ago), the indefatigable monster Samri (Ajay Aggarwal) terrorises Bijapur, the sultanate of Raja Hariman Singh. Samri frequently disrobes "*naujawaan, shaadi-shuda*" (young, married) women, kills children and disinters corpses to eat them. When he attacks the Raja's daughter, a royal decree is passed ordering his decapitation. Before he is thus executed, the monster makes a vow to return to life once again and curses the King's female heirs with horrible deaths in childbirth.

Cut to the 'present day' and the city. The latest descendant in the line of the Raja is Thakur Ranbir Singh (Pradeep Kumar), whose only child is the attractive Suman (Arti Gupta), a lissome girl of college-going age. Suman is in love with the strapping Sanjay (Mohnish Behl), and the two can barely keep their hands off one another, which sets alarm-bells ringing in the Thakur's head. Not having forgotten the curse that will strike Suman should she have a child of her own, he tries to break the couple up. Failing, the distraught father reveals the *shraap* (curse) that has followed their family all the way down the centuries from Bijapur. Convinced that the curse is nothing they can't overcome, Sanjay and Suman leave the city to return to the *haveli* (mansion) where it all began. Eventually, they overpower a back-from-the-dead Samri. The monster is burnt at the stake, the curse is lifted, and the lovers are married with the blessings of the Thakur.

As a narrative device, the curse at the centre of *Purana Mandir* is utterly unexceptional (an obstacle is created and then overcome), but its provenance is fairly interesting, a particularly instructive instance of the Brothers' ingenious deployment of horror film tropes. In countless American slasher films of the 70s and early 80s (*Friday the 13th, Prom Night, Nightmare on Elm Street*), sexual intercourse outside marriage is strictly prohibited, and trespassers invoke certain death at the hands of a knife/axe/machete/spear/impaling rod/electrocuting hotwire/scorching tongs-wielding maniac. In each film, we witness the bodies of young men and women enjoying sex away from the surveillance of their parents in an unpoliced and semi-rural environment where adolescent anarchy prevails. In each film, we witness the bodies of young men and women being yanked back under surveillance, 'disciplined' once again through torture. These grisly moments imbue the slasher film with the air of a parable or cautionary tale to warn against teenage illicit sex, cinematically converting it into taboo via an experience of Ripper-like horror.

Such repressive censoriousness means almost nothing in Bombay cinema, where it would be impossible to write a film in which teenagers are shown experiencing spectacular death, little or big. Graphic sex and frontal nudity are already taboo, anathema for an idiom which relegates them to a notional, invisible privacy somewhere beyond the end credits. No knives or axes are needed to temper sexual appetite in Bombay; there is already a series of tacit codes in place to make sure no one gets frisky. Institutionalised censorship is only one of these codes; consider equally the ever-present extended family, keeping a watchful eye within the diegetic world so that most unpoliced and parentless worlds remain dream locales.

In *Purana Mandir*, therefore, the curse of death is activated with childbirth: as a definite consequence of sex but sex within sacred marriage – almost like a side-effect of legitimate, productive and monitored sexuality. The *shraap* thus emerges in the rapprochement of fears – a kind of handshake in which both hands pocket something – serving as an instructive example of the way censorship doesn't just *happen* to a pre-existing text; rather, it looms always on the creative horizon, a phenomenal presence with institutional weight that challenges filmmakers in highly productive ways.

Further, the shraap also functions within the dominant syntax of monstrosity/sexuality popularised in British Hammer films (*The Brides of Dracula*, 1960; *The Curse of the Werewolf*, 1961) and serves as the means whereby the urban is displaced in favour of the backwoods. After the fashion of much horror from the American independent phase (especially *The Texas Chainsaw Massacre*, Tobe Hooper, 1974), this relocation provides the setting for a primitive ordeal from which a young woman, man or (as in the case of *Purana Mandir*) heterosexual couple escapes back to the order of the city. However, the exigencies of Bombay cinema require Suman's father to be witness to Sanjay's physical agency and

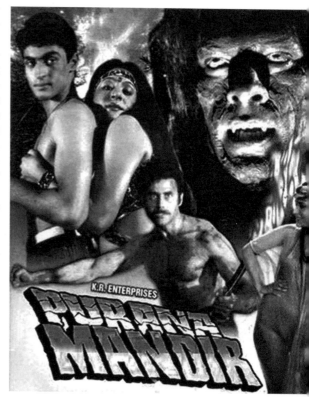

masculine prowess in subduing the monster and re-establishing harmony where there was once chaos. Therefore, in an unprecedented move for a horror film, *Purana Mandir* ends not with the bruised dyad but with a happy trio: boy, girl and girl's father. "I'm really proud of you, my son", the Thakur sniffs. The '*Purana Mandir*' of horror literally modulates into the *mandir* (temple) of the marriage ceremony as Sanjay and Suman are wed and 'The End' is hurriedly ushered in.

Inescapable here is the clunkiness of the Ramsay Brothers who, with their limited budgets and talents, only occasionally realised their ambitions. The frenetic camera movement of some sequences in *Purana Mandir* bears resemblance to the innovative cinematography in *Evil Dead* (Sam Raimi, 1981); the baroque, taxidermically-inclined space of the *haveli* recalls *The Haunting* (Robert Wise, 1963) or any number of Hammer films; the extremely tight composition into which something (a cat, a crazy woman) suddenly emerges to scare the living daylights out of Suman suggests *Halloween* (John Carpenter, 1978); the coffin and horse-drawn carriage are straight out of numerous Stoker adaptations; there are point-of-view shots that are akin to shots from *Black Christmas* (Bob Clark, 1974), as well as the Romero-style gait of the possessed man-servant. For the most part, though, these moments of 'horror' play out as incompetent hack-jobs and incomplete masteries. Night-time shooting was still a problem for the Ramsays, and *Purana Mandir* would have additionally called for a fairly complex choreography of darkness and lighting, silence on set and post-sync sound, not to mention a small army of technicians working with prosthetics, make-up, fog machines and other 'special effects'. It remains unclear what degrees of expertise were involved, given the general sense of workshop-improvisation prevailing with the family.

Where, then, does the horror inhere in a Ramsay film? The genre's conventions, forced into visibility by the yawning gap between aspiration and accomplishment – when the make-up is under-baked, or the camera doesn't move nearly fast enough, or when the cat looks less like it's jumping into the frame and more like it's being chucked into it by a spotboy – can be moments of unintentional hilarity, as globally circulating 'signs' of horror are shriveled to an embarrassingly inchoate generic language that cannot conceal its own manufactured-ness. These moments can also, however, cause shudders, involuntary r*ecoils at the excessive materiality of the image*; the Ramsay films often gain in stature as a result of this unexpected effect. Terror here is less a matter of slick technical virtuosity and more a

matter of something earthy and visceral. The vampire-overlord in *Bandh Darwaza* (Closed Door, 1990) has none of the ethereal, otherworldly quality of the early sound phase or the Hammer films; he is an affective, if inelegantly prosthetic monster. In *Aur Kaun* (Who Else, 1979), the corpse of a murdered woman rots in a refrigerator and is eventually sunk in a lake. The texture of every Ramsay film is heavy with the smell of bodies – the dread of corporeal finitude played out in a *mise-en-scène* of involute caves and subterranean dwellings.

Afterlife: Ramu, the Ramsays and the Haunting Problem of Genre

Without a doubt, the Ramsay films are indispensable today for the gauntlet they throw to connoisseurs of genre, even as recent work from the likes of Ram Gopal Varma (*Kaun?*/Who?, 1999; *Bhoot*/Ghost, 2003) accedes to a rapidly standardising idiom of horror, boasts top-of-the-line technical credentials and features a star-cast of appreciable order. If the Ramsay Brothers haunt Varma's work at all, it is as yesterday's awkward yet undisputed champions, a beloved and campy underground.

Having risen to international prominence as an essayist of urban desolation, Varma seems especially well-placed to articulate the postmodern sense of vulnerability that has overtaken city life. His films usually unfold in a cramped and intimidating world of high-rises and garbage, a "spatial topography of dread, decay and death" (Mazumdar, 2007), pushing a feeling that "the everyday social world and the world of terror are contiguous and threaten to overlap", a "strange sense of hyper-location" (Vasudevan, 2002). If his gangland films vibrate with the energy of individuals kicking to stay above the surface, his horror films telescope that energy into visions of possession, paranoia, and pain.

For *Kaun?*, Varma recruited Mazhar Kamran, a director of photography who had the previous year assisted on the steadicam-shot gangster film, *Satya*. Kamran brings everything he learned while shooting chase sequences and gunfights to *Kaun?*'s three-storey set. Complete with winding staircase and huge glass windows, the house swoops and shudders around Urmila Matondkar's already diminutive frame, scaling her isolation into relief. Varma is credited with introducing the use of the steadicam in India in the late 80s, and his incubation as a videoshop owner is crucial here.[6] Historically, the fortunes of the steadicam are tied up with the fortunes of the horror film, its effective execution canonised by *Halloween* and *The Shining* (Stanley Kubrick,1980).

In *Bhoot,* the camera's smooth insinuations, along with Varma's idiom of disorienting Dutch angles and strident synth sounds, give jump scares and boo moments their slickness. Aided by Adlabs on FX and Dolby on Sound, Varma freely trades in throwbacks to classics like *Chucky* while purloining from current Japanese horror like *Ju-on*. Clearly, Varma's appetite is as large as the Brothers'; only his ambitions are higher. Where the Ramsays managed a former Miss India for *Purana Mandir*, Varma gives us a Miss Universe in *Vastu Shastra* (2004). Varma doesn't play with the placeless hill stations and *havelis* of the 70s and 80s, nor do his films play there. *Bhoot*, for instance, "scared the daylights out of the city audiences, converting the shrieks and screams in the auditorium into the jingle of coins at the ticket-windows..." but never made it too far past the 'A'centres, as "revenues from circuits like Rajasthan, Bihar and UP came crashing down as the first week progressed" (*Film Information*, 14 June 2003).

Simultaneously, the Ramsay Brothers are entering a trans-continental fraternity of 'B' cinemas, positioned synonymously with such figures as Mario Bava and Georges Franju, other derogated practitioners of horror who have been revitalised by globalisation's enormous reach and recycling capacities. Long-forgotten as mindless Bombay bilge that wasn't even available with pavement hawkers, *Purana Mandir* is now being disseminated as intellectually affluent, global 'trash' cinema by the Mondo Macabro DVD series, a glossily packaged "walk on the wild side of Asian Cinema". The rehabilitation, however, has long roots, discernible in two divergent reviews of *Purana Mandir* that appeared in the year after its release. *Filmfare*, India's top-selling film magazine, had given the movie a pass in its opening weeks; in January 1985, however, testifying to *Purana Mandir*'s box office muscularity, the magazine gave its top critic, Pritish Nandy, a whole two pages to review it. Titled "Indiana Jones Returns to the Temple of Gloom" (*Filmfare*, 1-15 January 1985), Nandy's piece is an exercise in brutal belittlement. His observations are usually unkind ("the cardboard walls are falling off"), sometimes lazy (the repeated reference to the movie's monster as Shaitan; his name is Samri), and often unverifiable ("The results are predictable... Everyone wants the gate money back, while the ushers hide under the chairs"). Failing to mention even once that the film was a gargantuan success on any scale, the review concludes thus:

> One cannot but help admiring the sensitivity and intelligence with which this film has been made. It speaks volumes for Hindi cinema and the Ramsays, our horror movie moghuls, who have (with this film) graduated towards serious, thought-provoking cinema of a kind rarely seen before. (Nandy, 1985)

Six months after Nandy's review, another critic with *Filmfare* was also given two pages for an article on the Ramsays. In "Love at First Bite" (*Filmfare*, 1-15 August 1985), Roscoe Mendonza expressed boundless hope that a future re-evaluation would show the Brothers to have been *auteurs*. Mendonza's article is a half-winking, implicit but obvious rebuttal to Nandy's:

> We need such films. It may be fine for Mrinal Sen or Saeed Mirza to trumpet the ways and means in which their movies serve the needs of society. Likewise, the dukes of commercial cinema, who tout the need for entertainment in a weary society. But can either of these two cliques bring to their film-making a true understanding of the Indian Psyche the way Ramsay brothers have? (Mendonza, 1985)

Horror, writes Joan Hawkins, "is perhaps the best vantage point from which to study the cracks that seem to exist everywhere in late-20th century 'sacralised' film culture" (Hawkins, 2000). *Purana Mandir*, as it passed through the press mill, turned the pages of *Filmfare* into a cultural war-zone. In hindsight, it seems perversely appropriate that the Ramsays rose to prominence in the 70s, a period lit by the promises of the Indian New Wave and scorched by the anger of Amitabh Bachchan, and scored their biggest hits in the 80s, the decisive abyss of Bombay film history, a terrible time that produced few other memorable victories.

Virtuosos of the cinematic badlands of those years, the Ramsay Brothers challenge scholars of Bombay Cinema to take another look at its trash. The Ramsay Brothers – the men, the movies, the money, the mockery, the memory – have found altogether new channels via which to haunt the contemporary.

Notes

1. *Interview with Rahul Bhatia, "Future of the Ghost Movie". In* Open, *5-11 September 2009, pp. 42-43.*
2. *Tulsi Ramsay, interview with Kartik Nair, 16 July 2009. Andheri, Mumbai.*
3. **Purana Mandir**, *according to* **Film Information**, *27 October 1984, sold almost six lakh tickets in the first week of its release in Bombay alone. On 14 prints, the film ran to near full-house capacity at such subpar locations as Plaza, Filmistan and Jubilee. A week later, it registered 85 percent business on 11 prints in the city. Four weeks into its theatrical run, it was running in Bhopal; a week after that, it had dropped almost entirely off the radar, a mere blip in Delhi (two screens: Plaza, Jubilee).*
4. *Komal Nahta, Editor,* **Film Information**. *Interview with Kartik Nair, 3 September 2009,* **Film Information** *office, Bandra, Mumbai.*
5. *Ramsay, op. cit.*
6. *"The steadicam is usually used to capture chase sequences. In fact, Ram Gopal Varma was the director who first introduced the steadicam in India, with his film* **Shiva** *(1989)" (Mazumdar, 2007).*

References

- Hawkins, Joan. **Cutting-Edge: Art-Horror and the Avant Garde** *(University of Minnesota, 2000, Minneapolis).*
- Mazumdar, Ranjani. **Bombay Cinema: An Archive of the City** *(Permanent Black, 2007, New Delhi).*
- Mendonza, Roscoe. *"Love at First Bite". In* Filmfare, *1-15 August 1985, pp. 75-79.*
- Nandy, Pritish. *"Indiana Jones Returns to the Temple of Gloom". In* Filmfare, *1-15 January 1985, pp. 62-63.*
- *"Piracy Raids". In* Film Information, *27 October 1984.*
- Sathe, V.P. *"The Paradoxical Situation". In* Film Information, *27 October 1984.*
- Vasudevan, Ravi. *"The Exhilaration of Dread: Genre, Narrative Form and Film Style in Contemporary Urban Action Films". In* **Sarai Reader 02: The Cities of Everyday Life** *(Sarai, CSDS+The Society for Old and New Media, 2002, Delhi), pp. 58-67. Available online at http://www.sarai.net/publications/readers/02-the-cities-of-everyday-life/04dread.pdf (accessed 10 November 2009)*

"I Swear It's Not a Cow..."
The Eerie Glow of Television Screens in America's Heartland.

ANGELA ANDERSON

It's three o'clock in the morning, and despite the incredible silence outside, I find myself laying in bed, listening. I lie perfectly still, frozen in fact, incapable of moving even if I had to. I don't really know what I'm listening for – the sound of a twig breaking outside, the door of the garage slowly opening, a car coming up the driveway maybe. Wait, I hear something, I swear – a faint thumping. It's my own heartbeat resonating in my ears.

Given my hyper-attentive state of mind, you might think that I'm somewhere... in a conflict zone, maybe, or clandestine in hostile territory of some sort – somewhere where still and silence always have an uneasy undertone. Oddly enough, I'm in my childhood home in rural Northeastern Wisconsin, one of the states in the Midwest region of the US. The nearest town is five miles away, and there are at least as many cows as humans in this neck of the woods.

Having left Northeast Wisconsin immediately after high school and generally feeling more comfortable in urban environments, whenever I return to the dairy state (a.k.a. Wisconsin), I am subjected to the usual questioning: am I not scared of the big city – of shootings, of car jackings, of gang violence? For people here, fear means fearing the other – the racial other, the sexual other, the national other – the source of their fear is so transparent I can't help but answer with a stern, exasperated stare. No, I think to myself, being here scares me. When I find myself in Northeast Wisconsin in the middle of the night, I am gripped by an irrational sensation of fear that prompts me to make sure all the doors are locked and to constantly turn the lights off inside the house and on outside so I can peek through the closed blinds into the night to check that nobody's out there. Why, I wonder to myself, am I doing this? Where is this intense sensation of fear coming from?

Granted, it's not that there's nothing to be afraid of here – some fear has precedent. This includes the fear (for myself and others) of being killed by a drunk driver before reaching home, of being hit by a stray bullet during hunting season, of being chased by a deer or dog or bear while jogging, and the fear of freezing to death in a snow storm. These are transparent fears – unpredictable, but at least the potential threat presents itself clearly. The fear I'm referring to, however, kicks in after an evening of watching the local news, followed by major network television shows like *60 Minutes, 48 Hours, CSI* and *America's Most Wanted*. The barrage of stories of random crime ruthlessly committed against innocent victims, all delivered in an uncannily enthusiastic and excited tone, leaves me helplessly paranoid, imagining there's someone with an axe or a semiautomatic machine gun hovering outside, waiting for me to go to sleep.

In my very own, unscientific, personal survey of true crime television shows broadcast on the major commercial networks in NE Wisconsin, I've come to the conclusion that there are four particular crimes that get heavy rotation. These include a) kidnapped child either still missing or found dead – this is a standard, b) young woman disappears from a parking lot somewhere and is either missing or dead, c) an elderly woman is preyed upon in her own home – often ending up dead, or d) somebody breaks/forces/manipulates their way into the home of unsuspecting rural couple or family, sometimes taking advantage of their generosity – these people often end up dead. In theory, these are tragic stories – horrible stories – of events that theoretically shouldn't be repeated – and yet they are, in different variations, night after night. In isolation, these televisual 'events' could be considered crises – calamitous happenings that encourage people to reflect upon themselves and their communities – but the substantial and consistent flow of true crime programmes over what is now many years of televisual time places these shows, and thus these dramatically violent events, firmly in the realm of televisual information.[1] It could be called 'crisis information', actually – regular and even predictable, yet disturbing and destabilising, but never enough to actually stop the televisual flow.

Ever since the promise of Y2K delivered only disappointment to those hoping for something big, it seems like crisis information has become 'the' information in Northeast Wisconsin (and maybe the entire country). True to the old adage, 'if it bleeds, it leads', nothing that is not related to crime or violence seems to make it onto the local evening news. Instead, on a nightly basis, there's the report of the latest convenience store armed robbery or a shooting of some kind, intoned with a voice that implies simultaneous concern and anticipation that the world is going to hell in a handbasket. Couple the news with the true crime shows that follow, and basically what you end up with is a good reason to buy some guns and install a

CCTV setup around your house, and maybe build a bomb shelter while you're at it – all in the name of self-defence, mind you – and then wait for Armageddon to come because it's the only thing that's going to deliver you out of the terror of your monotonous, ordinary, 'normal' Midwestern life.

And this, of course, is the attraction of true crime television – the fact that these shows strip away the "fiction of normality" in a "sudden eruption of violence from beneath a therefore deceptively normal surface of things".[2] These shows remind you that there's always potential for action, even if that action is completely deranged.

I can't help but liken this type of television programming to the neo-conservative political agenda that still hangs over parts of the US like smog, with its preference for crisis and pure affect in the face of complicated economic and social problems. In Northeast Wisconsin – with its mostly White, Christian population of Northern European descent that has never come to terms with its colonial past, now facing both a shift in the social constellation of the region due to migration, and a new economic reality with the decline in manufacturing and the almost complete disappearance of small farming – crisis is attractive. It's attractive because it is a distraction from thinking about or thoughtfully dealing with a complex and threatening reality – crisis is almost as good as a crystal meth addiction or alcoholism.

Unfortunately for me, although I'm capable of intellectualising the attraction of true crime shows and the televisual flow of crisis information from the safety of my desk in Berlin, thousands of miles away, when I'm confronted by this disturbing realm of televisual violence in person, I lose all capacity to abstract, and become a ball of tightly wound nerves. I, unlike the people who watch these shows on a daily basis, am not numb to them. I've often hypothesised that if the content of mainstream television broadcasting in Northeast Wisconsin would shift from crime and violence to, say, something a bit less sensational, that viewers would suffer from a form of post-traumatic stress disorder due to a lack of the particular affective experience television currently delivers. I, on the other hand, suffer from an affective overdose that triggers excessively paranoid behaviour, which is otherwise, thankfully, dormant. Rule to self – no watching television in Wisconsin.

Notes
1. Mary Anne Doane. "Information, Crisis, Catastrophe". In (eds.) Wendy Hui Kyong Chun and Thomas Keenan, **New Media, Old Media: A History and Theory Reader** (Routledge, 2006, New York). Crisis, in a televisual sense, according to Doane, "is startling and momentous precisely because it demands resolution within a limited period of time", i.e. we have to find the killer, the body, etc. Televisual information, on the other hand, is the "steady stream of 'newsworthy' events characterized by their regularity if not predictability".
2. Mark Seltzer. **True Crime: Observations on Violence and Modernity** (Routledge, 2007, New York) p. 41.

IN CONVERSATION

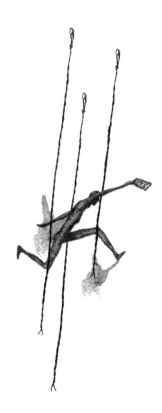

From Anxiety to Enthusiasm

SLAVOJ ŽIŽEK in conversation with Shuddhabrata Sengupta

Shuddhabrata Sengupta (SS): How does one begin looking at the phenomenon of fear?

Slavoj Žižek (SŽ): It's incredible, you know, what you discover when things shift, such as what happened when Communism fell. I read somewhere that the CIA was asked, when they bribed spies, why don't you spend more on intellectuals – because you don't need so much money. Intellectuals are cheap. It's incredible how, with a little bit of repression, how easy it is to corrupt the majority of intellectuals. Especially if you are in a little bit of a totalitarian country.

A model to be studied in this regard is the former Czechoslovakia after '68 – the so-called Brezhnev time – it was not 'big' terror. Let us say you were a little bit of a dissident in Dubček's Prague Spring – and the secret police would come calling and say, "We don't want to arrest you, make you lose your job", and then they would take you aside and in a friendly sort of way say to you, "We know that you are basically honest, and that you were seduced by these bad reactionaries. All we want is that you sign a text that says 'Unfortunately, I was seduced...'"

And so you put in a few names of the people who seduced you. And the secret police would stick to their word; they won't ever make either what you did or the names you named public. So if you do not sign, you not only lose your job... one of the ways to put pressure on intellectuals is through affecting the education of their children. You do not co-operate, your children never find a place in the right school or course or university. Your children become manual workers. And so you name names, you sign where they ask you to sign. And so it goes.

SS: Isn't it fascinating how intellectuals who can be very courageous in times of crisis by speaking truth to power can also give in at other times?

SŽ: I think it was Huxley or Orwell who said that most of the time when intellectuals speak about change, it has to be read as some kind of superstitious strategy, in the sense that if we talk a lot about change, then change will really not happen. And I think... I am not sure if this was true between the two world wars, but it is certainly true for the West European academic Left in the last decades.

The paradox is that to be critical of the state mechanism in a certain way is the best way to reproduce this mechanism. I think this is the best paradox of Western liberalism. It not only does not abhor criticism, it also thrives through criticism.

So, that is one thing.

The other thing is that, nonetheless, one should emphasise – and here I would like to celebrate intellectuals – theory, theoretical commitment, has a logic of its own. You can start developing a theory as a joke, or whatever, and all of a sudden, you take it more seriously. You fall into it.

So it is more ambiguous. I always like the story of Giordano Bruno. He wasn't a heroic person. He was a coward, he usually came to a city, stirred up things, provoked and then escaped and so on. All of a sudden, everybody was shocked. In the end, he said, no, I will not escape, I will stick to my positions, even if I die, or whatever.

So this process, I think, is much more interesting. This is how intellectuals occasionally become authentic. It's not that originally you are authentic, and then slowly you get corrupted. I claim, you start corrupted. I like very much the novel by Eric Ambler, the great detective writer; it's called *Journey into Fear*. In this novel, he has a wonderful sub-story of a guy who is a Communist, and he explains how this guy became a Communist. He is married to a rich woman, whom he hated. And to annoy his wife, when they received guests, he would advocate Communism, to embarrass his wife and the guests. Then, through playing this game, he started to really believe in Communism, dropped his wife and became a revolutionary.

I love this story. This is how it works, and I like really this idea that authenticity is not about throwing off the wrong glasses and looking deep into your self. No, if you look deep into your self, you find shit. Authenticity is something you have to work hard on. Even to be naïvely dedicated to a cause, you have to work really hard.

Part of the story also is how intellectuals can get caught in their own game. Which is why this would be the big lesson for me. Let's say, I am developing a theory, a radical, good theory. And you play the critical analyst. And you say, "Look, look, he is preaching this theory, but privately", let's say, "he is flying business class". But I don't think that this kind of *ad hominem* argument works. There can be more truth in theory. Which is why I like what Jacques Lacan says, when somebody accused, "Look, you're breaking your rules", to which Lacan remarked, "Don't look at what I am doing; listen to what I am saying".

I hope I am not personally corrupt, but I hope that my theory is worth the while, even if I am not.

SS: You have recently called for people to learn. To *study*. You take the example of Marx writing to Engels in the 1870s: "Can't the revolutionaries wait? I have not finished with writing *Kapital*".

SŽ: Truly, it is a wonderful letter.

SS: It is an interesting statement, because the other temptation of intellectuals is to be categorical, when in fact the grounds are for greater uncertainty. And the 'call to action', which intellectuals often make as 'tribunes to the people', may also be reflections of their own fear of admitting to their own uncertainties. And by asking intellectuals to actually attend to their study, which you have done, as an almost 'militant' invocation, you are, to my mind, asking for a return to a recognition of uncertainty as central to the intellectual's calling.

SŽ: Of course this uncertainty does not mean a kind of opportunism. First, I always hated this patronising self-humiliation of intellectuals. Terry Eagleton once told me a wonderful story about something that happened, I think, to Eric Hobsbawm. He wanted to do the 'proper thing' to prove that he was a leftist. And so he went to some modest workers' gathering, a trade union meeting or some such thing, to give a talk to them, and he started in this patronising, pseudo-populist manner by saying to the workers, "Listen, I don't know anything more than you, I came here just to talk with you as an equal", and so on. And then, a wonderful thing happened: one of the workers who was present immediately interrupted him and said, "This is fakery, fuck off, it's your duty to know more than us, that's why you are here to teach us", and so on. This, you see, is the authentic voice.

First. As intellectuals it is our duty and privilege, if we have a chance, to know and to teach others what we know. We should not be ashamed of this. Second thing, what you call 'uncertainty'. I totally agree with you, and it also fits nicely with psychoanalytic theory that 'a call to act' or sometimes even an 'act', as such, is often a desperate strategy to avoid uncertainty. I spoke with some American psychologist who did some stuff on terror. He is a nice guy because he told me he started as a CIA employee, he studied terrorism for them, and then he saw so much despair among ordinary Arab people that in the end, it was not that he became sympathetic to terrorism, but just that he decided to quit the CIA because he did not want to play their game.

He told me about the so-called 'suicide terrorists'. He said, "It's not as simple as the media presents it – they are not idiots who believe that they will get their 70 virgins in heaven or something like that once they blow themselves up – no, it is not like that often. They doubt. They are shaken by doubt, and they think that by blowing themselves up they will prove their faith.

[Phone rings]

SS: Sorry, that is my phone.

SŽ: Now, you know how my wicked mind is working? This is God calling to say, "No, no, no, I do have 70 virgins waiting, you blasphemer!"

So, let's go back to what we were talking about. You put it very nicely. Today, I claim, more than ever before, we do live in an era of uncertainty. What do I mean by uncertainty? Not this bit of post-modern jargon – "Everything is a construct that can be deconstructed", and so on. No. I am thinking of uncertainty in another sense.

I cannot emphasise this enough: traditional theorists, liberals and Marxists, insist that we know where we are and the same story goes on. For liberals, capitalism goes on, and for Marxists, also, capitalism goes on. Yes, basically they agree here. And then, we have many of these 'post' theories. Post-modernism, post-risk society, post-industrial society. They say that something new is emerging, but they have basically journalistic decryptions of this new thing that is emerging. I don't think they propose new theories. And I stand here like Pascal. You know, Badiou taught me this lesson: when something new is emerging, the dialectical paradox of history, the only way to get it, is to try to be faithful to the old, and then you get what it is that is new... For example, Pascal did that with early modernity. There were all these stupid liberals who had just embraced the Enlightenment. Nobody reads them today. But Pascal. Ah, he is different. Pascal's problem was how to remain Christian in modernity. We still read him more today because he saw much more.

Or let us turn to cinema theory and practice. It was precisely those authors who at the very beginning of sound film resisted sound who realised much more deeply the true potential of sound. The early Russians, Eisenstein, and Chaplin. Chaplin's history with sound is very instructive. It happens in stages. It starts in *City Lights*. Chaplin puts in just a few sounds of objects. In *Modern Times*, you hear, very nicely, only mediated speech. You hear something when someone listens to the radio. You don't hear any direct speech. And it is only with *The Great Dictator* that you get to hear voice, you first hear the gibberish of the dictator. Chaplin was somebody who, in this sense, was conservative. He saw much more clearly the dark potentials of the new.

I am not saying that we should forget about Marxism. I am just saying that we should know that we don't yet know where we are today. Even Badiou once said, "We all know what is happening around us, we know imperialism and so on, we simply don't know how to mobilise people around what we know". No, I don't agree with this. The problem is not simply a political one. I don't think we really know what is really going on.

SS: Is the problem you are hinting at deeper? More embedded in the structure of contemporary capitalism? And is the search for an answer to this question something that occupies you?

SŽ: This is what I will try to do, desperately, in my next few books. For example, the critique of political economy – I know that there are nowadays some very good Marxist analyses which claim that they predicted the crisis of the financial economy, and they may be right. But there is this still, a totally basic question that needs to be asked.

Marx has a certain model of exploitation. Does it still hold today? Can we still repeat the kind of critique of political economy that Marx was doing? Because, if you immediately apply Marx, you get some strange results. It does not work. Sometimes, to annoy my leftist friends, I say, "Take Venezuela; if you directly apply Marx, then you have to say that Venezuela is exploiting the United States". Because for Marx, emphatically, natural resources are not a source of value. And you know what is the irony? You know which example Marx takes for natural resources not being a source of value? It is oil! Oil itself!

What the leftist populists usually do is to simply avoid this problem and talk in these vague terms – "The natural/national resources should be owned by the people", and so on. They do not ask or answer the precise question about natural resources. One answer I have for this comes from an Italian economist, who talks about the need for us to turn our attention, in terms of looking for an answer for this question, from profit to rent. It's not that I like this, it's just that it is the only good theory that I know of at the moment. It explains both the question of the exploitation of natural resources and that Bill Gates question, intellectual property. Bill Gates' money is not profit. It is rent. This is why I try (against Marx) to rehabilitate the question of the relationship of the general intellect and the intellectual substance (intellectual property). Bill Gates monopolised, privatised, part of our general intellect, and now we are paying rent to him.

SS: What else do you think we have reason to be uncertain about?

SŽ: For example, China. Do we really know what is really going on there? And I don't mean some kind of orientalist statement about the 'inscrutable Chinese'. No, the question I am interested in is about whether or not there is something new emerging. To put it in simplistic terms, are we seeing the emergence of a new form of capitalism, which, contrary to the fond hope of the liberals, will not only not usher in democracy, but which may in fact survive even better and thrive without democracy. And the worst and most dangerous thing that Western liberals can do is to attribute this to cultural differences by saying that "the Chinese (because of cultural reasons) are incapable of democracy".

No, no, no, no.

We, in the West, are inventing our own mode of so-called 'capitalism with Asian values'. Look at Sarkozy and Berlusconi. Alain Badiou showed me what they share, despite their differences – this kind of comical authoritarian capitalism, where the authoritarian structure is not the old familiar authoritarianism. It's not as if Berlusconi will proclaim one morning an emergency state – the Italians still retain their personal freedoms, their sexual freedoms, consumerism, blah, blah – but the worrying things is that political life proper in Italy is gradually disappearing, dying down. The truly interesting thing in France and Italy is not the vigour of Sarkozy and Berlusconi, it is the demoralisation of the opposition. The Left simply does not know what to do.

My hypothesis is: the West was usually characterised by the presence of some extreme parties: radical Communists and parties targeting some marginal populations; the centre was occupied by two big parties addressing the entire population: Left-of-centre social demo-crats and, on the Right, a moderate conservative tendency. Now, I think something different is happening. The centre is occupied by a pure, neutral technocratic party, which may be even socially vaguely Left-of-centre. But the only alternative to it is a populist Right, and these are also not mutually exclusive. Berlusconi, or Putin, can be a populist and at the same time a technocrat. I think this is a very dark development because we are witnessing, more and more, even in Western Europe and the United States, an unease, a discontent (following Freud) in culture, and a discontent with liberal culture. But the tragedy is that the only big power that articulates this discontent is that of populist nationalism. We have to break out of this. And it is very difficult. This is why I am an optimist for the same time as a pessimist. Things cannot go on for a long time as they are going on. I am not a short-term catastrophist. I am not saying (like that shitty movie *2012*) that things will end in 2012. But I am also not saying that we have to wait another 200 years. I am saying that maybe in the next ten or 12 or 20 years, things will have to happen. And that is why I call our times uncertain.

SS: You've said that it is easier for us to imagine the end of the world than it is to imagine the end of capitalism.

SŽ: I took this thought from Frederic Jameson. I copied him in saying this, let me be honest. But now, I want to write a long text on this. I want to say that this is the lesson of 2009. Let's take two events of the last year. The financial crisis and the summit on climate change in Copenhagen. We all know that the climate issue is really serious, that we can all die, the planet is at risk – but what did they produce at Copenhagen? A purely verbal agreement, which is, to paraphrase the Hollywood magnate Samuel Goldwyn's (he was a genius) famous statement, "an oral agreement that isn't worth the paper it is not written on". The Copenhagen agreement is something like that.

Here, the survival of humanity is at stake, but who cares! But look at what they did with the financial crisis. Immediately, they were able to act. Here, the problem was whether or not they could commit to giving 50 billion to poor countries in ten years to help them out with the transition to less energy-intensive economies; there, they could immediately find thousands of billions to help out the banks and the financial markets. So you can see precisely that this is the attitude of capitalism. When the fate of life on earth is at stake, we must negotiate. But when the normal functions of capitalism are at risk, there is no room for negotiation even.

It's not as people say (and here psychoanalysis enters), as if the conflict is between ethics and egotism. Ecological moralists like to claim that we are obsessed with short term con-sumerism, and that causes us to forget larger ethical concerns. No; it is as if capitalism is some kind of evil, demoniac god which demands that we do our duty. You know, the definition of duty is, as they put it in Latin, *fiat justitia, pereat mundus* [justice will be done even if the world is imperilled]. This is what capitalism does: even if we all drop dead, this fact is just an empirical, utilitarian consideration and detail, we must still follow our duty towards the maintenance of capitalism.

Something very interesting is happening here which tells us a lot about how ideology functions. Here, we can also see how wrong the conservative characterisation of capitalism as something utilitarian is. No, there is nothing utilitarian about capitalism. Capitalism is perverted duty. The message of capitalism is, "I must follow it, even if we all die following it".

SS: And the role of ideology is to love what we do in discharging that duty?

SŽ: Yes, I almost admire the trick of ideology. Let us say that we two are mobilised into some ethnic cleansing operation, we have to kill and rape people. People who are moderately decent don't generally like doing this. And the function of ideology is to make us, moderately decent people, convince us to do this. For example, Himmler, the Nazi, provided a wonderful formula for this. It doesn't ignore the uneasiness that moderately decent people have at the prospect of doing terrible things, but it interprets my attempt to act against my spontaneous ethical instinct as the true sign of patriotic greatness. Himmler says somewhere, "Nazi officers killing the Jews, they are doing horrible things, but it is their being able to withstand what they are doing that is true evidence of the true love that they have for their country". The formula recognises that your ability to suppress your spontaneous ethical repulsions for a patriotic cause must be interpreted as a sacrifice.

SS: In this way, aggressors begin seeing themselves, and not their victims, as martyrs, and their violence as somehow spiritually noble.

SŽ: I am an atheist, but I have a great appreciation of the social logics of certain religious practices. But, nonetheless, to respond to what you just said, I would quote Steven Weinberg, a cosmologist, who said something very vicious. And I like what he said. He said, "In a society without religion, good people would be doing good things, bad people would be doing bad things, but in order to make good people do bad things, you need something like religion". This is a clear example of the trick of ideology. The very spontaneous decency, and the fact that you have to violate it, is sold to you as your greatness.

SS: In fact, Himmler was a great admirer of the Bhagavad Gita.

SŽ: I know; the solution to Arjuna's problem is not so different to what Himmler proposed.

SS: That Arjuna should overcome his human decency, his spontaneous repulsion and anxiety in the face of the war, and participate in the slaughter in order to do his duty dispassionately as a warrior.

SŽ: This is why it is more and more interesting for me to consider debates in the Indian traditions. And I now want to write about this. Because here we have the site of this basic ideological tension at its purest. On the one hand, you have the *Laws of Manu* and all the traditions linked to it, which is for me, together with the other big example, Confucius, the foundational ideological text. But then you also have with early Buddhism, despite its ambiguities, the extremely forceful egalitarian counter-attacks. This is the site of the struggle. What interests me here is how the old lessons of Manu were revived and in some senses re-invented during colonialism.

I read, in one of the books published by Navayana press [http://navayana.org], how manual scavenging and shit-cleaning by untouchable castes went through an explosion in the 19th century with the expansion of cities. So here is an example of how modernisation, urbanisation, actually gave new life to what we would think is the stuff of tradition. So this is a very good lesson to teach us that ideology can work in many ways. And capitalism and modernity can in fact revive and give new strength to the oppressions of the past.

I am thoroughly fascinated by the *Laws of Manu*. And I claim that it is the fundamental ideological document because it not only spells out the prohibitions and taboos, but it also tells you what will happen if you violate the laws. In fact, it lays down the laws of how to violate the laws. In other words, it lays down an extreme prohibition, knowing fully well that most people will not be able to follow it to the letter. Then it lays down what you can do to compensate for your violation. In other words, for every rule, it states the conditions of the exception.

So, if you are a brahmin, you should not sell rice. But if you are a brahmin who sells rice, at least you should not sell it on a Monday. And if you are a brahmin who sells rice on a Monday, at least you should not wear this or that garment. And so on.

The whole point of regulation is to regulate violation. So that every instance of dissent is also already scripted. Everything, every response, is already insured, already managed. This is ideology.

SS: Are you saying this anxiety about constantly negotiating violations of violations leads to a pervasiveness and a generalisation of fear? The thin spread of fear on the surface of our lives.

SŽ: Precisely. This is also what I call the politics of fear. You are never escaping fear. In societies where everything is managed technocratically, the only way to mobilise people is on the basis of fear. The fear of taboos, of pollution, of outsiders, of who knows what.

In the West, we have no longer the capacity to produce a positive vision. Everything is predicated on the technocratic management and mobilisation of fear. And Left and Right are united on this. You have rightist fears – immigrants, homosexuals, etc; you can have leftist fears – ecological devastation…

SS: So, if not fear, then what?

SŽ: Badiou and I have been debating this thing privately, and we are now going to write about it. There is one place where Lacan should be theoretically corrected. You know, Lacan, following Freud, says that the only emotion that does not cheat is anxiety. The idea is that all others can be masks, so even love can be a mask of hatred and so on. But not anxiety. With anxiety, you encounter the Real. To this one should add: enthusiasm. Already Kant, while talking about the French Revolution, hinted that enthusiasm (as in the sublime) is where you touch the noumenal, the thing in itself.

And in politics, with enthusiasm you cannot cheat. Now, you might say, what about the fanaticism of racists, of Nazis? But that is not enthusiasm, and I can prove this. Enthusiasm is not fanaticism.

SS: How do we distinct enthusiasm from the fanaticism of the fanatic?

SŽ: By its inherent structure. My reproach to Nazism is that it is negative, it is based on fear. How should I put it… enthusiasm does not need a Jew. When you talk with an anti-Semitic racist, it is already wrong to frame the discussion on the terms of 'what Jews really are like'. Anti-Semites have no interest in finding out what Jews are really like; in fact, they were strongest in Germany in the very places where there were almost no Jews.

SS: So what is enthusiasm?

SŽ: We know that it is not fear. In a Badiou-Kantian sense, it is a commitment to an idea. The idea, in my understanding, is a Communist idea. For example, in politics, you cannot have enthusiasm for your nation. It has a universal dimension. You can have enthusiasm for equality, justice. For something greater than the particular. A certain kind of enthusiasm.

Now, you might say, what about the enthusiasm of an élitist artist? Is that universal? I would say, even in the case of a very difficult poet like Mallarmé, composers like Schoenberg, their work, despite its élitism, has an underlying enthusiastic dimension. In enjoying it, in enjoying its enthusiasm, you want to share it with everyone. It has this universal dimension. Of sharing.

I am crazy, and an old-fashioned dogmatic. I think that every form of enthusiastic politics has to be, in some sense, Communist. Now why Communist? Why keep this crazy word? I follow Badiou in this.

Badiou claims (and I agree) that '89-90 was a kind of necessary historical break. I have no mercy for 20th-century Communism. It has its own greatness, here and there, in the beginning, but it was a mega-tragic failure. But still, even in this, I insist there remains a distinction from fascism. Communism was still a properly tragic failure. There is nothing tragic about the failure of fascism, to simplify it to its utmost. They were bad guys, they said that they wanted to do bad things, they came to power and – surprise, surprise – they did some very bad things. But there is nothing tragic in their failure. This is why there are no dissidents within fascism. But with Communism, there is a genuinely tragic dimension. My god! Look at what we wanted to do, and look at the shit we produced. So it is a proper tragedy.

Now, that story is over, and we must begin from the beginning again, as Lenin would have said. So why Communism? When we were young, we used to dream of Socialism with a

Human Face; nowadays, the mainstream of the Left only basically dreams today of capitalism with a human face. Most leftists talk nowadays like Fukuyama, as if history has ended, and only some 'adjustments' have to be made.

But it is clear to me that capitalism cannot adequately address the question of the ecological crisis. The other thing that capitalism cannot solve is the question of intellectual property, and then there is bio-genetics. The market can work maybe at the city level; it cannot work at the global level. The melting of the ice at the poles cannot be solved by market forces. All these problems are problems of the commons. Nature is our commons, as is that which is called intellectual property today and our bio-genetic heritage. All these are problems of the commons. That is why I want to keep the word 'communism'. I know it has a problematic heritage. But at least we are not saying, "Oh, all we need is some more solidarity, some more kindness". Even Tony Blair wants that. No, we need a radical break, and that is why it is important to reclaim an idea that proposed a radical break. You have to signal that there is a need for real change.

The first part of the struggle is to define the co-ordinates of the struggle. It is not, as the media says, a struggle today primarily between enlightened capitalist development and fundamentalism. To me, these are two sides of the same coin. I like what Benjamin says: "Whenever you see fascism, look for a defeated revolution". Whenever you see fundamentalism, it should be seen as the sign of the failure of the Left.

The struggle is actually between Socialism and what is potentially Communism. And here, by 'socialism' I mean a kind of authoritarian, market-centred but state-managed capitalism – which is what we have and will increasingly have, and China is a great example of what this means.

The distrust of this authoritarian capitalism can make one a fundamentalist, and one becomes a fundamentalist if no other vector of critical politics is any longer available.

You know Afghanistan was once a very socially liberal place. And Kansas (in the USA) was once known for its radical political culture. You should read that book by Thomas Frank, *Whatever Happened to Kansas*. Today Kansas is the Bible belt. Today, the nature of global politics has made fundamentalists dominate both Afghanistan and Kansas.

SS: But maybe fundamentalism, which requires a lot of funding, is also on its way out, because it is too threatening to the liberal capitalist order. It is not being bankrolled any more. But that does not mean our problems are over.

SŽ: So what do you see as its replacement?

SS: You could have the choice between enthusiasm and despair.

SŽ: Despair. Yes, we should take this seriously.
Burkina Faso, Mali, Niger (not Nigeria). They no longer even dream about change. People simply accept that life is bad and it is getting worse. They no longer have space even for the

millenarian catastrophe of fundamentalism. The total resignation of an entire population.

SS: And this is much scarier than fundamentalism. It is the transition from the suicide bomber to suicide.

SŽ: Yes. Without bomb. So the alternative is to bomb or not to bomb, no? Maybe we can construct, following Jameson, a semiotic square or triangle, no? So you have one axis, suicide, another axis, bomber, and the third axis, despair. So the fundamentalists are on the suicide axis, the revolutionaries are on the bomber axis, and where are the liberals?

SS: I think the liberals are on the bomber axis. They bomb, without the suicide.

SŽ: You are right, the liberals are the bombers. And ordinary people? What about them?

SS: In despair?

SŽ: Yes. But where does that leave people like me? Neither suicide, nor bomb. But I want arms. I am going to want to keep that option open!

Based on a visual angle
of one minute

$\frac{20}{200}$	E	200 FT. / 61 m	**1**
$\frac{20}{100}$	N T	100 FT. / 30.5 m	**2**
$\frac{20}{70}$	H U Ž	70 FT. / 21.3 m	**3**
$\frac{20}{50}$	I A Ž M	50 FT. / 15.2 m	**4**
$\frac{20}{40}$	P E C F D	40 FT. / 12.2 m	**5**
$\frac{20}{30}$	E D F C Z P	30 FT. / 9.14 m	**6**
$\frac{20}{25}$	F E L O P Z D	25 FT. / 7.62 m	**7**
$\frac{20}{20}$	D E F P O T E C	20 FT. / 6.10 m	**8**
$\frac{20}{15}$	L E F O D P C T	15 FT. / 4.57 m	**9**
$\frac{20}{13}$	F D P L T C E O	13 FT. / 3.96 m	**10**
$\frac{20}{10}$	P E Z O L C F T D	10 FT. / 3.05 m	**11**

Without Fear or Favour

ASHIS NANDY in conversation with Shuddhabrata Sengupta

Shuddhabrata Sengupta (SS): Professor Nandy, I have been reading two essays of yours recently, again and again. One is "Welcome to the Age of Fear", and the other is "Narcissism and the Age of Despair", on terrorism.

Both of these texts seem to me to be speaking very directly to the theme of *Sarai Reader 08 – Fear*. In fact, they are like a kind of conspectus of the emotion, and I want to start by asking you how you think we learn to be afraid. Because what's interesting in your conception of fear is the place you give, not just to physical, bodily fear, but also to the fear of things we may never experience, and I am quite curious to know about what you think we learn to be afraid of in that which may not even touch us.

Ashis Nandy (AN): I suspect that fear is a quasi-biological, human, learned response to various kinds of danger. A child is not fearful of fire. Unless and until a child gets singed, or associates attempt to go and hold anything on fire by his or her parents, he lacks fear.

Animals have fear. Animals may not have other sentiments associated with fear, but that's a different story. So the first point in response to what you are asking is that we don't have to learn to fear, fear is given to us as a tool of human survival. And perhaps because of that, fear in the normal sense, in everyday life, is a normal sentiment. Nobody gets anxious if your son shows fear of things. Unless and until it goes out of the range of normality – and this happens under two or three circumstances. One is being perpetually afraid of something because that thing has gotten associated with something, it has acquired a symbolic load in the mind, it in a sense hampers your social life or social relationships. People begin to fear you if you are always fearful of certain things. This is not normal or natural.

There is no clinical profile for normal fear because it is part of human normality. There will be clinical profiles for certain kinds of exaggerated fear. Indeed clinicians fear, psychiatrists and psychoanalysts and psychologists fear, things more about anxiety and panic much more than fear.

For a long while, the excess of fear was seen as – not always, but generally, there was a tendency to view the excess of fear as a feature of less developed societies. Fear of ghosts, for instance – that will not be called pathological, it may be a part of a community's belief system, but the belief system itself will be seen as pathological.

SS: At the beginning of "Welcome to the Age of Fear", you speak of an almost sense of relief with which Auden and Erikson announce the age of anxiety. And you talk now of a return to the age of fear. As if you, Ashis Nandy, are standing at the threshold as a doorkeeper and saying, "Welcome, welcome to the Age of Fear". What, then, makes those who had this confidence of being sophisticatedly anxious, suddenly fearful again?

AN: This sensitivity was directly a byproduct of the Freudian revolution. Fromm was a psychoanalyst and a Marxist; Auden was deeply influenced by Freud, and indeed wrote a wonderful poem about him, one of his best.

One byproduct of this relationship was the distinction between fear and anxiety that was spelt out. Anxiety is a more diffuse sense of discomfort, with no fantasy in it. Fear usually has a concrete reason of fear, and even when it is vague, even when it is the fear of ghosts or witchcraft, has a clear-cut fantasy beneath or within it. So diseases which had this kind of fantasy were seen as particularly characteristic of more primitive societies, which had not gone through the process of disenchantment that the Enlightenment prescribed.

SS: So is the re-entry into the age of fear in advanced, industrial societies, in some way a paradoxical return to an age of enchantments?

AN: Yes, exactly; and there are clear fantasies. Entry into the age of anxiety – vague, diffuse anxiety, which does not have fantasies but rather has psycho-somatic expressions, such as cardio-vascular diseases, skin allergies, asthmas – these are the things that prompted the declaration of the age of anxiety.

Now, according to that theory, we are in a regression. We have not only fear, but one wonders what are the specific fantasies – fantasies may change, from area to area, person to person, there may be a plethora of fantasies, and these may vary.

Some may have the fantasy of meeting the Islamic hordes at the walls of Europe – crusader fantasies are being recreated. Some may have fantasies about hidden agents, sleepers possessed of inner secrets, who cannot be identified by their looks, who can look like you or me, who can look like anyone else.

For a long time, European and North American society was blind to the presence of their own Muslim minorities. There has been a long history of African American Muslims, for instance, who were like other African Americans, but suddenly, now, people in America have woken up to them because (as Muslims, after September 11) they are surfaces on which their fears can be projected. And now they have to think about them, and they have to think about people who do not necessarily look any different from them. You cannot necessarily make them out by their skin colour or the presence or absence of an epithelial fold. This awareness has come back. And it has brought fears back with it.

SS: A return to the culture of the Inquisition, perhaps, where people were suspect not because they showed outward signs of difference. In fact, the person whom you feared most was the one who may have looked exactly like you, behaved exactly like you, but who was suspected of responding to the commands of some secret power.

AN: Traitors within – the fears of traitors within, and the concomitant wish or desire for an exorcism, is a very important feature of modern life. It had been pushed out of modern life without a recognition of the enormity of the passions that it contains. But now it has returned in full force.

The Nazis were reacting to similar passions in the case of the Jews, also in the case of homosexuals. Of course, you know that Adorno and Horkheimer found in their study of the Authoritarian Personality that people who scored high on their 'F' Scale also exhibited a tendency towards sado-masochism. Even a certain kind of hypermasculinity is associated with a vague sense of homosexual fantasies of various kinds. You fear what you fear not only because it is strange, but also because it reminds you of yourself.

SS: Let us invoke another kind of fear – the fear of annihilation. We are living in Delhi, the capital of a nuclear power, which has gone to war more than once with its neighbour, which is also now a nuclear power. If there is a city that should be the locus of this fear of annihilation, it should be here; and yet, there is a happy or unhappy deferral of the fear of annihilation. In modern metropolitan India, we are beset by many fears, but annihilation does not seem to be one of them.

The fear of the nuclear holocaust was a part of the folklore of contemporary urban life in post-Second World War Europe or Japan or the United States. We are more or less in the same position today. We are exactly where the United States or Europe were in terms of the nuclear arms race in the 1950s, but we don't seem to have the same generalisation of this fear. Though there are a few exceptions, there are comic books and the odd Hindi film, which do seem to obsess with nuclear holocaust fantasies, but there does not seem to be a generalisation of this fear. How do you explain that?

AN: No, I will have to disagree with you here. I think just because you cannot see this fear, it doesn't mean it doesn't in fact exist. Even in Europe and North America, in public life and in public rhetoric, this fear was fully disowned. Everyone went about their business as if nothing had changed, and yet you saw it in fantasy, in novels, in movies, and they were successful by being provocative, they did attract a lot of viewers and readers. Also, that which was hidden by and from adults was not hidden in the case of children, and studies do show that younger children often lived with this fear of annihilation. They had internalised it. And they had not internalised it only from their peers, they must have internalised it from the fears and anxieties of their parents, which in fact were not expressed or communicated but were present all the same. Often these children were very small, and when you asked them to paint and draw, it would express itself directly. I suspect that children in this case were acting as the unconscious of the society as a whole, and so were the artistic and literary products of the time.

Yes, in India, I do see a lesser expression of this fear, partly as a result of the fact that there is always an attempt by modern states to use these weapons as instruments of statecraft, which leads to a tendency to underplay their reality and the fears associated with them. The way, in India, in which nuclear accidents have been well-hidden, including the one that happened recently, say, for instance, the one that happened at the reactor at Narora, on the banks of the Ganga, some of the scientists concerned were sure that they would all die. Even scientists!

So, it is not what the politicians claim, and not what the manifest public culture in this country allows for that we must consider alone. Indeed, I will go further to say that this absence of anxiety is becoming a typical feature of a kind of 'Festive Style' which is the present form of capitalism's attempts to generalise all over the world.

SS: You mean the pressure to be always cheerful and confident?

AN: Yes, the demand that all unhappiness, pain and even the sorrow of death must be immediately forgotten. Such that you are normal, even if your parents die, you act as if nothing much has happened, that you must get on with life as usual, You are required to behave, if you come out of a major surgery which has probably reduced your life-span by three or four years, as if it is a small thing, and you say that you are going to join work in three or four days.

So this style, this 'Festive Style', where you have nothing to mourn and nothing to lament, is something that we have adopted whole-heartedly. And perhaps because this city, Delhi, as we know it today, which is a Punjabi refugee city (not the city that it was before 1947), this city has a cultivated style, which is perhaps a reaction to the suffering and uprooting that people here have had once to go through during Partition, and that memory, they (the inhabitants of Delhi) have been trying to work through rather aggressively. In that process, they have acquired this style, and they found this festive style of capitalism a nice endorsement. It has come as a godsend.

SS: At the same time, nowadays on television, we see public service announcements issued by the Ministry of Health and Family Welfare which talk about depression as a clinical symptom. They used the Hindi word, '*avasad*' to describe an unhappiness without reason. They are often directed at parents, and ask parents to be vigilant about the unhappiness of children and young people; they say there is a cure, that you can take the person concerned to a doctor at your nearby health centre. It is interesting to note that along with the rise of the 'Festive Style', just as the pressure to be happy mounts, there is an acknowledgement of depression as a public health issue.

AN: There is no doubt about that. Data show that depression has become much more common in India than before. Previously, the majority of Indian psychiatric referrals generally featured two common categories: obsessive-compulsive disorders (OCDs) and hysteria. This is understandable; hysteria has psycho-somatic implications underpinned by specific fantasies; with the decline of these specific fantasies, the symptoms also became less common. Freud's first patients were hysterics, but hysteria declined first in Europe, and people teaching psychiatry in European institutions found it difficult to find appropriately hysteric patients to demonstrate to their students. But in India, it was very common.

Of course, OCD was considered to be a typically Indian disease, and it was often explained away; the middle class was very small, and, in upper-caste contexts, it was passed over, it was, how should I put it, not under-emphasised, but incorporated into everyday normality by saying, such-and-such a person has... in Bengali, we would say '*suchibai*', the compulsive and exaggerated observance of purity and pollution taboos and caste-linked prohibitions. It was the standard way of referring to the obsessions of widows. Every upper-caste Bengali household had somebody who suffered from OCD.

Now, the largest number of referrals comes from the sector we call 'depressed'. And many of them are clinically depressed. It is not mere sub-clinical melancholia, which you can easily explain away by referring to incidents and biographical details. But 'depression' per se is a much more serious matter, and maybe part of the load it carries has to do with the kind of issues that you are raising.

SS: Of being already in the age of anxiety even though fear is very much around us? Living in India, you have access to a diachronic sensibility, the experience of living in more than one time at once, which is very uncomfortable for people more used to living in one time at a time. Hence this layering of anxiety with fear, which is now a part of our general life here, which you say the West has to get used to again, but which we have lived with, both fear and anxiety.

AN: You are very right, but this has what I might call a robust side to it also. I remember Ravi Mathai, a former director at IIM [the Indian Institute of Management], Ahmedabad, once told me an anecdote about innovation. There was a cobbler in a village that Mathai was interested in who resisted all attempts to use new methods, techniques and technologies.

Even though his own brother was an 'early adopter'. So Mathai asked him, why don't you do like your brother, and take to the new methods, so that you too can earn more and be more productive. The cobbler said his brother's productivity may have increased, but his needs have also expanded, and that is why he needed all the money he could get, whereas he was content with what he had. "My brother cannot do without the things which I do not need", he said, implying in a way that he was in fact more prosperous, because his needs were more fully met, than his more 'productive' and 'innovative' brother.

As a final gambit, Ravi Mathai said to him, but people are saying that you are backward, traditional, unchanging, that you are stuck in the last century. To which, the cobbler replied by saying, "I decide which century I want to live in".

I thought this was a lovely reply. In India, this option is still available. From the 6th century to nearly-Stone Age aborigines, like the Onges of the Andamans, to fully modernised sectors of society, we have everything, the whole bloody range. This allows an enormously diverse range of experiments to go on, in Indian cities, in villages too, in Indian society as a whole. This diversity, this experimentation, can only make this society more vigorous and creative without threatening its basic styles, its basic algorithms of life.

SS: At the same time, we are beginning to get more instances of what we might call the psychopathologies of contemporary life. I have always thought that one can measure capitalism and development itself by the instances of serial killing. That serial killers, people who kill for no reason other than the enjoyment, pleasure or the drive to kill, are peculiar features of contemporary capitalism. As we know well from watching American slasher movies, they are, generally, single White men who live alone, are often highly successful, they are not necessarily social outcasts, but are often quite well integrated into society, and that they nevertheless channel the darkest drives of society and are able to camouflage them through their apparent normality. The veneer, or performance, of normality of the psychopath is I think now beginning to present itself in our newspapers.

AN: There is a lovely essay by George Orwell, "The Decline of the English Murder", you must have read it, which, for the first time, argues this case, in non-technical language, and I like it because of that. It conveys everything without using technical language. But if you will allow me to digress a little bit, then I will say that this is a very good measure you are suggesting, because you have in some way captured the spirit of a society where conformity is not demanded explicitly but is always extracted. Indeed, in no other society can dissent be as expensive, especially if dissent does not conform to the standardised, dominant modalities of dissent.

Regardless of the fact that people might make fun of Leninism today, we must remember that Leninism is a product of the modern age. A person who calls himself or herself a Leninist is a natural ally of the state, of society, of the family and the workplace. He might be seen as somewhat old-fashioned, but nobody will see his dissent as infantile or irrational. Whereas certain forms of dissent which do not meet this criteria, which seem insane, infantile and irrational, have very little space in contemporary society. This exclusion cuts across ideological boundaries too. There is a consensual affirmation of normality. So some kinds of dissent are almost taboo.

And, as it happens, this is the kind of dissent that many artists and writers, without necessarily knowing it, have taken to, partly because it is acceptable that they should do so. It is not allowed if you are a scientist or a social scientist or a philosopher. I think that these sectors, I mean the sectors of art and fiction writing, remain virtually the only spheres where this kind of dissent has a place. In fact, there (in the arts) you can experiment with the immature, the infantile and the irrational much more openly and dramatically today than you could earlier. Earlier, the conformity extended there too.

Now, the controls are so tight that only in the imaginary can you play with these sensibilities, but in analytical writings, and in your thoughtful writings, you are forbidden access to these dispositions. Only rarely, maybe in the likes of Gandhi, maybe, perhaps partially, in Nelson Mandela or the Dalai Lama, you find an example of that.

There is a kind of strange split. You admire these persons and yet think that they have nothing to say about real, live politics. And that split is within you. And there is an almost desperate attempt to incorporate them in the culture of the state, as iconic figures who are 'too good' to be of any relevance to everyday life.

SS: So they are in a sense domesticated by placing them on a...

AN: On a pedestal... Absolutely!

SS: I'd like to bring you back to the question of normality, violence and pathology.

AN: Let us take the case of the present discomfort with the Naxalites (Maoists). It is almost becoming a sin to mention any larger issues, or think about any long term motivational factors or vectors when considering their opposition. The moment you bring up such matters, you are told, "We are not concerned with that, we are concerned with the immediate threats to India's security and its developmental programme".

The fact of the matter is, that in their irrationality, in their immaturity, and what is the third expression I used? Yes, infantilism...

SS: Infantilism? Lenin's expression, 'the infantile disorder'?

AN: Yes, infantilism. Now they too, the Naxalites (Maoists), I mean in all their immaturity, irrationality and infantilism, have nevertheless hitched upon something which has served them well. Namely, our record vis-à-vis our tribal population. What we have done in 60 years to them has created an enormous reservoir of bitterness and anger. The Naxals have simply stumbled upon that base. They (the Naxals) might have their own motivations for doing so. They might have discovered an ideological vantage point that allows them to vent their anger as legitimate. They might have taken advantage of it to meet the needs of their anger and hostility, which were looking for a target of a different kind. In other words, this might have become a vehicle of their own private psycho-pathologies, but this does not detract an iota from the fact that they have found a hearing in a very large sector of our tribal population. And I suspect, I am convinced, why should I say suspect, I am indeed convinced that the bitterness and anger of the tribals is not unjustified.

Look at our developmental profile. Look at the way in which our factories and our dams have displaced people, and find out the proportions of tribals displaced as compared to the proportions of others displaced in these ventures, and you will always find that we have been ruthless with them.

And even this present nervousness and anxiety and fear centering on the Naxal uprising or upsurge (whatever you would like to call it) is partly born out of the feeling that the tribals are sitting on a goldmine which they cannot use and nor will they let others use. And the best that we would like them to do is to politely, obediently and gracefully vacate their place in history and enter the textbooks of history, so that we can celebrate them as people who were 'once staying here', and whose creativity and colorful life can become remembered exemplars of what India could have been.

Their only crime is that they are, in fact, our next-door neighbours. We would like to talk about them in the past tense.

SS: You have written eloquently about the narrowing space of anguish as some sort of an epi-phenomenon of the expanding space of fear. Perhaps what you are expressing is that the narrowing of the space for the expression of the anguish that these 'neighbours' feel probably transforms them into the vectors of our fear, and the objects of our fear.

AN: Yes. You are probably right. I suspect that we are seeing the beginning of the end of our tribal population. We have always been unhappy that we have not been able to do to them that which the Americans did to the American Indians and what the Australians did to the Australian aboriginals. America and Australia are the best examples of what settler societies can do. And we are psychologically becoming like settler societies. We, urban, middle-class, metropolitan Indians, are becoming like a 'settler society', confronting around us a huge population of people we have consigned to the category of the 'primitive', the 'sub-human', about the existence of whose souls we can debate endlessly, like some European evangelical groups did in the 18th century.

That is exactly the situation which we are in today. I am afraid I see very little sensitivity to this. Only yesterday, I received news of a Gandhian ashram being sacked (by agencies allied to the state) in Chhattisgarh. This is not surprising to me at all. But it is pathetic. It is pathetic on compassionate grounds, but it is also pathetic on intellectual grounds. It shows the utter poverty and shamelessness of the metropolitan culture of India as it is functioning today.

SS: If we relegate a population to a position outside our constructed horizon of humanity, then they become the repositories of all our favourite fears?

AN: Not only of fear, but even of all the categories which we love. They also become the repositories of purity, of honesty, of simplicity, of austerity – of all kinds of things that we have disowned. We feel the need to have them around as 'categories' that can act as balancing forces against our greed, our consumerism, our individualism. So, after we have made them extinct, after we have pushed them into the Indian Ocean, after we have ensured that they exist only in the textbooks of history, then we will be invoking them as reminders of possible checks on our lifestyles.

SS: I want you to talk briefly about the absence of fear. That specific kind of absence of fear which translates as impunity.

AN: Impunity in Indian public culture is primarily based on the fact that if you have big money, no one can touch you. The regimes that are central to the system cannot be persecuted, cannot be held accountable. But there is another kind of impunity. And that is, I think, a trickier thing. It is the feeling that you are invulnerable because you are on the side of progress and development, and thus have nothing to fear.

That cultivated sense of invulnerability is constantly threatened by a tacit awareness, a latent awareness, that you are actually very vulnerable. Vulnerable in two senses: one, that electoral fortunes cannot be predicted with certainty, and that this time there are large enough sectors of the population who have paid for the kind of progress, development and modernisation that you have opted for, and these sectors are now demanding an equality that you cannot give them, or a form of representation which can be very threatening. Very threatening. I am afraid that this entire Naxal upsurge is a test of Indian democracy. My feeling is that Indian democracy will emerge triumphant, though it will make a compromise with the elites, and also try to keep its developmental journey unhindered.

SS: To come back now to a different question. When you were growing up, there was fear of social crises erupting and so on and so forth. But I think a recognition needs to be made of a different kind of fear. The fear that somewhere in a market place, a bomb may go off. This identification of the very material structure of urban life – dustbins, cars, tiffin boxes. Now we are told a camera can be a bomb, a tape recorder can be a bomb, phones can be bombs. So what does it do to our ordering of our desires and our ability to construct a day-to-day rationality and commodities?

AN: I think there is a new kind of contamination that is coming in. Anyone, you, me, anyone can be contaminated. Like this man who shot his colleagues in America. We have a fear of contamination of things in cultural terms, in emotional terms.

The kind of anxiety that people had about contamination in earlier times centred on diseases. Now, that fear of contamination is lessened, but it has been displaced on to the idea of 'secret enemies' who are like you (us) and therefore cannot be distinguished. My suspicion is that the global middle class culture will have to live with this fear, because this culture did try to close all options, imagining (to use that buzz word) an 'end of history' and that human beings have at long last found the final answer to problems of social and political arrangements. I think that the human quest for a perfect public life has not ended and cannot end. That (quest) is in the nature of human beings. Many things that in the past looked as if they were final answers turned out after a point of time to be hollow options that were not worth pursuing. We live in times when, after 70 years of a revolution, the revolutionary regime collapsed, and despite all the violent means at its disposal, this superpower could not sustain itself, what to speak of sustaining an alternative world. The vulgarity of that enterprise was so enormous that you do not find enough numbers of vestigial followers in the societies that they ruled. I mean, the number of Leninists in India is far higher than the number of Leninists in Russia.

SS: Yet Stalin is very popular in Russia nowadays...

AN: That is a nationalist thing. It is seen as a marker of greater certainty. It's like Peter the Great being popular in Russia. Russians would not like to live either under Peter the Great or under Stalin, but still they are popular. Exactly just as Mrs Gandhi or Subhash Bose are popular, posthumously. Their ghosts are popular. That is part of human nature. A desire for a fantasy Stalin or a fantasy Indira Gandhi attracts people because they are safely dead.

SS: I want you to help me think about something you hinted at earlier – the therapeutic possibilities of anguish and despair. You say that the diminishing of space for anguish and fear expands the space of fear. This is an unorthodox thought, one would normally think that anguish and despair are emotions that you would like to avoid in your life, and yet you insist on a place for them.

AN: In fact, they are thought to be psychiatrically marked – anguish and despair – but I would like to see some possibilities there, and I feel (to use the expression of Laing), "Breakdowns can also be breakthroughs". I guess I am more optimistic than others, because I feel that something more creative will come out of this, all these sacrifices will not go in vain, and often the carriers of new messages are not as likable as persons as we would like them to be, but that is okay.

SS: Before we began our interview, in the conversation leading up to it, you spoke of the childhood sources for learning about the unhappiness of the world, and you spoke about the Bengal famine of 1942, you spoke about communal violence, and the World War. What lessons did being very young, in the face of extreme abjection, give to you that you carry through your life?

AN: I think I learnt human cruelty to human beings can be limitless, provided you can close your mind and find in it a larger purpose. Because we have lost faith – because, to use those much-used words, we have 'killed god' – we feel that we have acquired almost god-like power in dispensing life and death. You might remember, Stalin prohibited any alms, any help, to the famine victims in the Soviet Union (in the Ukraine). It was a man-made famine, everyone knows that. And people swallowed that prohibition. I do not think that it was because it was a police state, but I think it was because, in some sense, it was seen as a 'normal' blood sacrifice for the making of a great nation. One of the tacit messages of development in our times is this, an unsaid formulation of state formation: 'You do to your people what we have done to our people to become what we are today'. And that is why the Indian and Chinese effort to 'equal' the West involves an unacknowledged acceptance of hard statecraft and the glorification of a hard state which will navigate the turbulent waters of international and domestic politics.

SS: Is that something you fear, personally?

AN: Yes, and no. Because I am also fully aware that this cannot pass in India. It cannot pass in India. It has to give way. In the case of China, it will be an enormous struggle. But in India, it just cannot sustain itself. Things have to go to the people for whatever reason (that's another discussion), they will have to go to the people, and ultimately their fate will be decided not the way the Naxals would like it, but the way the fate of despots has been decided earlier in this society, through the ballot box.

The Naxals, though they might think of themselves as the agents of history, have actually stood in the way of a more preferred and more acceptable solution of the problem, in the sense that if, for instance, 12 or 13 percent of Muslims in India are said to affect the results of 110 or 113 constituencies in the general elections, it is unthinkable why you could not think of the tribal population in a non-violent democratic way making a huge electoral impact. It would probably have taken lesser sacrifices, and lesser effort.

SS: In that sense, would you agree that the hard state would always prefer its enemy to be someone like the Maoist insurgent?

AN: Absolutely. For example, the Israeli state is the harshest with those who have opted for non-violent resistance to it, they are the ones who are arrested first, and they (the Israeli state) have taken great pains to ensure that such movements do not take off because they know that, in the present global situation, that could be really dangerous for their power.

SS: Thank you, Professor Nandy, for taking this time out to talk at such length about Fear, without fear or favour!

AN: I am afraid it's been my pleasure.

ALT / OPTION

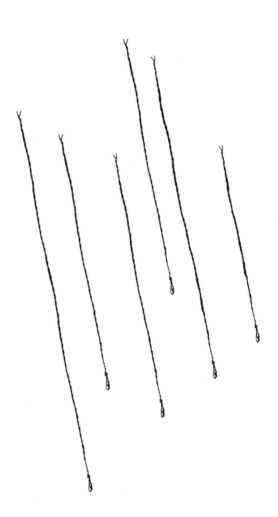

Fearless Speech, Fearless Listening

CYBERMOHALLA ENSEMBLE

I was cleaning my room. One by one, I shifted all the things out. I took the posters off the wall, the cooking pots off the shelf, shifted out of the room the television set and the refrigerator, the fish tank and all the gifts that had been kept on it. The room became as still as a picture and entirely soundless. Without the toys and gifts, it looked incomplete, like a 'thing'. My eyes roamed the room, from one corner to the other. I imagined faint outlines of the objects that were no longer there, and tried to remember when they had been brought home, who had brought them; I wondered about who would have made them. But even as I thought about the things that had been in here, all my eyes could see were the different corners of the room, now no longer concealed by those objects. Bare now, it was as if the room was looking back at me. As if it wanted to reveal to me something about itself. I felt an unknown feeling, something akin to happiness, brimming up inside me. But more recognisably, I felt a fear. I felt as if I was standing not in one, but in two rooms.

①

A friend of mine from childhood had recently started working. When I met her, I asked her, "Do you like it? Are you enjoying the freedom that comes with stepping out of the house everyday?" She looked at me for a long moment, then smiled and said, "The strangest thing about going to work is that everyone wants me to talk about it, but it seems to me no one really wants to listen". When she saw I was a little confused about how to tell her I sincerely wanted to know, she elaborated:

> One person asks me about freedom, another about exhaustion, someone else about the difficulty of working, and yet another about the exhilaration of finding my own way in the world. It is as if the frames through which I can speak are outside of me. I keep talking, but it seems to me that whatever I say to someone, he or she already knows it. Moreover, if I become inward at home for a few hours, my family thinks I'm hiding something, and if I intervene confidently in any debate in my own house, my visiting relatives object and say that I've become a loud-mouth ever since I started working. So, if there's one thing I can say with absolute certainty about my going out to work, it's this: it has affected and changed what I can say and how much I should speak.

It seemed to me my friend was telling me something very fundamental – that whenever we start something new, or make a departure from our routine in even small ways, the first thing that happens is a shift in how we encounter speech. This set me thinking. *Are there thresholds of speech in daily life that we are not permitted to cross? What would happen if we crossed them?*

I started paying attention at home. I filled notebook after notebook transcribing conversations; I wrote down everything anyone said. Simple conversations my mother had with us, conversations between us and our guests, what someone said after a visit to a doctor or to her son's teacher at school, at weddings, when someone was born, when a stranger knocked at the door, when people gathered to offer condolences for someone's death. Months passed. My notebooks, and my mind, filled with words.

It was festival season. One evening, my friends and I stepped out into the streets of the neighbourhood to watch the magic that travelling magicians were performing. Everywhere, the audience stood mesmerised; many requested the magicians for certain tricks, each more difficult than the last. It suddenly struck me: *A magician can't say, 'It's impossible!'* My mind raced through my notes from the last few months. I thought: *My mother can't say to me or to my brothers and sisters, 'I forgot'. A doctor can't say to her patient, 'I don't know, I'm still learning'. A teacher can't say to her student, 'I don't understand'.*

As I turned back home, I remembered how once there had been a bitter fight between my mother and my eldest brother, and he had said, "I would have told you, but you wouldn't have been able to bear it". Things didn't remain the same at home after this. Hadn't my friend poignantly said, "...it seems to me no one really wants to listen"?

The more I thought about it, the more it seemed to me we create thresholds of listening which determine what and how much we will hear, and, in turn, what speech we will allow around us. *What is my capacity to listen?* I wondered. *How and when is it challenged?* As I lay in bed, I thought, *Are there people around me who might want to say something to me but hesitate because they think I don't have in me the capacity to listen?*

I switched on the light, opened my notebook to a fresh page and wrote:
Fearless speech requires fearless listening.

①

I would write everyday. I liked writing, liked the way my words would take shape, liked the way my hand looked as I wrote. I'd put *mehandi* on my hands or wear bangles, and then sit down to write. But very soon I would also want to stop thinking about the characters I was writing about. That is why each of my stories was half a page long – my characters would die in half a page.

I wasn't alone in this. I was with many others who were, like me, beginning to experience their forays into thinking through writing. And it took us some time to realise all of us were killing our characters – if not of an incurable disease, they'd die of heartbreak; if not in a road accident, they'd meet their end in a calamitous earthquake. The turning point came when we were trying to compose a text together, where each person contributed a line by turn to build the narrative. In this text, one character died after every three lines! It was as if we were all flinching from thinking, and so committing a sort of 'thought *hara-kiri*'. We resolved that day to stop killing our characters.

But then we started on a different track. We'd have long discussions every week about what we had written. Usually these resulted in the voicing of differing points of view, and examples – both from personal experience and from the experiences of those around us – would be cited to corroborate arguments. Slowly, everyone's texts started beginning with the refrain '*hamare yahan*', that is, 'this is how it is where I come from'. End of discussion. The fall in the decibel level of our discussions soon produced concerned enquiries from the neighbours, and so it can be said that circumstances forced us to ignore this repeated refrain, and eventually each of us was compelled to drop it altogether from our texts.

For some time, however, the more ingenious among us continued to invent and evoke different boundaries to restrict being pushed by others to think in ways other than the one we had chosen. I, for instance, continued to fight thinking by saying, "But I'm not permitted to think about this". And if I was still pushed, I'd get provoked and say, "*Meri marzi*" – I'll do as I wish. I did everything in my power to push thought away.

One day, Azra read out a beautiful text she had written about a cycle rickshaw ride. It was elegant in its description. Yashoda still says, after so many years, that she was very inspired by it, and it changed the way she approached writing. But I was moved by it for an entirely different reason. After Azra finished reading out her text, someone asked her to read again the lines she had written about the rickshaw puller. They were:

He was a handsome young man. So fair, that he may have been Kashmiri. He also looked educated. 'Poor thing!' I thought to myself. 'Surely he can get a better job than this...'

"Do you remember anything else about the man?" we asked Azra.

But Azra didn't. She was quiet for a long time. We were all waiting. Then she looked up from her notebook and said, "By calling him 'poor thing', I pushed him away from my thought. Maybe he attracted me, and I used those words to produce a gap, a kind of thought full-stop".

I think now that if each of us had set out in search of our 'thinking self' alone, it would have been a tall order indeed. But in the co-presence of many others, this search started finding a language and a craft. Babli says that her repeated encounter with others – all of us – in a search similar to her own caused a loosening of her 'I'. From this emerged an inchoate search to produce a new 'we'. That's probably how it was for us all. For many of us, thinking started with this 'I' which was fearful of thinking, fearful of how we thought and how we would be received by others. But as time passed, this 'I' got complicated and, I would even say, started searching for a deeper relationship with the world.

☾

Everyone had started telling me to emerge out of myself and write. I had taken to saying to everyone that I had no thoughts, that nothing came to my mind. It was true; that's how I really felt. But, after repeatedly hearing from everyone "emerge out of yourself", I slowly wondered if I was really in self-love after all.

I opened my notebook to a fresh page and wrote:
I am in self-love.
Then I leafed through some blank pages and wrote again on a new page:
Listen to others.
That week, I made time to get together some people for tea and snacks at my house. Instead of constantly deprecating my own self, I would praise others. Therefore, there was to be a simple rule for this evening of storytelling. I explained it:

> Someone will begin by telling a story. Everyone has to listen carefully. After he or she finishes, the person next to her will praise her by saying *'Wah! Wah!'* (Bravo! Bravo!), and then tell a story which follows from the story she has just heard.

There was a slight restlessness in the room. But then Faisal began. His story was about skipping class to go watch a play. "Bravo! Bravo!" said everyone. Soon there were stories about running away from the village to come to the city, "Bravo! Bravo!"; someone's travels through the city ticketless, "Bravo!"; getting out of home to look for someone in the middle of the night, "Bravo!"; taking help from a postman to locate the address of a long-lost friend, "Bravo!"; long-distance phone calls by a young girl to her mother telling her of the new places she went to every day since she left home...

I was listening carefully. With every story told, there was anticipation for the next story one would hear, and also a challenge to oneself to find a story which matched and built on the daring pitch of the previous story. I realised that without intending for it to be that way, everyone's stories were about one question – how far would you go to listen to me? In a flash, I remembered a woman I knew in my neighbourhood, who had taken in and raised a girl who had wandered away from her elders during a rally. After that evening, I went and met her several times.

☉

For some days, Shamsher had been meeting and holding long conversations with Babu Baba, a man who travels a lot, who is famous in the neighbourhood for his fearlessness, a soothsayer, a practitioner of black magic. Shamsher would come back from his conversations thoughtful. There was something about these conversations which went beyond storytelling. Shamsher would say, "Babu Baba doesn't talk about his life at all. He doesn't think of his life as a series of events, or something that needs to be narrativised". It seemed to me Babu Baba was challenging Shamsher to rethink how people narrate themselves, and this is what drew Shamsher to him day after day, and that Shamsher was struggling to find a way of narrating his encounters with Babu Baba back to us. But every day, there would be one image or the other of Babu Baba that Shamsher came back with. One day, he said Babu Baba had said to him:

> Do you see my hands? With these hands, I can hold someone I love close to me. With them, I could kill someone. If I raise my hands, I can reach god. If I spread them out, I could make the entire world my own, travel from here to anywhere.

With a gesture of his hands, Babu Baba could extend himself from where he stood to infinity.

This set me wondering. Writing and sharing with others what I had been thinking, for days, weeks, months and years, knowing that others had been reading and listening to me, my words, for very long, I had slowly begun to feel a strange fear taking hold of me. A fear of proximity. I feared my listeners may hold on to one or a few of my words and define me through them. I feared that someone, after reading what I had written, might say one day, "I have understood you". I feared being caged forever in my own words. I feared I might soon begin to feel fearful of my own words, begin to distrust them.

But like Babu Baba, am I too not limitless, constituted by infinite things, small pieces that don't seamlessly join to make a whole? If that's how I perceive myself, how will it affect what

I write, how I write it? I decided to do an experiment with myself. Starting that day, I would write not long texts but small pieces, of one paragraph or two, on index cards. I'd write 500, no 1,000 index cards, then shuffle them up and make different sequences of them, to construct innumerable narratives that would be about myself, about others. I wondered if in this way, it would become possible to find an expression that does not exhaust surprises, for me and for others around me. I started that day. For my first entry I wrote:

> I am not being stubborn when I say we must break the moulds that are made for us and demand that the limits of what is acceptable be pushed. I'm not being stubborn when I say we must participate in different contexts as if they were our own. I wasn't being stubborn when, some years ago, I refused to leave the job I had in hand for months, even though every passer-by made promises to me about getting me a better, bigger job. I'm not being stubborn when I refuse to see myself the way everyone else says they see me. I'm not being stubborn when I continue to do that which everyone around me, near me, thinks is dangerous for my future, because I believe in it. I know I must test myself in terms I choose myself.

⊙

One morning, I pasted a sheet of paper on the door of the room in which we meet to discuss our questions and thoughts and share our notes. I had intended it as a kind of announcement about what our meetings were about. A sort of self-definition. Everyone stopped at the door to read it before entering, and really appreciated it. But I noticed that Nasreen was spending the longest time reading my text. Her face was very thoughtful. I went up to her to ask her what she was thinking. Then I saw she had cut out some words in the text and replaced them with others.

She travels   *herself*   *she*
~~We travel~~ from place to place, trying to connect people to ~~us~~. And sometimes ~~we~~ as

   curls   *hides*   *her*   *her She doesn't*
if ~~curl~~ up and ~~hide~~ in a corner hoping someone will find ~~us~~, discover ~~us~~. ~~We don't~~ have

                  she   *she*
any fixed social definition, that is why ~~we~~ can take on different roles. Sometimes ~~we~~ can

be like a bright shower of lights that sparkles up the night sky. And sparkles in the sky

belong to no one; in the sky no one can tame them or claim them as their own. Stitching

                                         her she tries
together myriad scratches of images of different people around ~~us~~, ~~we try~~ to breathe

                      She isn't
life into them through thinking them. ~~We aren't~~ some scrap of paper that has accidentally

blown into this context with a gust of wind. ~~We are~~ *She is* part of our environment. And ~~we seek~~ *she seeks*

nurturing from our environment. ~~We are~~ *She is* like a membrane rather than a door ~~we attempt~~ *she attempts*

to keep destabilising separations between ideas of 'inside' and 'outside'. ~~We try~~ *She tries* to keep

the threshold of entry of others into ~~our midst~~ *her life* simple and welcoming.

She turned to me and said, "I was thinking that to all the puzzles that personalities around us are, we must add this personality too, to think with".

CONTRIBUTORS (in alphabetical order)

Aarti Sethi is currently working as an urban researcher with the Sarai Programme at the Centre for the Study of Developing Societies (CSDS). Her interests include political theory, and the history and anthropology of city spaces and media cultures. <aarti.sethi@gmail.com>

Adnan Hadzi is undertaking a practice-based Ph.D., "The Author vs. the Collective", that focuses on the influence of digitalisation and the new forms of (documentary) film production, as well as the author's rights in relation to collective authorship. This interdisciplinary research combines sources and expertise from the fields of media and communication, computer studies and architecture. The practical outcome is Deptford. TV, an online database drawing on the current regeneration process in Deptford, South/East London. The database serves as a platform for artists and filmmakers to store and share the documentation of the urban change of S/E London. <a.hadzi@gold.ac.uk>

Agat Sharma completed his undergraduate degree from the National Institute of Fashion Technology (NIFT), Gandhinagar, in 2007 and is currently a Master of Design student at NIFT, New Delhi. <agatsharma@gmail.com>

Agon Hamza is enrolled in Ph.D. studies in Philosophy and Visual Culture, Primorska Univerza, Slovenia. He was a co-initiator of the DKS (Department for Social Critique) and is currently engaged in the Group for Research in Sociology and Philosophy (GRSP). He publishes articles in the politics section of daily newspapers, and is the assistant editor of the *Kritika dhe Shoqëria* magazine, published by the GRSP. <agon.hamza@gmail.com>

Ambarien Alqadar is currently a Fulbright-Nehru Fellow at the School of Communications and Theatre, Temple University, Philadelphia. She previously taught Video and Television Production at the AJK Mass Communication Research Centre, Jamia Millia Islamia, New Delhi. As a documentary filmmaker, her works include *Who Can Speak of Men; Elsewhere* (Best Documentary, the Digital Film Festival, Mumbai 2005); *Barefoot* and *Four Women and a Room* (Silver Award, Best Documentary, Indian Documentary Producers' Association (IDPA) Awards for Excellence, Mumbai, 2008). She is one of the founding members of the Jamia Teachers' Solidarity Group, New Delhi, a body of activists and teachers formed after the September 2008 police encounter at Batla House, demanding a free probe of the event and a fair trial for those still in custody. <ambarien@yahoo.co.uk>

Amitabh Kumar is an artist based in Delhi. He has researched extensively on Raj Comics at Sarai. He is a co-initiator of the Pao Collective, an ensemble of graphic artists. <amitabhkumar84@gmail.com>

Andrés de Santiago Areizaga graduated from the Glasgow School of Art in 2002 and has since been active not only as a designer, editor and artist, but has also been involved in the private and public spheres of art museums and galleries, architecture, photography and in communication and archiving. He runs the arts and culture platform, Skorpion, and has exhibited and participated in artist residencies and workshops in Spain, the UK, Athens, Tokyo, Holland, Paris, Beijing and New York. With interests in economics, linguistics and semiotics, institutional critique, and the politics of value and exclusion, he works mainly in art direction and editorial design, and contributes regularly to magazines and publications. <skorpiongrafik@gmail.com>

Andrew Goffey is Senior Lecturer in Media, Culture and Communications at Middlesex University. He writes about issues crossing the domains of philosophy, science and culture and, apart from the Evil Media project, is currently working on a monograph on the politics of software. He has published essays on a range of topics, including immunology and sophistry, and has translated work by Eric Alliez, Barbara Cassin and Isabelle Stengers. <a.goffey@mdx.ac.uk>

Angela Anderson grew up in Northeastern Wisconsin, leaving for the University of Minnesota immediately after high school. After extensive travelling, she now lives in Berlin, where she works as a videographer and multi-purpose art tech. She returns to the Midwest now and then for occasional family visits (and unintentional yet unavoidable cultural anthropological research). She is currently completing her M.A. in the Media Studies programme at The New School, New York City. <andea580@newschool.edu>

Angana P. Chatterji is Convener of the International People's Tribunal on Human Rights and Justice in Indian-administered Kashmir (IPTK), and Professor of Social and Cultural Anthropology, California Institute of Integral Studies. **Mihir Desai** is Legal Counsel of the IPTK and Lawyer in the Mumbai High Court and Supreme Court of India. **Parvez Imroz** is Convener of the IPTK and President of the Jammu and Kashmir Coalition of Civil Society (JKCCS). **Gautam Navlakha** is Convener of the IPTK and Editorial Consultant with the *Economic and Political Weekly.* **Khurram Parvez** is Liaison of IPTK and Programme Coordinator of JKCCS. **Zahir-Ud-Din** is Convener of IPTK and Vice-President of JKCCS.
<achatterji@ciis.edu>, <kparvez@kashmirprocess.org>

Ashis Nandy is a dissident thinker and commentator on all things from politics to cinema to cricket. He is currently a senior honorary fellow at the Centre for the Study of Developing Societies, Delhi. Trained as a sociologist and clinical psychologist, Nandy is also known for his work in political science, social theory and future studies. However, during the last three decades, he has travelled through some of the less familiar territories of social knowledge, such as scientific creativity, future studies, post-developmental and post-secular visions, cities of the mind, myths of nation-states, and alternatives. He has written several books, including: *Alternative Sciences; At the Edge of Psychology; The Intimate Enemy; The Tao of Cricket; The Illegitimacy of Nationalism; The Savage Freud and Other Essays in Possible and Retrievable Selves; An Ambiguous Journey to the City; Time Warps; The Romance of the State and the Fate of Dissent in the Tropics* and *Traditions, Tyranny and Utopias.*

Atul Mishra is a doctoral candidate in international politics at the Centre for International Politics, and Disarmament, School of International Studies, Jawaharlal Nehru University (JNU), New Delhi, India. His doctoral research tries to interpret partition as a process of state formation and examines the impact of the 1947 Partition on sovereignty regimes in India and Pakistan. <anticontic@gmail.com>

Claudia Roselli is a researcher, town planner and architect. She is studying for her Ph.D. with joint research at the Faculty of Architecture, Department of Urban and Territorial Planning, Florence, and at the School of Planning and Architecture, New Delhi. Her fields of interest are: the contemporary city, third urban spaces, the dynamics of urban transformation linked with artistic processes, and extra-institutional practices able to promote a dialogue with institutions. She has worked in theatre as part of an international team, and was co-founder of Svarnet, an artistic collaboration between art and theatre. <roselliclaudia@gmail.com>

Cybermohalla Ensemble is a constellation of young people in different neighbourhoods in Delhi who pose and engage with questions of how to think about the urban in our present times. They bring their thinking between each other and into the public through writing, conversing, making books, art works, soundscapes, images, blogs, events, etc. The ensemble draws within it practitioners who have, for different durations since May 2001, been associated with Cybermohalla, a collaborative project of Sarai-CSDS, and Ankur Society for Alternatives in Education. Their recent writings, *Trickster City*, a book about the city, has been brought out by Penguin India (February 2010). <www.sarai.net/practices/cybermohalla>

F. Zahir Mibineh is a writer and independent curator based in Beirut. He has curated exhibitions in Tehran, Cairo and London and he has written for *ARMOIRE, Free Press, Alphabet Prime* and *Muhtelif: Magazine for Contemporary Art*. <f.zahir.mibineh@gmail.com>

Francesca Recchia is a researcher and lecturer, currently teaching at the University of Kurdistan, Hawler, in Northern Iraq. Her work intersects the fields of Urban, Social, Postcolonial and Visual Studies with a particular attention to the geo-political dimension of cultural process. <kiccovich@yahoo.com>

Ivana Franke is an artist based in Zagreb and Berlin. She often works with transparent materials and light to create situations that convey a sense of the ephemeral. Her installations probe the relations between appearance and materiality, questioning our sense of spatial dimensions. By introducing unstable forms at the margins of perception, they are opening up moments of inaccuracy in human perception. <ivana@ivanafranke.net>

Jamie Cross is a social anthropologist. His book, *Dream Zones: Promise and Loss in India's Economic Enclaves*, is due to be published in New Delhi by the Social Science Press in 2011. <jamiejcross@gmail.com>

John Armitage is Head of the Department of Media at Northumbria University, UK. He is co-editor, with Ryan Bishop and Douglas Kellner, of the Berg journal, *Cultural Politics*. <j.armitage@northumbria.ac.uk>

Jonathan Watkins has been Director of Ikon Gallery since 1999. Previously he worked for a number of years in London as Curator of the Serpentine Gallery (1995-1997) and Director of Chisenhale Gallery (1990-1995). He was Artistic Director of the 1998 Biennale of Sydney, and was guest curator for Quotidiana, Castello di Rivoli, Turin (1999-2000); Europarte: La Biennale di Venezia (June 1997); Milano Europa 2000; Palazzo di Triennale, Milan (November 2000); 'Facts of Life' at the Hayward Gallery, London (Autumn 2001) and 'Days Like These', the Tate Triennial exhibition of contemporary British art (London, 2003). He was on the curatorial team for the Shanghai Biennale (September 2006), the Sharjah Biennial (April 2007) and the Palestinian Biennial (December 2007). Recent essays by him have focused on the work of Giuseppe Penone, Martin Creed, Semyon Faibisovich, Yang Zhenzhong, Noguchi Rika, Caro Niederer and Cornelia Parker. He was the author of the Phaidon monograph on the Japanese artist, On Kawara. <j.watkins@ikon-gallery.co.uk>

Kartik Nair is in the second year of his M. Phil. at the School of Arts and Aesthetics, JNU. His dissertation will focus on the work of the Ramsay Brothers. In 2007, on a student research fellowship from Sarai-CSDS, he worked on the history of Appu Ghar, India's first amusement park. In 2008, he produced a research paper titled "Hanging out at the Multiplex" for the Public Service Broadcasting Trust. He has also previously freelanced as a copy-editor with Sage, written film reviews for *Campus 18*, and served as an editor on the 9th Osian's-Cinefan Film Festival Bulletin. Kartik currently serves on the editorial board of the online journal *Wide Screen* and is a recipient of the James Beveridge Media Resource Center Junior Research Fellowship, 2009-10. <kartiknair@gmail.com>

Kaushik Bhaumik is Senior Vice President at Osian's – Connoisseurs of Art. He is a historian by training and the co-editor of the recently published *Visual Sense: A Cultural Reader*, brought out by Berg, Oxford. His monograph on early Bombay cinema is due this year from Clarendon Press, Oxford. He has published extensively on Bombay and World Cinema and has recently started writing on modern Indian art. <bhaumikenator@gmail.com>

Kuhu Tanvir holds an M.A. in English Literature from the University of Delhi. Having worked until recently as a sub-editor with New Delhi Television, Kuhu is also one of the editors of *Wide Screen*, an international, open-access journal of cinema. <kuhutanvir@gmail.com>

Maja Petrović-Šteger is a Research Fellow and Director of Studies for Anthropology and Archaeology in Peterhouse, University of Cambridge. Her research explores various contexts where bodies – whether living, dead or in the form of medically usable remains – become the sites of economic, legal, political, scientific and artistic attention. She also translates poetry and drama from Serbian into Slovenian. <mp333@cam.ac.uk>

Markus Miessen is an architect, spatial consultant and writer. In 2002, he set up Studio Miessen, a collaborative agency for spatial practice and cultural analysis, and in 2007 was founding partner of the Berlin-based architectural practice, nOffice. In various collaborations, Miessen has published books such as *East Coast Europe* (Sternberg, 2008), *The Violence of Participation* (Sternberg, 2007) and *With/Without – Spatial Products, Practices and Politics in the Middle East* (Bidoun, 2007). He is currently a Harvard fellow on a research project in Iran/Iraq and is a Visiting Professor at the Berlage Institute (Rotterdam). His forthcoming book, *The Nightmare of Participation*, is due in 2010. He is now a Ph.D. candidate at the Centre for Research Architecture (Goldsmiths, London) and an editor of *ARCHIVE* (Berlin/Turin). <studiomiessen@gmx.net>

Matthew Fuller works at the Centre for Cultural Studies, Goldsmiths College, University of London. Books he has authored include *Media Ecologies: Materialist Energies in Art and Technoculture*; *Behind the Blip: Essays on the Culture of Software* and, with Usman Haque, *Urban Versioning System v1.0*. He is editor of *Software Studies: A Lexicon* and is a co-editor of the *Software Studies* series at MIT Press. He is involved in a number of projects in art, media and software. <www.spc.org/fuller>

The Media Lab at Jadavpur University was set up by the Department of Film Studies in 2008. As a centre for experiments with digital forms of knowledge and art, it seeks to extend the work of the Department in a direction where scholarship and hands-on work can come close to each other. The Lab works as a digital resource centre with its main activity consisting in building digital databases on the history of Indian cinema, and organising inter-disciplinary short-term workshops around archiving, art and critical practices. It is supported by the Navajbai Ratan Tata Trust, Mumbai. <medialabju@gmail.com>

Mohammed Khidar is the photographer of the image on the back cover. Khidar, from Aligarh, was formerly a *mela* photographer and owner of Bombay Studio. He has since changed his profession and now runs a shoe shop, which bears resemblance to a photography studio. His image was provided by **Sameena Siddiqui**, who is studying for her Masters in Art History from Kala Bhavan, Santiniketan. During her summer internship in Sarai, she embarked on building a collection of photographs from various neighbourhood photo studios in North India. <sameena42@hotmail.com>

Moinak Biswas is Reader in Film Studies at Jadavpur University. He writes on Indian film and culture. One of his recent books is *Apu and After, Revisiting Ray's Cinema* (2006). Biswas co-edits *Bio-Scope*; *Screen South Asia* and the *Journal of the Moving Image*. He is also the initiator of the Jadavpur University Media Lab, a centre for experiment with digital art and knowledge. He has recently finished a feature film in Bengali with Arjun Gourisaria, titled *Sthaniya Sambaad* (Spring in the Colony, 105 min). <moinak.biswas@gmail.com>

Naeem Mohaiemen is an artist and writer working in Dhaka and New York. He uses text, photography and video to explore histories of the international Left and utopia/dystopia slippage. Projects have shown at Dhaka Shilpakala Academy, the Finnish Museum of Photography, Kolkata Experimenter, Dubai Third Line, etc. Working between two countries, Naeem also explores contradictions between Bengalis in marginal migrant status, and majoritarian (and authoritarian) roles in their own country. He writes on Bangladesh's religious and ethnic minorities for the Ain Salish Kendro Annual Human Rights Report (www. askbd.org) and on activist blogs (www.unheardvoice.net/blog). As part of this work, *Muslims or Heretics: My Camera Can Lie (*2004) was a film about multiple audiences. His writings include "Islamic Roots of Hip-Hop" in *Sound Unbound* (MIT Press, 1998), "Adman Blues Become Artist Liberation" in *Indian Highway* (Serpentine Gallery, 2008), "Everybody Wants To Be Singapore" in Carlos Motta's *La Buena Vida* (Art in General, 2008), and "Collectives in Atomised Time", with Doug Ashford (Idensitat, 2009). <www.shobak.org>

Nandini Sundar is Professor of Sociology, Delhi School of Economics, Delhi University, and Co-editor, *Contributions to Indian Sociology*. Her publications include *Subalterns and Sovereigns: An Anthropological History of Bastar* (2nd ed. OUP, 2007), published in Hindi as *Gunda Dhur Ki Talash Mein* (Penguin 2009), and *Branching Out: Joint Forest Management in India* (OUP, 2001). She is editor of *Legal Grounds: Natural Resources, Identity and the Law in Jharkhand* (OUP, 2009) and also co-editor of *Anthropology in the East: The Founders of Indian Sociology and Anthropology* (Permanent Black, 2007), and *A New Moral Economy for India's Forests: Discourses of Community and Participation* (Sage Publications, 1999). Her current teaching and research interests include citizenship, war and counterinsurgency in South Asia, indigenous identity and politics in India, and the sociology of law and inequality. <nandinisundar@yahoo.com>

Nanna Heidenreich works with film/video on various levels, mainly within the context of Arsenal – Institute for Film and Video Art (www.arsenal-berlin.de), specifically focussing on experimental cinema and video art. She was part of the curatorial team for the programme, Forum Expanded, at the International Film Festival Berlin. Her focus areas in her research, teaching, writing and curating include: migration, theories of racism, visual culture and queer cinema. She is also part of the anti-racism network, Kanak Attak www.kanak-attak.de) <nn@kanak-attak.de>

Nicole Wolf researches, writes, teaches and occasionally curates with moving images, mainly with documentary and experimental work, and with a specific focus on the contextual productions of the political and the public. She has a particular interest in the South Asian documentary and the varied histories and presents of international aesthetic alliances. She currently teaching at the Visual Cultures Department of Goldsmiths College in London. <nicole.wolf0@googlemail.com>

Nupur Jain is currently associated with Sarai-CSDS, New Delhi, and is writing a biography of the multiplex in India. She has worked for four years in the Bombay film industry as a freelance writer/assistant director on film, documentary and advertising projects. In 2008, she co-organised the *DNA* Jaipur Film Festival. She is also associated with Jawahar Kala Kendra, Jaipur, holding film screenings. <nupurjn@gmail.com>

Padam Sherman has an M.A. in Public Administration and a Bachelor's in Library Science. A regular contributor to travel magazines, Padam is also part of a group of photographs at www.imi.in. His photography ranges from travel to street art. <shermanpadamjpr@gmail.com>

Priya Sen is an artist and filmmaker based in New Delhi. She works in the Media Lab and the Cybermohalla project at Sarai-CSDS. She is currently on an artist residency at Gasworks, London. <priya@sarai.net>

Rahul Govind was educated in Yangon and Delhi. Completing his undergraduate and Master's degrees from St. Stephen's College, Delhi University, he went on to do his Ph.D. at Columbia University, New York (2008), after which he spent a year as a Visiting Associate Fellow at the CSDS (2008-09). He is at present Assistant Professor at the History Department, Delhi University. <govind.rahul@gmail.com>

Rahul Mukherjee is a graduate student in the Department of Film and Media Studies at the University of California, Santa Barbara. His research interests involve looking at alternative media and new social movements, and national cinemas and media citizenship studies. Rahul's academic preoccupations often meander into imaginings about the media's role with(in) alternative futures for/of politics and technology. <mukherjee.rahul@gmail.com>

Raqs Media Collective (Jeebesh Bagchi, Monica Narula and Shuddhabrata Sengupta) has been variously described as artists, media practitioners, curators, editors and catalysts of cultural processes. Their work, which has been exhibited widely in major international spaces and events, locates them at the intersections of contemporary art, historical enquiry, philosophical speculation, research and theory – often taking the form of installations, offline and online media objects, performances and encounters. They live and work in Delhi, based at Sarai, the Centre for the Study of Developing Societies, an initiative they co-founded in 2000. <raqs@sarai.net>

Roberto Cavallini is a writer and Ph.D. candidate in Visual Cultures at Goldsmiths, University of London. His research interests include the works of Derrida, Arendt, Bataille and Blanchot and the films and poetry of Pier Paolo Pasolini. He is coordinator of InC, a research group in continental philosophy at Goldsmiths, and is a member of the organisational team of Reloading Images, a research network for the arts. As an independent curator, his projects have taken place in Venice, Bologna, Spain (Waste Art Biennial), Damascus, Istanbul and Tangiers. <rcavallini@gmail.com>

Sandhya Devesan Nambiar is presently writing her doctoral thesis on Conceptualism at JNU. She has worked on American Beat Poetry for her M.Phil. dissertation. She is a published poet and editor, and has been associated with the Shastri Indo-Canadian Institute as well as with publishing concerns like Katha and Sage. She has contributed to the book, *Translating Power*, published by Katha, with more works forthcoming. <sandhya24.7@gmail.com>

Shuddhabrata Sengupta is an artist and writer with the Raqs Media Collective and one of the editors of the Sarai Reader.

Shveta Sarda is a writer and translator based in Delhi. She has been working in Sarai-CSDS since 2001. Her translations have appeared in the Sarai Readers and other publications. She is the translator of a collection of writings about Delhi by Cybermohalla practioners, *Trickster City*, brought out by Penguin India (2010). <shveta@sarai.net>

Slavoj Žižek is a philosopher and critical theorist working in the traditions of Hegelianism, Marxism and Lacanian psychoanalysis. He has made contributions to political theory, film theory, and theoretical psychoanalysis. Žižek is a senior researcher at the Institute of Sociology, University of Ljubljana, Slovenia, and a professor at the European Graduate School. He is the founder and president of the Society for Theoretical Psychoanalysis, Ljubljana. He has written several books, including *The Invisible Reminder*; *The Sublime Object of Ideology*; *The Plague of Fantasies*; *The Ticklish Subject* ; *In Defence of Lost Causes* and *On Violence*.

Subuhi Jiwani is a writer and researcher based in Mumbai. She has a Master's in Media and Cultural Studies from the Tata Institute of Social Sciences, Mumbai, and is currently pursuing a postgraduate diploma in Indian Arts and Aesthetics at Jnanapravaha, Mumbai. She has worked as an arts journalist and critic, and writes about the visual arts, theatre, film and poetry. <subuhi.jiwani@gmail.com>

Sukanya Ghosh is an artist and designer based in Kolkata. She has studied Animation Film Design from the National Institute of Design, Ahmedabad after completing a B.F.A. in Painting from M. S. University, Baroda. <skinnyghosh@gmail.com>

Svati P. Shah is an Assistant Professor of Women's, Gender and Sexuality Studies at the University of Massachusetts at Amherst. Her book on sex work and migration in Mumbai's informal sector is being published by Duke University Press. Her work on on the politics of sex work and sexuality has appeared in academic and non-academic venues. Svati works with a number of feminist, queer and sex workers' organisations in the US and in India. <svatipshah@gmail.com>

Zainab Bawa is a Ph.D. scholar at the Centre for the Study of Culture and Society, Bangalore, working on politics and economy in contemporary Indian cities. She is associated with the India-South Africa (ISA) comparative research project with the Centres de Sciences Humaines (CSH), New Delhi. She is currently authoring a monograph on the history of Internet, Transparency and Politics in India with the Centre for Internet and Society (CIS), Bangalore, and is also involved with a study of technology, communities and participation with Servelots, Bangalore. <bawazainab79@gmail.com>

Editorial Collective

Awadhendra Sharan is a historian and Fellow at the Centre for the Study of Developing Societies. He is currently leading a project on *Peri-Urban Interface and Sustainability of South Asian Cities*, in collaboration with the Institute for Development Studies, Sussex. <sharan@sarai.net>

Jeebesh Bagchi is an artist with the Raqs Media Collective, and one of the initiators of Sarai. He coordinates the activities of Sarai's Cybermohalla project in collaboration with Ankur, Delhi. <jeebesh@sarai.net>

Monica Narula is an artist with the Raqs Media Collective, and one of the initiators of Sarai. She is the coordinator of the Sarai Media Lab. <monica@sarai.net>

Ravi Sundaram is a Fellow of the Centre for the Study of Developing Societies, Delhi, and one of the initiators of Sarai. He coordinates the *The Social and Material Life of Media Piracy* project at Sarai in collaboration with the Alternative Law Forum, Bangalore. He is the author of Pirate Modernity: Media Urbanism in Delhi (Routledge, 2009, London). <ravis@sarai.net>

Ravi S. Vasudevan is a Fellow of the Centre for the Study of Developing Societies, Delhi, and one of the initiators of Sarai. He has edited *Making Meaning in Indian Cinema* (2000). He is the author of The *Melodramatic Public: Film Form and Spectatorship in Indian Cinema* (Permanent Black, India, 2010) <raviv@sarai.net>

Shuddhabrata Sengupta is an artist with the Raqs Media Collective, and one of the initiators of Sarai. He writes regularly in kafila.org and the reader-list on contemporary media, politics and culture. <shuddha@sarai.net>

Acknowledgements

1. "The Cow Ate It Up" by Amitabh Kumar was made during a residency at Watermans Gallery, London, summer 2009

2. Jonathan Watkins' essay "Bethlehem" was previously published in *Pure Consciousness*, a catalogue of an exhibition by the artist On Kawara that was installed in kindergartens all over the world.

3. "*Otondro Prohori* : Guarding Who? Against What?": Portions of this project were installed at Dhaka Shilpakala Academy, with assistance from Zaid Islam, as part of Chobi Mela V (2009) curated by Drik/Shahidul Alam

4. "Graves: Buried Evidence from Kashmir" by Angana Chatterji et al. is a re-published version of Chapter 1 ("Graves") of *Buried Evidence : Unknown, Unmarked and Mass Graves in Indian-administered Kashmir – A Preliminary Report*, published by the International Peoples' Tribunal on Human Rights and Justice in Indian-adminstered Kashmir (IPTK)

5. "Police States, Anthropolgy and Human Rights" by Nandini Sundar is adapted from a text by her (with the same title) that was posted on blogs and email discussion lists such as Kafila.org and the Reader List.

6. "Fear, Inequity and Time" by Raqs Media Collective is excerpted and adapted from an interview with Ashok Mathur that appeared in *Boot Print* 3 (1), Summer 2009.

7. The interview with Slavoj Žižek was facilitated by Žižek's publisher in india, Navayana Books, during a lecture tour through India by Žižek in January, 2010

Image and Photo Credits

pp. 8, 9, 12, 14, 15 and 16 Claudia Rosselli

p. 32 Large California gold nugget on display and Wells Fargo Center as viewed from the Foshay Tower, Minneapolis, provided by Andrés de Santiago Areizaga

p.34 Photograph from the mid-1870's of a pile of American bison skulls to be ground into fertiliser, provided by Andrés de Santiago Areizaga

p. 52 Subuhi Jiwani

p. 53 Ambarien Alqadar

pp. 84-89 Naeem Mohaiemen

p. 98 photograph by Wolfgang Troger of Hansa Thapliyal's intallation 'His City' at 'Rest of Now', Manifesta 7, Bolzano

pp. 130, 135, 137 and 139 courtesy, International Peoples' Tribunal on Human Rights and Justice in Indian-adminstered Kashmir (IPTK)

pp. 214-222, Padam Sherman

p. 242 screen grabs from *A Wednesday*

p. 257 poster for *Purana Mandir*, courtesy Sarai Archive

pp. 258 and 259 screen grabs of *Purana Mandir* provided by Kartik Nair

p. 261 detail poster for *Purana Mandir*, courtesy Sarai Archive

p. 262 Angela Anderson

p. 278 Shuddhabrata Sengupta

pp. 290, 296 Cybermohalla Ensemble

Inside Back Cover *Petromechanophobia or Fear of Flying*, by Sukanya Ghosh